FIRST WORLD HUNGER

Also by Graham Riches

FOOD BANKS AND THE WELFARE CRISIS

UNEMPLOYMENT AND WELFARE: Social Policy and the Work of Social Work (*co-edited with Gordon Ternowetsky*)

First World Hunger

Food Security and Welfare Politics

Edited by

Graham Riches
Professor of Social Work
University of Northern British Columbia
Prince George

First published in Great Britain 1997 by
MACMILLAN PRESS LTD
Houndmills, Basingstoke, Hampshire RG21 6XS and London
Companies and representatives throughout the world

A catalogue record for this book is available from the British Library.

ISBN 0–333–64525–1 hardcover
ISBN 0–333–64526–X paperback

First published in the United States of America 1997 by
ST. MARTIN'S PRESS, INC.,
Scholarly and Reference Division,
175 Fifth Avenue, New York, N.Y. 10010

ISBN 0–312–16107–7

Library of Congress Cataloging-in-Publication Data
First World hunger : food security and welfare politics / edited by
Graham Riches.
p. cm.
Includes bibliographical references and index.
ISBN 0–312–16107–7
1. Food relief. 2. Hunger. 3. Public welfare. I. Riches,
Graham.
HV696.F6F545   1996
363.8—dc20   96–15979
                                                        CIP

This book is printed on paper suitable for recycling and made from fully managed and
sustained forest sources.

10   9   8   7   6   5   4   3   2   1
06   05   04   03   02   01   00   99   98   97

Printed and bound in Great Britain by
Antony Rowe Ltd, Chippenham, Wiltshire

Contents

Tables and Charts

Tables and Charts

Preface and Acknowledgements

A collective work is the result of many people's ideas, labours, support, hospitality and financial contributions. The idea for this book germinated during a trip to New Zealand in late 1992 when I was fortunate to meet Helen Walch, Director of the Wellington Inner City Ministry, who was deeply involved in the issues of hunger and food banking. My conversations with Helen had many parallels with those I had held with Ed Bloos, Director of the Regina Food Bank in Saskatchewan, Canada, and they both provided the initial impetus for writing a comparative study of first world hunger. Wayne Sanderson, Director of Brisbane's Lifeline organization, furthered the idea when he and his staff were struggling over whether or not to start a similar organization.

Gráinne Twomey, my editor at Macmillan, in accepting the proposal for the book, moved the project to the next stage. Special thanks are due to her for being so supportive of the project and for never failing to provide the right advice and encouragement when they were needed.

I would also like to thank each of the contributors for willingly accepting the task of writing their respective chapters, for sharing their insights and expertise and for keeping to the deadlines. Not only do they have busy teaching and research agendas but each is engaged in a range of progressive work in the community.

Each contributor would like to acknowledge others who have contributed to the writing of their respective chapters. Gary Craig would like to thank Liz Dowler for a new and fruitful collaboration at a time of considerable pressure. Jan Poppendieck wishes to thank the Professional Staff Congress-City University of New York Research Award Program and the Asper Institute Non-Profit Sector Research Fund for partial support of the research reflected in the chapter on the USA. In addition, she thanks Richard Ryan for careful review of the helpful suggestions concerning the manuscript, and John Cook at the Center on Hunger, Poverty and Nutrition Policy for help in sorting out measurements and definitions. As well, she thanks Mimi Abramovitz, Lynn Chancer, Sarah Breenblatt, Ruth Sidel and Woody Goldbert for fruitful discussions and consistent encouragement. Stephen Uttley would like to acknowledge financial support towards background research for the New Zealand chapter from the Internal Grants Committee of

Victoria University and the invaluable assistance of research students Jean-Paul De Reed and Michèle De La Cour. John Wilson would like to thank Mary and Gordon Wilson for their important contributions to the Australian chapter as well as Belinda Wilson for typing the manuscript and the financial support of the Department of Social Work and Community Welfare at James Cook University of North Queensland.

Research for the Canadian chapter was made possible by two grants for which I am particularly grateful: a Faculty Research Award made available by the Canadian High Commission in Canberra in 1993 and funding from the National Welfare Grants Division of Human Resources Development of Canada which was administered by the National Anti-Poverty Organization. It should be noted that National Welfare Grants was eliminated in the recent spending cuts and will be badly missed in the Canadian Social Welfare Community.

Those who contributed their ideas, support and hospitality are many and I would like to thank Rod Macrae, Lynn Toupin, Rosemary Spendlove, Gary Bellamy, Sue Cox, Wardie Lepan, Ed Bloos, Marjorie Bencze, Bruce Moore, Tom Taylor, Evariste Therrault, Philip Hepworth, Dorothy Hepworth, Loralee Manning, John Stapleton, Leah Cohan, Ernie Lightman, Debbie Field, Peter Reble, Heather Coffin, Laura Kalina, Dorothy Moore, Duncan Cameron, Pat Kerans, Marion Kerans, David Ross, Peggy Teagle, Martha Jackman, Patrick Johnstone, France Asselin, Yussuf Kly, Bob Britten, Patricia Riply, Gerrard Kennedy and Barry Davidson. It should be noted that the views expressed in this publication do not necessarily reflect those of any of the funding agencies or individuals with whom the authors consulted.

Thanks are also due to David Fish, Dean of the Faculty of Health and Human Sciences at the University of Northern British Columbia, and Gordon Ternowetsky, former Chair of Social Work, for supporting this endeavour and to my new colleagues, Barbara Herringer, Barbara Isaac, Glen Schmidt and Kwong Tang, for bearing with me during a very busy period in the development of a new programme of social work education. Special thanks must go to Joann Kennedy, Catherine Foster, Vicki Lunz and particularly to Vicki McKendrick, the Social Work Programme Secretary, who expertly and conscientiously provided the final manuscript.

Finally I must thank Mary, with whom I live, without whose support from the very beginning this project would never have materialized. Mary knows far more about food, nutrition and diets and their essential importance in the physical and social lives of all of us than I could ever know and I owe a deep debt of gratitude to her for enabling me to work on this text.

Graham Riches
30 September 1995

Contributors

Gary Craig worked in several community development projects in the North of England for 13 years before researching and teaching social policy within the British university system. He has been editor of the *Community Development Journal* for 12 years and is currently Secretary of the UK Social Policy Association. He is now Professor of Social Policy at the University of Humberside. He has written widely on community work and social policy issues and his most recent book, jointly edited with Marjorie Mayo, is *Community Empowerment* (London: Zed Books, 1995). His current research interests cover social security, poverty, local government and community development issues.

Elizabeth Dowler, a nutritionist by training, is currently a lecturer in the Human Nutrition Unit, Department of Public Health and Policy, London School of Hygiene and Tropical Medicine (University of London). Her interests have long been in the social and policy aspects of human nutrition rather than the biological. She has worked with social and political scientists as well as nutritionists in many parts of the non-industrialized world, and in the UK. She has been a regular consultant for international agencies on nutritional surveillance, nutrition in agriculture and nutrition curriculum design. More recently she has worked on nutrition and poverty in the UK and the rest of Europe, looking particularly at the nutritional consequences of poverty, influences on food choice, and potential for policy interventions at the local and national level. In 1995 she published a seminal study, with Claire Calvert, *Nutrition and Diet in Lone-parent Families in London* (London: Family Policy Studies Centre).

Janet Poppendieck is Director of the Center for the Study of Family Policy and an Associate Professor in the Department of Sociology at Hunter College of the City University of New York. She is the author of *Breadlines Knee-Deep in Wheat: Food Assistance in the Great Depression* (New Brunswick: Rutgers University Press, 1986) and articles on hunger, food assistance and public policy. She is chair of the Board of Directors of the Community Food Resource Center in New York City and is active in the Association for the Study of Food and Society. She is currently at work on a book on emergency food in the United States: *Reinventing Charity: Emergency Food in American Culture* (New York:

Penguin, 1996, forthcoming). She lives in Brooklyn, New York with her husband and daughter.

Graham Riches is Professor of Social Work at the University of Northern British Columbia. He was previously Foundation Professor of Social Work and Community Welfare at James Cook University of North Queensland, Australia and has taught at the University of Hong Kong and the University of Regina in Canada, where he was Director of the Social Administration Research Unit. He was a co-founder and joint editor of the *Canadian Review of Social Policy*. Previous publications include *Food Banks and the Welfare Crisis* (Ottawa; CCSD, 1986) and *Unemployment and Welfare: Social Policy and the Work of Social Work* (Garamond, 1990), co-edited with Gordon Ternowetsky. He has practised community development in South East Asia, London and Liverpool.

Stephen Uttley is Senior Lecturer in Social Policy at Victoria University, Wellington, New Zealand. Born in England, he worked as a social worker in Manchester and taught social policy in a social work training programme at Manchester University before moving to New Zealand in 1976. His research interests include theoretical explanations for welfare state development and in particular the impact of technological change on such developments. He has authored a book on these issues entitled *Technology and the Welfare State* (London: Unwin Hyman, 1991). He is also a member of the Overseas Editorial Board of the *Journal of Social Policy*.

John Wilson is currently the Health Services Coordinator at Nganampa Health Council, an Aboriginal-controlled, community-based primary health care service in remote Australia. Previously, he taught in the Department of Social Work and Community Welfare at James Cook University, Townsville, Australia. He is the author of several social welfare texts about the Australian welfare state and social service provision. He is the author of a biographical novel, *Lori*, published by Australia's first indigenous publishing house, Magabala Books (Broome, Western Australia, 1989). He has published a seminal study of Australian single fathers, *Single Fathers: Australian Men Take on a New Role* (Melbourne: Macmillan, 1990). More importantly, he has ongoing responsibilities as a father, grandfather, brother and son, and a great passion for detective fiction and Australian Rules football.

A serious commitment to charity and beneficent action requires commitment to material justice and so to political change. Practical reasoning about hunger has an audience only when it reaches those with the power to bring about that change.

(O'Neill, 1986, p.163)

1 Hunger and the Welfare State: Comparative Perspectives
Graham Riches

This book is about hunger and the politics of welfare reform and food security in affluent first world societies. It addresses the nature and causes of hunger, explores government and community responses and examines what can and should be done about it. Its focus is the re-emergence of hunger in five advanced industrial states with developed welfare states: Australia, Canada, New Zealand, the UK and the USA, and how as the twenty-first century fast approaches the governments of each of these countries have sought to reform their public welfare systems whilst at the same time neglecting the growing issue of hunger and food insecurity. It is about understanding hunger as a political issue and the possibility of liberal welfare states being able to break their mould and guarantee basic human rights to food, adequate incomes and remunerative employment in the broader context of social justice and economic renewal. Essentially, the questions posed in this text ask whether the real litmus test for any welfare state is its capacity to guarantee the basic rights of its most vulnerable citizens.

During the 1980s and 1990s hunger and absolute poverty have re-emerged as a significant social issue in many rich industrial countries. Yet along with continuing high levels of unemployment and underemployment, it has become publicly acceptable and attracts little government attention, despite the fact that its existence stands in stark contrast to increasing economic prosperity and common standards of human decency. Not only is hunger economically inefficient, it violates the domestic and international human rights obligations of first world nations. It is testimony to growing vulnerability and inequality and the erosion of the social and economic rights of millions of people. In Canada 2.5 million people a year are receiving food from charitable food banks yet this has provoked little sense of collective outrage or positive government action (CAFB, 1994). The Bread for the World Institute reports that 'In the United States an estimated 30 million people cannot afford to buy enough food to maintain good health. One of every five children lives in poverty and sometimes goes hungry' (BWI, 1995, p. 2). In New Zealand food banks have proliferated in recent years (McGurk and Clark, 1993) and at the opening of the Melbourne Food Bank in Australia in March 1993 it was claimed there were 10 000 people in that city who did not have enough to eat (Council for Homeless Persons, 1993). Prime Minister Major in Britain recently felt able to condemn beggars on the street, doubtless because he did not fear public approbation or political fall-out. Whilst UN conventions require ratifying governments to meet the basic needs of their citizens, in the New World Order hunger is again a matter for charity and not for state or collective action. Hunger in western wealthy societies, it would seem, has effectively been depoliticized with profound personal, moral and social consequences.

The purpose of this text is to understand, through comparative policy analysis, and the use of national case studies, why hunger, absolute poverty and food insecurity have again become prevalent in particular first world countries with established welfare states and social safety nets; to examine its nature, incidence and personal and social consequences; to explore the policy responses (and non-responses) of government and the community to the growth of hunger, and to anticipate strategies for public action particularly in terms of the respective roles and responsibilities of government, non-government organizations (NGOs) and pressure groups in promoting and guaranteeing food security as a basic human right. The book explores the relationship between the politics and practice of food security and welfare reform by examining the types of policies and programmes that are most likely to succeed in combating hunger and the kind of community work and political action which will result in governments according the issue their highest priority (Hall *et al.*, 1975).

COMPARATIVE POLICY ANALYSIS

Cross-national studies commend themselves for a number of reasons. As Jones (1985, p. 3) has suggested, they help us to learn more about our own domestic policies, they broaden perspectives and suggest 'lessons from abroad', and they help advance the development of social welfare theory free from narrow chauvinistic concerns by drawing on a broader array of case-study material. As a project in comparative analysis this collection of national studies is intended not only to contribute to the debate about hunger and poverty but help articulate what can and must be done to eliminate hunger in advanced industrial societies.

The five countries studied in this book were selected for a number of reasons, the main one being that there are lessons that each could learn from the others. Clearly, one must treat with caution the idea that lessons from abroad can be neatly transposed to other societies for, as Jones (1985) has observed, 'social policies do not exist in a vacuum from each other and independent of the society within which and as part of which they have developed. They are not therefore available for export with 'satisfaction guaranteed' (*ibid.*, p. 5). Yet there is a great deal to be learned. If the New Right agenda of Thatcherism and Reaganism could be so diligently studied and advanced in the 1980s in Australia, Canada and New Zealand, as well as in the UK and the USA, there is no reason to suppose that the lessons of progressive public policy and community action cannot be similarly applied.

This much became clear to me in the early 1990s when I was living and working in Australia, having previously spent many years in Canada where I had researched the rise of food banks and the collapse of the social safety net in the early 1980s. I also had the occasion to visit New Zealand and speak with food bank staff in the Inner City Ministry in Wellington. I was both alarmed and intrigued. I was struck both by the similarities of the hunger situation in New Zealand compared to Canada, the common dilemmas facing the churches and non-government organizations as they confronted the vacuum in welfare policy created by government neglect and the thought that there was much to be learned by reflecting on the ways in which different societies were responding to the hunger issue, both in terms of meeting immediate needs and the possibilities for longer-term progressive public action.

This experience spawned the idea for this book, later confirmed when attending the inauguration of the first food bank in Melbourne, Australia. What concerned me most about this event was not the endorsement by corporate Melbourne of the charitable food bank idea and the privatization of welfare, but the comment of Hazel Hawke, Australia's erstwhile first lady as partner of the former Labour Prime Minister Bob Hawke, who, in declaring the food bank open, called it an 'exciting development'. It seemed as if there was a yawning chasm between the expectations and understandings of the political elite and the experiences and realities confronting hungry people. One wanted to ask whether the movers and shakers behind the Australian food bank movement were fully aware of their actions. Had they thought through what the rise of food banks meant in terms of the stigmatizing of poor people, the failure of public welfare, the legitimizing of public begging and the erosion of the social rights of citizenship? Why not look to Canada, New Zealand and the USA to consider the consequences of food banking before starting down this course? What would the experience of public begging in the UK have to tell us about the failure of state welfare and the need for alternative courses of collective action? Perhaps there were lessons to be learned.

From the standpoint of social welfare theory and welfare state development these societies and their responses to the growing issue of hunger also merit attention because they each confront the issue of whether they can break out of their current welfare state moulds and find new ways of meeting basic human needs free from the requirement always to be satisfying the dictates of the marketplace. Australia, Canada, New Zealand, the UK the USA have been described, along with Ireland, as constituting 'liberal' welfare state regimes in contrast to the corporatist welfare systems of Austria, France, Germany and Italy and the social democratic model of the Scandinavian countries (Esping-Andersen, 1990, pp. 26–7, 52). This cluster of Anglo-Saxon societies, Esping-Andersen suggests, comprise residual welfare states lacking any commitment to full employment and seeking to maintain a state/market dualism in which the state defers to the market. Their welfare arrangements are characterized by

> means tested assistance, modest universal transfers or modest social insurance plans.... Benefits cater mainly to a clientele of low-income, usually working class, state dependants. In this model, the progress of social reform has been severely circumscribed by traditional, liberal work-ethic norms: it is one where the limits of welfare equal the marginal propensity to opt for welfare instead of work. Entitlement rules are therefore strict and often associated with stigma; benefits are typically modest. In turn the state encourages the market, either passively – by guaranteeing only a minimum – or actively – by subsidizing private welfare schemes. (*ibid.*, 26–7)

In this context people's entitlements to welfare assistance are directly related to their capacity to sell their labour-power as a commodity in the marketplace. The point which Esping-Andersen makes, and which is entirely germane to the subject matter of this book, is that the commodification of labour-power means that 'people's rights to survive outside the market are at stake' (*ibid.*, p. 35). This struggle to survive in terms of the right of individuals and families to be able to feed themselves and their children (as one of a number of interrelated basic human rights), whether or not people are gainfully employed, is a key theme of this book. The evidence of minimalist and frequently punitive public welfare policies buttressed by government denial of the existence of hunger presented in this study supports his residualist classification of the countries studied. A central concern therefore arises with the capacity of 'liberal' welfare states to promote the decommodification of social rights, that is, 'the degree to which individuals, or families, can uphold a socially acceptable standard of living independently of market participation' (*ibid.*, p. 37). If the right to food security is to be constrained by people's ability to participate fully in the marketplace, particularly in societies which show little inclination to support full employment, the future is one of increasing risk and vulnerability. The essential challenge is to move beyond the doctrine of less eligibility, the idea that no one 'on welfare' should earn more than the lowest paid wage-earner, in order to establish rights of citizenship which are inclusive and guarantee freedom from hunger.

It would however be a mistake to insist that the 'liberal' or residual model precisely fits each of the Anglo-Saxon welfare states. As Esping-Anderson (1990, p. 49) himself notes, there are no pure cases and historically each of these countries at different times in its welfare history has demonstrated commitments to universality and decommodified social rights. We should also take note of the warning by Ginsburg (1993, p. 18) that 'The very suggestion of "comparative analysis" of social policy is problematic because it conjures up the point that social scientists have developed rigorous methods and established schools of thought for comparing welfare states. Nothing could be further from the truth.' Nevertheless, in terms of qualitative comparative analysis, Ginsburg argues the merits of adopting a 'structured diversity' approach, which emphasizes the need to appreciate the uniqueness of each welfare state in its national, social and historical context. The diversity may be structured by domestic political processes, cultural values, economic forces, demographic factors or whatever' (Ginsburg, 1993, p. 23). He provides a helpful approach for comparing the national case material discussed in this book when he cites Castles, who argues that 'Learning from a particular national experience will always take particular forms, but patterns of human action and purposes, especially as moulded by the fact of living in societies constrained by common structural parameters, are likely to manifest intrinsic similarities as well as residual differences' (1989, pp. 12–13). It is from these that we can hope to learn.

Perhaps the most significant of the structural parameters linking Australia, Canada, New Zealand, the UK and the USA, as Taylor has noted in his study of the social effects of free market policies on these five societies in the 1980s, is 'their common heritage – not least in their use of the language which is the common language in use of the international and economic and financial communities' (1990, p. 20). The idea of a common heritage refers also to shared history (conflicts and co-operation) and democratic traditions, styles of representative government, systems of law, religious ideas and institutions, capitalist economies and systems of social welfare. Of course, differences must be recognized. Canada officially is a bilingual country and Quebec, currently engaged in the politics of independence, could by no stretch of the imagination be described as Anglo-Saxon in its origins. Similarly, the historical demographic characteristics of each of these societies are shifting in response to changing patterns of immigration and growing ethnic and cultural diversity. Indigenous populations, the Maori in Aotearoa/New Zealand, the First Nations in Canada and the USA, Aboriginal and Torres Strait Islander peoples in Australia, the Welsh, the Scots and the Irish in the UK must also object to the classification of their societies as being English-speaking, let alone Anglo-Saxon.

There are other differences, which make welfare policy comparisons difficult: Australia, Canada and the USA are federal as opposed to unitary states, a fact which has significant implications in terms of the constitutional responsibility for heath, education and welfare, and the complexities of social policy-making in divided jurisdictions; the fact that each welfare state, whilst similar to the others in many respects, has grown out of a particular national context and demonstrates a unique array of social welfare programmes; and, as Taylor has observed (1990, pp. 20–1), their responses to the development of the free market economy in the 1980s has taken different forms: in Britain it involved a 'headlong assault, at the ideological level and also in terms of individual policy innovation, on the institutions of organized labour and the welfare state'; in Australia and New Zealand these changes seem to have been orchestrated 'through the political parties and institutions representing organized labour'; in the USA, lacking a strong 'tradition of labourism or social democracy influential at the government level, the project of the free marketeers has perhaps been rather more straightforward: an attack has been mounted on the notion of Big Government'; in Canada 'the development of "free market solutions" occurred almost invisibly in the early 1980s' until its full impact was made clear in the announcement of the Free Trade Agreement in 1988 with the United States. This has been referred to by Canadian analysts as 'social policy by stealth' whereby during the Mulroney regime 'arcane and poorly understood technical changes to programs, such as partial de-indexation and clawbacks... were imposed on the Canadian people without their knowledge or consent' (Battle and Torjman, 1995, p. 9). It is evident that the shift to privatization and selectivity in each welfare state in recent years has been marked by harsh and adverse effects for the poor and hungry.

HUNGER IN ADVANCED INDUSTRIAL SOCIETIES

In addressing the topic of hunger in technologically advanced industrial societies with long-established welfare states it is necessary to consider possible objections to using the term to describe the problems people are experiencing when confronted with inadequate welfare benefits and lack of access to food. Clearly one should distinguish first world hunger from the starvation and malnutrition brought about by famine and endemic undernourishment in developing countries (Dreze and Sen, 1989) where it is estimated that in 1990 nearly 800 million people, or 20 per cent of the developing world's population, are chronically undernourished (BWI, 1995, p. 10). Yet hunger and undernutrition caused by lack of access to food is a growing phenomenon in affluent first world countries, certainly not on the scale that exists in developing countries, but as the data presented in this book suggest, its prevalence is a major public policy issue. There are, of course, causal links between the poverty and hunger experienced in the 'developing' and 'developed' world not the least of which are the policies and practices of transnational corporate agribusiness and the structural adjustment policies favoured by such international bodies as the World Bank and the International Monetary Fund, and applied domestically and overseas by governments of countries such as Australia, Canada, New Zealand, the UK and the USA. Indeed, it is a matter of some irony that the Global Assembly on Food Security, organized to mark the fiftieth anniversary of the Food and Agriculture Organization, was held in Quebec City in autumn 1996 at a time when governments in North America were systematically dismantling their social safety nets, thereby increasing the possibility of more extensive hunger and poverty.

We might also wish to ask whether it is morally appropriate and politically wise to speak of hunger in the affluent first world when the same term is used to describe the plight and desperation of those suffering from lack of food in famine-stricken Somalia or in the war-

ravaged Rwanda or the former Yuogslavia. Television images of despe-
rate and starving people establish benchmarks in viewers' minds about
the subjective experience of hunger which are difficult to shake. Yet the
beggars on the streets of London, New York and Toronto, or those
seeking hand-outs from food banks in Wellington or Sydney, are also
destitute and in need of help. Their hunger is often unrecognized or, as
Wilson comments in relation to Australia, the response is that of a
'hungry silence'. Indeed, such images may deaden our responses for in
not knowing what we can do about the tragedy of war so many miles
away we also close our eyes to the problems in our own neighbourhoods.

It may even appear to be highly contradictory to be writing about
hunger in wealthy industrial societies when, as Dreze and Sen (1989, p.
4) have noted, 'the *typical* person in Europe or North America tries to
reduce – rather than increase – calorie intake'. In other words, overconsumption and the specialized diets needed to contain it vie with
hunger as a health and social issue, and certainly absorb acres of news-
print in journals and magazines to persuade us that we are all eating
too much. In this context hunger has a hard time competing for public
and political attention. By the same token how possible is it to persuade the public that hunger is a critical issue when, as Ormerod
(1994, p. 25) has observed, 'in the United States around $60 billion a
year is spent on personal beauty care' and in 'the United Kingdom
over £1 billion is spent on pet food. Yet in both countries the public
has been told repeatedly that there is no money available for the provision of better public health care or better public education'? Clearly
there are choices to be made.

A key problem is that governments of advanced industrial nations
refuse to acknowledge the existence of hunger. They are assisted in their
denial when, for example, the United Nations Development Programme (UNDP) reports on the problem of global poverty without
providing data on hunger and poverty in industrial countries. The
UNDP ranks the countries of the world according to their socio-economic progress and uses a Human Development Index (HDI) which
is a more comprehensive measure than GDP. Its key indicators are
longevity (increases in life expectancy), knowledge (advances in literacy
and mean years of schooling) and standard of living (as measured by
purchasing power) (UNDP, 1994, p. 91). Yet while data on absolute poverty are included for developing countries, there is no mention of the
incidence of poverty in the industrial world though data are provided
on unemployment and income distribution. In 1994 Canada came first

of 53 'high development countries' on the HDI index. Australia and the USA were seventh and eighth, and the UK and New Zealand ranked tenth and eighteenth respectively (*ibid.*, p. 129). The troubling fact is that each of these countries confronts significant issues of hunger and poverty.

It has, of course, often been observed that hunger is a difficult concept to define (Dreze and Sen, 1989, pp. 35–45; Cohen, 1990, p. 23; Chelf, 1992, p. 41). It is not intended in this introduction to present a concise definition of hunger to be used as a criterion for assessing the degree of hunger prevalent in the five countries being studied. Each author has determined her or his approach to the topic and some have engaged in a useful debate about the nature and definition of hunger in their particular societies. Rather, the intention is to provide a framework of ideas for thinking about the phenomenon of hunger in wealthy societies which have the capacity to feed themselves and for anticipating the possibility of progressive reform and the elimination of hunger. Three approaches are suggested: hunger as a key element of absolute poverty and significant consequence of relative deprivation; hunger and its relationship to the broader question of food security and healthy well-being; and hunger understood as a political problem and matter of fundamental human rights necessitating progressive intervention by the state and civil society in ways that move it beyond an immediate issue of welfare.

Dreze and Sen (1989, p. 15) have argued that hunger is 'a many headed monster' related to 'a wide range of deprivations': biological, economic and social. While the focus of their studies is global hunger in the developing world it is also important to recognize that first world hunger in the 1990s should be understood *both* as an attribute of absolute or primary poverty and a key attribute of relative deprivation. In 1899 Rowntree in his studies of poverty in the UK defined people as living in primary poverty where 'total earnings are insufficient to obtain the minimum necessaries for the maintainence of merely physical efficiency' (Townsend, 1979, p. 33). A century later this physical concept of need still applies. It means that individuals and families do not have enough money to pay the rent, heat their homes, buy clothes, afford transport and generally take care of themselves. As a consequence, as the evidence of the national case studies makes clear, it is the food budget, being the most elastic, which suffers, and individuals and families, including many children, go hungry. The situation is absolute in that hungry people require immediate practical and material assistance without which their physical capacity to lead normal healthy lives and also to survive is threatened. Indeed, even in first world countries, some may die from lack of food as the chapter on Australia reveals. Hunger clearly requires prompt and direct responses, but its day-to-day alleviation is related to a range of other issues such as unemployment, inadequate housing and sub-poverty level welfare benefits, which governments today refuse to acknowledge.

Clearly, a broader approach to the problem of hunger is required and, following Townsend, we should understand it in terms of a social conception of need or as a consequence of 'relative deprivation' where

> people lack the resources to obtain the types of diets, participate in the activities and have the living conditions and amenities which are customary or at least widely encouraged or approved in the societies to which they belong. Their resources are so seriously below those commanded by the average individual or family that they are, in effect, excluded from ordinary living patterns, customs and activities. (*ibid.*, p. 31)

In other words, people's experience of hunger and poverty is directly related to the societies in which they live and the standards of living which are customarily enjoyed. If citizens of affluent industrialized countries cannot afford to purchase food in the supermarket or local corner store, and are dependent on intermittent food bank handouts, whilst they may still be better nourished than hungry people in the developing world, they are still hungry. Moreover, their experience of having to obtain food in such a humiliating way is personally undermining and stigmatizing. From this perspective hunger must be understood as a function of inequality.

Another useful framework for thinking about hunger in the context of the national case studies presented in this book is that suggested by Radimer and her colleagues (1992, pp. 36S–44S) in their discussion of the broader issue of food security. Hunger in their view is 'the inability to acquire or consume an adequate quality or sufficient quantity of food in socially acceptable ways, or the uncertainty that one will be able to do so' (*ibid.*, 39S). This operational definition is derived from a study of low-income women in upstate New York as part of a nutrition surveillance project to develop more precise indicators of hunger experienced by women and children. The women described hunger existing at two levels: the individual and the household, and each level comprised quantitative, qualitative, pyschological and social components (*ibid.*, 36S). At the individual level the responses of the women were labelled as insufficient food intake, nutritional inadequacy, lack of choice and feelings of deprivation and disrupted eating patterns; at the household level the problems were those of food depletion, unsuitable food, anxiety about the food supply and having to acquire food in socially unacceptable ways (*ibid.*, 37S–39S). Hunger, therefore, was not only being without food but being unable to acquire it through normal channels. It was experienced as a 'managed process' in which the women adopted a range of coping mechanisms in their attempt to keep hunger at bay. Hunger provoked anxiety and uncertainty about where the next meal was coming from. In other words, the central issue for the women of upstate New York, as for millions of hungry people elsewhere, was one of food security.

In 1983 the United Nations defined the goal of food security as being 'to give populations both economic and physical access to a supply of food, sufficient in both quality and quantity, at all times, regardless of climate or harvests, social level or income' (FAO, 1995). This definition, whilst comprehensive, appears to rely on an assumption of aid and charity rather than people having control over their food production and distribution systems. A more empowering definition is that provided by the Ontario Public Health Association, which states that the challenge of food security is when people 'can get enough food to eat that is safe, that they like to eat and that helps them to be healthy. They must be able to get this food in ways that make them feel good about themselves and their families' (OPHA, 1995, p. 2). How such food security might be achieved is a central theme of this book. It is related to the debate about welfare policy and social security reform, but moves beyond it and engages questions of basic human rights, community health, food policy, agricultural reform, community development and local control of the food supply.

The concept of food security also invites us to think about food as a social good which plays a central and intimate role in our lives. Winson (1993, p. 4) has correctly observed that 'If food and drink have become commodities, they are "intimate" commodities like perhaps no other. In the process of their consumption we take them inside our very bodies, a fact that gives them a special significance denied such "externally" consumed commodities as refrigerators, automobiles, house paint or television sets.' If hunger, like poverty, is to be abolished, it means moving beyond residual responses such as food banks and soup kitchens, which have become necessary adjuncts of the failing welfare state, to engage more difficult questions of inequality, powerlessness and the economic and social rights of citizenship, which must include being able to produce, obtain and consume food in socially acceptable ways as well as understand its social and cultural significance in the lives of people.

It should also be noted that the United Nations recognizes that the 'overall availability of food in the world is not a problem... there is enough food to offer everyone in the world around 2500 calories a day – 200 calories more than the basic minimum' (UNDP, 1994, p. 27). If that is the case, it is essential that we understand hunger primarily as a political issue. If it is to be eliminated in first world countries, to say nothing of its abolition in developing countries, the roots of hunger must be acknowledged to be man-made (the term is used advisedly). As Fernand Braudel (1985, p. 31), the eminent French historian, once said, 'Today's society, unlike yesterday's, is capable of feeding its poor. To do otherwise is an error of government.'

In Australia, Canada, New Zealand, the UK and the USA nutritious food is not equally available to all, and joblessness, low wages and inadequate welfare benefits act as almost insurpassable barriers to people, many of whom are children, needing access to life's most basic resource. Historically, governments of these countries have sought to address issues of hunger, nutrition and poverty through a range of direct and indirect policies though it is unclear how co-ordinated such approaches have been. They have included agricultural and fisheries policies food and nutrition standards, community health programmes, employment creation, minimum wages and income subsidies, fiscal and social welfare policies and public safety nets designed to provide a modicum of social rights for protecting the most vulnerable and hungry members of society. It is this glue which has now come unstuck, not as the result of lack of food but because the ideological preferences of the governments in power (of both the Right and the Left) in each of these countries from the early 1980s have followed the New Right economic agenda which champions individual acquisitiveness at the expense of the poor and collective well-being.

Governments have not simply been cutting welfare programmes in the interests of mere efficiency, rather they have deliberately been using welfare reform policies to create new categories of the deserving and undeserving poor dividing claimants into employable and unemployable groups thereby using the spur of poverty and the ache of hunger as tools for disciplining labour and increasing the profitability of the private sector. Legitimate concerns about social justice have been thrown out of the window with the sole message being that unless or until deficits are cut and economic growth is restored, those in receipt of welfare will have to wait. The idea that distributive justice should apply, whether or not an economy is growing, remains static or is in decline, seems lost on the politicians of the day. People have become expendable and collectivist values set aside. Yet hunger as an outcome of high unemployment is a persistent and growing issue which will not easily disappear. Politicians may choose to disregard it and treat it as a matter of charitable concern, but there are forces at work which suggest that sooner or later governments will be required to respond.

One such force, which is discussed in the pages that follow, is the idea that food *is* a basic human need and that people everywhere have an inalienable right to adequate nutritious food. In terms of international law the countries studied in this book, with the exception of the USA, have ratified the United Nations' *International Covenant on Economic, Social And Cultural Rights* (1966) and the *Convention on the Rights of the Child* (1989), both of which recognize the right of people 'to an adequate standard of living for himself and his family, including adequate food, clothing and housing, and to continuous improvements of his living conditions. The States Parties will take appropriate steps to ensure the realization of this right' (Article 11: 1, UN Doc. A/6316, 1966). Each country has also committed itself to furthering the aims of the *World Declaration on Nutrition* (Rome, 1992) and the *Declaration and Programme of Action of the World Social Summit* (Copenhagen, 1995), which invite member states to draft national programmes of action, respectively, to improve nutrition and defeat poverty. These are all international instruments waiting to be used in the battle against hunger not only in developing countries but also in the presumed first world. It would be naive to expect immediate action, but at the very least these instruments provide important mechanisms enabling the struggle against hunger to be advanced by progressive peoples and their organizations.

Lastly, it should be noted that each of the national case studies can be read as informed analyses which stand on their own. Each author was asked to build her or his contribution around the themes identified at the beginning of this chapter but each has interpreted these guidelines in her or his own way. Whilst this makes systematic comparsion of the national case studies difficult, there are however a surprising number of common themes which emerge in terms of the incidence of hunger and its causes in first world countries and the responses of governments and the community. These are discussed in the final chapter, which explores the question whether there are lessons to be learned and considers the possibilities for public action and the elimination of hunger in today's liberal welfare states.

2 Australia: Lucky Country/ Hungry Silence

John Wilson

We were a poor family and frequently went for several days at a time with little or nothing to eat. Consequently hunger is one of the most enduring memories of my childhood. If we were lucky, our daily diet would consist of a bowl of porridge in the morning before school, one slice of bread with dripping or golden syrup for our school lunch, and occasionally damper for tea. We ate whatever we could find – kangaroos, wallabies, snakes run down by passing cars, snakes killed in the yard, and fruit and berries from the trees. Very few Aboriginal children could ever afford to bring a lunch to school and when the bell began to ring for the beginning of afternoon class and the end of lunch time, we would gather around the rubbish bins and hastily pick out any crusts or a half-eaten apple or other leftovers. (Wilson, 1989, p. 16)

INTRODUCTION

Whilst the hunger of Aboriginal Australians, such as that recalled above, continues to be both a national and international scandal, hunger experienced by many other Australians is best described as hidden or silent hunger, not readily acknowledged publicly.

Thirty years ago, Horne (1964, p. 220) coined the phrase 'Lucky Country' to describe Australia as a 'nation more concerned with styles of life than with achievement' and where the principal goal was that 'everyone has the right to a good time'. And still today, most Australians experience standards of living well in advance of those of nearly all other nations, and we are currently ranked seventh in the world on the United Nations Human Development Index (1994) as reported in the Human Development Report of the United Nations Human Development Programme. With a century of uninterrupted liberal democracy, plentiful natural resources, relatively little pollution, extremely low population density, one of the best health-care systems in the world, high levels of home ownership and a culture which values the pursuit of leisure above nearly all else, most Australians can be regarded, relatively speaking, as prosperous, healthy and free.

Yet despite the claims by some commentators and academics such as Travers and Richardson (1993, p. v) that most Australians are 'living decently' and that 'material affluence [is] at an all-time high', Australia has a hungry underbelly. Many Australians are poor and many of the poor are hungry, and the available evidence suggests that hunger is on the increase in the Lucky Country.

This chapter begins with a historical overview of hunger in Australia since colonization including an overview of the dimensions and extent of hunger in Australia today. Drawing upon the research literature and interviews with key informants, several examples of programme responses to the problem of hunger are described. Finally, these programmes (which are illustrative rather than representative) are discussed in the context of current federal government policy settings which, directly and indirectly, bear upon the problem of hunger in Australia.

The main argument presented is that whilst the concept of hunger *per se* is politically useful in drawing attention to the daily subjective experience and nutritional needs of many disadvantaged Australians, it has limited value alone for progressives or activists who wish to focus on political action for structural change and social justice.

HUNGER IN AUSTRALIA: A HISTORICAL OVERVIEW[1]

Whilst receiving scant attention from historians, hunger has been a persistent theme in Australia since European colonization began in 1788.

In the beginning, hunger was closely related to the tyranny of distance from Europe. The motives behind colonization were complex, but essentially this new outpost was seen as a source of raw materials for Britain (flax for rope and linen; timber for shipbuilding) and a depository for convicts from Britain's overcrowded prisons. In addition, following the American War of Independence in 1776 it was no longer possible to send convicts to North America. The immediate concern of those (mainly convicts and soldiers) who arrived on the First Fleet in Botany Bay (now Sydney) was to grow enough food to survive and 'all eyes turned to the earth, watching for the first shoots of wheat' (Blainey, 1966, p. 41). Due to poor soil and the deterioration of seed on the voyage out, the first attempts to grow wheat, fruit and vegetables

were unsuccessful, and many men and women fell sick from scurvy.
From the beginning, everyone was allocated a weekly ration of food,
which by 1790 had been halved to a diet of slow starvation. Ships were
sent to Cape Town and China to purchase provisions, without which
the colony would not have survived. Even then according to Blainey
(*ibid.*, p. 45) 'many convicts were no longer strong enough to hoe the
soil'. Thanks to the arrival in 1791 of the Second Fleet and subsequent
supply ships, this early experience of famine was never repeated,
although meagre rations were the common experience for the next
quarter-century.

The search for pastures and arable land was the driving force behind
the earliest exploration of the interior. The first colony, located on relatively poor soil in a narrow strip of land between the sea and the Blue
Mountains immediately west of Sydney, could not possibly support the
increasing population and it became 'a matter of necessity to penetrate
beyond the mountains' (Scott, 1966, p. 77), a task achieved in 1813.

By this time it was known that Australia was an island continent, but
widely believed that the interior contained a vast inland sea, and exploration with a view to settlement of the interior was motivated, especially by a desire for water following the severe drought of 1825–8.
Explorers experienced severe hunger and some died of starvation as
they found it difficult to harvest water or food from the land. Indeed,
as Reynolds (1990) has shown, many more might have died from starvation were it not for the practical assistance of indigenous people
who possessed the necessary knowledge and skills to live from the
land.

It was of course the Aborigines themselves who most experienced
hunger in this period. Dispersed from their traditional lands and deci-
mated by disease and massacre, food sources and supplies rapidly diminished, and thousands died from starvation. Others were forced
ultimately to survive on charitable rations, which were both meagre
and disease-promoting; the heritage of sugar, flour, tea, tobacco and alcohol being their high rates of diabetes, hypertension, obesity and heart
disease today.

Peel and Stirling's experiment in the 1830s to establish a new colony
without convict labour in the far south-west corner of the continent
was a failure. This settlement, some 3500 kilometres from Botany
Bay, clung to the edges of a land area (now Western Australia) four and
a half times as big as France – a country of large forests and bush
land and of immense waterless plains. Hunger was rife in what was
described as 'the scarecrow of civilisation' (Scott, 1966, p. 138), and

in 1855 Western Australia was forced to begin accepting convicts at the very time that transportation was ending in the other Australian colonies.

The discovery of gold in the 1850s brought a huge influx of immigrants and free settlers to the goldfields in Victoria and New South Wales and then in the 1860s to those in Queensland. The 'Gold Rush' diversified the economy, greatly strengthened the middle class and had a profound influence on the development of the 'mythopoetic' Australian – egalitarian, anti-authoritarian, racist and nationalistic (McQueen, 1970, p. 146). On the goldfields most miners did not succeed. Few made their fortunes whilst many were impoverished, and those who did best were the food producers and merchants who supplied the vast of army of 'diggers'. Self-government was achieved in Victoria, New South Wales and Queensland by 1859 and with the rapid increase in population demands for new land for small-scale farming became pressing. Selection Acts in the eastern colonies opened up new tracts of land for selectors with very different class consciousness, resources, manners and aspirations from those of the squattocracy – the large wealthy landowners who had hitherto controlled access to the land and the legislative processes prior to the 1850s. Selectors, who were drawn from the urban middle class, could take up a small block at a nominal price and there were incentives offered for improvements made. Many selectors, however, lived in appalling squalor, due to the hostility of squatters, the vagaries of climate and price, lack of capital or equipment, ignorance and isolation from markets (Clark, 1963, p. 135).

Many of the bigger landowners, with large flocks of sheep or droves of cattle, also experienced harsh deprivations as they battled to seek out a living establishing introduced species across foreign and treacherous landscapes. The wealth of the huge pastoral industry which developed in the north and northwest of Australia in the latter part of the nineteenth and early twentieth centuries could not have been built without the largely forced labour of Aborigines, who worked on the sheep and cattle properties for meagre rations.

Many who originally took up selections were forced by poverty and drought to return to the towns and cities for waged work or to work as drovers (horsemen who took cattle to market or from one grazing area to another) or as hired hands for large landowners. Poverty and hunger were a common experience for these men and their families. Henry Lawson, Australia's best known poet, wrote in Queen Victoria's Jubilee year of 1887 of the steady tramp of thousands in the cities whose 'hands clutched in vain for bread' (Clark, 1978, p. 31) and described the condition of settler farmers thus:

> Land where gaunt and haggard women live alone and work like men.
> Till their husbands, gone a droving, will return to them again;
> Homes of men! if homes had ever such a God-forgotten place,
> Where the wild selectors children fly before a strangers face,
> Home of tragedy applauded by the dingoes dismal yell...
>
> *(ibid.*, p. 50)

Many men were forced to take to the road as 'swaggies', carrying their possessions as they roamed from town to town seeking work and charity.

Waltzing Matilda, Australia's informal national anthem and best loved song, commemorates the swagmen and the practice of sheep stealing to assuage hunger, which had grown into a commonplace outback strategy in nineteenth-century Australia. A severe depression, prompted by the collapse of international financial markets, struck Australia in 1890. Clark (1963, p. 159) reports that in Sydney on Sunday, 19 November 1893, a large procession of unemployed was led by someone carrying a cross upon which was nailed the effigy of a downtrodden man clad in rags and on his back the words 'Murdered by the rich!'

In Australia, the 1890s were characterized by intense cultural and political activity. They witnessed the birth of the Australian Labour Party and the emergence of a genuine working-class consciousness and a nationalism concerned to protect Australian industry and exclude non-British people and especially Asians from Australia. There was a growing desire on the part of both capitalists and workers to develop a national economy that would ensure that the depression experience of the early 1890s would never be repeated. All of these factors combined to produce what Gollan (1960, p. 112) terms a 'radical nationalism', which culminated in the federation of the colonies and the establishment of the Commonwealth of Australia in January 1901.

The Australian welfare state thus emerged from a trade-off between capitalists and workers. Workers (largely male) benefited from strong unions and a minimum wage. Capitalists were guaranteed protection from cheap labour and imports. The Immigration Restriction Act of 1901, enshrining the White 'Australian Policy', was one of the first pieces of legislation enacted by the new Federal Parliament. The concept of a basic or minimum family wage, regarded as sufficient to support a working man, his spouse and three children, evolved from the Commonwealth Arbitration and Conciliation Act of 1904, and was enshrined in the Harvester Judgment of 1907, which laid the basis for Australia's unique system of wage arbitration and a minimum (male) wage. This policy of 'New Protection' (Gollan, 1960, p. 165), the aim of which was both to protect industries and to ensure that the workers benefited from the growth of those industries, remained the foundation stone upon which the Australian welfare state was built, and its key organizing principle until the deregulation of the labour market under Labour governments in the 1980s. This early optimism that accompanied the building of a new nation was shattered, however, by the national experience of World War I. Sixty thousand Australians died. Of the 330 000 Australians who fought in World War I, two-thirds were killed or wounded, and the economic burdens of interest due on war debts and repatriation costs were severe.

Through the 1920s, Australia was governed by a conservative coalition of liberals and the newly formed Country Party, which represented the interests of the primary industry sector. Protection policies in this sector were further strengthened, a factor which added considerably to Australia's economic vulnerability and rapid decline when the Great Depression struck in 1929. Ex-servicemen were taking up blocks of land allotted to them by the Soldier Settlement Schemes of the Commonwealth and state governments. Their experiences, for the most part, were miserable and degrading, as the following case example, quoted in Clark (1987, pp. 179–80), illustrates:

> In the middle of the summer of 1920 one soldier settler arrived [at his block] to find that all the stuff he had read in the literature about being supplied with a tent and stretcher on arrival was hot air. He and his wife and two children spent the night under the shelter of a big tree. For weeks he and his family had to depend on the hospitality of other ex-diggers for shelter... many diggers who had gone on the land were... on the borders of starvation.

The Great Depression of 1929–33 brought near-starvation to a large proportion of the population. Unemployment exceeded 30 per cent, and real wages fell. 'Susso', or sustenance payments made in cash or kind by governments, was the most common form of relief, undermining dignity and morale. The Secretary of the Melbourne Charity Organization described the situation thus: 'Government sustenance, relief works and voluntary charity are powerless to stem the tide of hardship, eviction and hopelessness which is sweeping over Melbourne. The habit of steady work is becoming dangerously undermined in countless people' (Anderson, 1972, p. 20).

Old army uniforms were taken out of storage and dyed black for those on 'susso'. Ironically, returned servicemen from World War I were put to work cleaning or restoring memorials earlier erected to their courage. George Johnston's (1967, p. 159) *My Brother Jack* describes graphically the misery of these years and has bequeathed for future generations lasting images of a depression for which Australia was unprepared and which filled the nation with 'shabby figures shambling along suburban streets'.

Renewed optimism following World War II was accompanied by social and economic reconstruction, mass immigration, the development of the modern welfare state and full employment. Australia entered a period later termed 'the long boom', and the conventional wisdom until the late 1960s was that poverty no longer existed. The most intense and systematic study of poverty in Australia was conducted by the Henderson Commission of Inquiry into Poverty 1972–5, from which emerged the Henderson Poverty Line (HPL) a calculation of the minimum income required by families to cover basic living costs and to have an austere living standard. Despite its numerous methodological and ideological limitations, the HPL remains Australia's only (quasi-official) measurement of poverty and is updated quarterly by the National Institute of Economic and Industry Research.

POVERTY AND HUNGER IN CONTEMPORARY AUSTRALIA

There is some evidence that absolute poverty exists for some members of particular disadvantaged groups in Australia. Aboriginal infants are three times more likely to die in infancy than non-Aboriginal infants. They have a lighter birth weight on average and rapidly fall further behind average developmental milestones after the first six months of life. Average life expectancy at birth is nearly 20 years less. Mortality from preventable infections and parasitic diseases is 12 times that for the population as a whole (Thomson, 1991). A recent paediatric study in the Northern Territory suggests that up to 20 per cent of Aboriginal children under 2 in that Territory are malnourished (The Bulletin, 17 April 1995, p. 7). Hunger was an often-mentioned experience of homeless young people in evidence presented to the 1989 Burdekin Inquiry into Homeless Children and Young People. They often reported sleeping on the streets with nothing to eat for days at a time (Human Rights and Equal Opportunity Commission, 1989, p. 235).

Poverty in Australia is more usually, however, a relative phenomenon. Most Australians in poverty are in no immediate danger of starvation. The amount, quality and range of food they can afford, however, will often fall well below that which average Australian families enjoy.

Being Aboriginal, being unemployed or living in a sole-parent family are key factors associated with poverty. In addition, since 1976 there has been an increasing proportion of jobs which are low-paid, casual and which attract relatively little occupational welfare, and there has been a fall in real earnings for low-paid workers since 1985. Amongst non-Aborigines, sole-parent families (overwhelmingly headed by women) have the highest incidence of poverty in Australia. In 1990, over 40 per cent of these families lived below the poverty line. At the beginning of 1994, a sole-parent welfare recipient with three children had a weekly income A$36 below the HPL (Brotherhood of St Laurence, 1994a, pp. 10–11).

Over the past 15 years the material circumstances of Australian families have become more unequal and there has been a polarization of family incomes (Harding, 1993). Well-off families have become better-off and there are a large number of families on very low incomes. There has been a growing division between, on the one hand, the many families who have more than one member highly skilled and in secure well-paid work, and on the other, those families where all or most members have less education and few recognized skills, and where unemployment is either prolonged or any job obtained is insecure, short-term and poorly paid (McClelland, 1993; Probert, 1993).

Raskall (1992, p. 9) considers that, in terms of income, Australia is one of the most unequal societies in the world. He states that in an 18-nation comparison of income, where the share of the top 20 per cent in the society was compared with that of the bottom 20 per cent, Australia was considered the least equal society. The bottom 50 per cent of Australian society has less than 10 per cent of the nation's wealth with approximately 80 per cent of income units receiving less than average weekly earnings (Harris, 1989, p. 27).

At the start of the 1990–2 recession, an estimated one in eight Australian households were living on incomes on or below the poverty line. Yet during the 1990–2 recession, the income of the lowest 50 per cent of households fell by 2.6 per cent, while the income share of the top 50 per cent of households increased by the same amount.

Saunders and Matheson (1992, pp. 5–6) consider that these factors have worked together to produce what has been called a 'new poor', mainly consisting of working-age families without jobs, many of whom are caring for children. They comment that both economic problems and family breakdown have combined to expose the greatest proportion of the community to poverty since the Great Depression.

The Brotherhood of St Laurence, a large non-government welfare organization (NGWO) in Melbourne has been undertaking research about poverty in Australia since the 1940s. Under their auspice, Trethewey (1989) published a study of families with children living on low incomes in the 1980s. In the foreword to the study, titled *Aussie Battlers*, the then Executive Director of the Brotherhood wrote:

> The families who are the subject of this book do not fit the traditional stereotypes of irresponsibility that the poor are supposed to manifest. Their diaries reveal a common lifestyle that revolves around daily survival. It is a lifestyle of collecting food vouchers and parcels, going to material aid centres for clothing, receiving Christmas hampers and gifts of money and hand-me-down clothes from family and friends. It is a lifestyle of being forced to move from one house to the next, threatened with eviction, going without food to pay the rent, or having to beg for help. (Trethewey, 1989)

Currently, the Brotherhood's Life Chances Study is gathering longitudinal data on 161 children born in inner Melbourne in 1990, 35 per cent of whom are living in low-income families. These families report various costs for their children that they find difficult to meet, in particular clothing, food, medications and child care. Cost of food and having to miss meals were issues for a significant number of these families (Taylor and McClelland, 1994, pp. 5–6). Studies of low-income families indicate that towards the end of the fortnightly (two-week) social security benefit period, expenditure on food declines rapidly (Trethewey, 1989; Crotty, Rattishauser and Cahill, 1992; McDonald and Brownlee, 1992). Before the introduction of the Victoria Food Bank in 1992, relief agencies in that state were spending over 10 million dollars annually on food relief (Kaye, 1991).

Frederick (1994, pp. 36–45) has reviewed the recent research into the effects of poverty on people in Australia which shows that the poor have very little in the way of assets, savings or material possessions and lack adequate resources for everyday living, including food. Food was a basic necessity found lacking in a number of studies, with findings showing that food was a discretionary item in respondents' budgets; after paying bills there was often not enough to buy food;

respondents cut back on food, clothing and basic necessities. A significant finding among these studies was the widespread need for emergency relief. Many families required emergency relief; used emergency relief as an income supplement, mainly for food; and depended on emergency relief to meet basic needs for food and clothing.

All of the above indicates that in Australia there are significant numbers of low-income families who experience subsistence living standards and face an ongoing battle to make ends meet.

THE AUSTRALIAN WELFARE STATE

The federal system that came into being in Australia on 1 January 1901 was preceded by over 40 years of self-government in five of the six colonies, all of which had developed strong individual traditions of government. Australia has developed a system of government characterized by state autonomy, bicameralism and entrenched constitutions. The policy environment has been shaped by tensions between the state governments and the Commonwealth government – tensions generated by constitutional limits on Commonwealth policy initiatives and at the same time increasing Commonwealth financial control (Lester, 1994, p. 11).

The Australian welfare state is often said to be particularly distinctive in its relationship to the economy. An employment-based approach to welfare has been reflected in the pursuit of full employment, the determination of wages through a centralized arbitration system, supplemented by a social safety net for these falling outside the workforce (Castles, 1985). Australia has developed a residual, 'safety net' welfare state. The federal government is responsible for income security (pensions and benefits, etc.) and fiscal welfare, whilst the states deliver health, education and welfare services, which for the most part are federally funded. Pensions and benefits are increasingly selective and targeted and have developed historically in a piecemeal and incremental fashion as reactive devices to ameliorate the most obvious aspects of disadvantage.

The Federal Department of Social Security, whose charter is to deliver social security benefits 'with fairness, courtesy and efficiency', administers a range of income support programmes (Department of Social Security, 1992). Income-support levels take into account rental, telephone and education expenses, but there is no specific consideration of food costs.

Australia is also characterized by a mixed economy of welfare and NGWOs, or the charitable sector, which plays a crucial and central role in addition to governments in the delivery of social welfare. This sector pre-dates any form of government intervention and has its roots in philanthropic, humanitarian and religious convictions. The current Industry Commission Inquiry into Charitable Organizations in Australia, established in 1993 to overview the sector and recommend future funding and accountability parameters, has attempted to quantify key characteristics of the sector. There are over 11 000 NGWOs in Australia, with a total annual expenditure in excess of $4.4 billion, of which governments fund about 60 per cent. The sector employs about 100 000 people, mostly women who work part-time. It is estimated that 1.3 million Australians contribute their time and skills as volunteers, estimated at some 95 million hours of voluntary time per annum, or equivalent to 50 000 persons working a 40-hour week. In addition, Australians contribute in excess of $500 million per annum by way of donations to the sector (Industry Commission, 1994, pp. 4–7). NGWOs are represented in the political area by a large number of peak councils (representative lobby groups), many funded by governments.

Federal Health Strategy

At the federal level, the issue of hunger is subsumed within the broad parameters of health policy. In 1990 the federal government commissioned a major strategic review of health – the National Health Strategy. The health portfolio is highly concentrated on medical and hospital services; questions of health promotion and illness prevention, through such strategies as appropriate nutrition policies, are well down the list of funding priorities. Australia has not yet developed a comprehensive nutrition monitoring and surveillance system and is one of the few developed countries not to have done so. However, towards the end of 1992, the federal government announced the National Food and Nutrition Policy, with the equitable improvement of nutritional status as its goal. The policy is aimed at the needs of population subgroups at risk of nutrition-related disadvantage and includes a commitment to equitable availability of appropriate foods (with particular reference to remote locations), to improved affordability of nutritious foods, and to equitable access to education and information about food and about nutrition. Priority objective 3 of the policy and strategies for implementation are set out in Chart 2.1.

Chart 2.1 National Food and Nutrition Policy: Community-based Initiatives

---

Objective 3: Support for community-based initiatives to improve the diet of people with special needs.

Strategies:

(a) Support will be provided for research and development projects on barriers to the availability, accessibility and cost of nutritious food for communities which have either socio-economic and/or geographic disadvantage with a view to action to overcome these barriers. The needs of lower socio-economic groups and older people need to be particularly considered.

(b) In line with recommendations contained in the report from the National Conference on Aboriginal Nutrition in Remote and Rural Communities (1991), models for community-based food and nutrition programmes for Aboriginal and Torres Strait Islander people will be developed, and appropriate curriculum material will be made available for nutrition components in Aboriginal health worker (and other professional) education, training and employment programmes.

(c) Support appropriate and ongoing training for nutrition advisers for special needs groups.

Whilst not questioning the necessity for and importance of statistical benchmarks of nutrition, their current value would appear to be somewhat limited for several reasons. First, as already pointed out, there is to date a dearth of research related to the nutritional intake of people with special needs; secondly, the subjective and individual experience of hunger and the consequences of this cannot be captured by such benchmarks; and thirdly, there is official denial of the need to address hunger and undernutrition as a genuine priority within Australia, with the policy and programme emphases firmly and almost exclusively directed at health problems associated with overconsumption.

For example Australia's Health 1994, the health report of the Australian Institute of Health and Welfare, states (p. 46):

Nutrition is an important contributor to health, and the evidence linking diet with the chronic, preventable, non-communicable diseases is sufficiently strong for public health initiatives to include improved nutrition as a major component. These diseases and their risk factors arise from overconsumption. Although there are less than optimum intakes of some nutrients in some groups, under nutrition is uncommon in Australia.

Some benchmark evidence does exist that some Australians experience dietary deficits. Analysis of Australian household food expenditure

data suggests that a substantial proportion of the population (in the order of 10 per cent) is severely restricted in its capacity to make healthy
food choices and to achieve a healthy lifestyle. Low-income households
can neither gain optimal nutritional status nor match the nutritional
status of the 'better off' (Lester, 1994, p. 15). As discussed elsewhere in
this chapter, persistent mild to moderate levels of undernutrition have
been documented in some groups of Aboriginal children and homeless
youth.

THE EXPERIENCE OF HUNGER

As indicated earlier, however, there is a great deal of both quantitative
and qualitative data to suggest that the *experience of hunger* (as distinct
from statistical measures of undernutrition) is widespread and persistent among a large number of Australians. Such evidence, which is illustrative, includes the provision of emergency relief, responses to
hunger in a regional city, the impact of natural disasters, child hunger
in remote Aboriginal communities and the rise of food banks. It is to
that evidence that we now turn.

Emergency Relief Programmes

Emergency relief is the provision of assistance to people in need which
is in addition to the provision of normal, front-line benefits and pensions. There are two types of assistance: first, financial and/or material
aid to address an immediate need, such as the provision of food vou-
chers, food parcels, clothing, furniture, transport and accommodation
or cash; and secondly, 'the provision of a service which assists people
with basic advice and advocacy and links them with specialist community services to address the cause of these needs' (ACOSS, 1993, p. 1).
Emergency relief was originally regarded as temporary or one-off help
in a financial crisis. However, research indicates that on-going assistance is increasingly being provided to people experiencing recurring
financial crises (McCaughey, 1992, p. 50). It is estimated that 85 per
cent of the emergency relief distributors are voluntary organizations
(ACOSS, 1993, p. 7), including a large number of very small rural and
localized groups and community-based agencies, such as neighbourhood centres and Citizen's Advice Bureaux.

   The main source of funds for emergency relief are donations and
fundraising by church and charitable groups, the federal government,

through the Department of Human Services and Health Emergency Relief Programme, some state governments, court funds and local government grants. Some limited data have been collected on emergency relief between 1978 and 1990. The most recent national survey was conducted in 1990 and revealed that approximately 90 per cent of people requesting emergency relief obtained their income from Department of Social Security allowances or pensions. Of these people, the largest groups were the unemployed, sole-parent beneficiaries and people receiving sickness/disability payments (ACOSS, 1993, p. 9). As Frederick (1994, pp. 42–5) in his extensive review of the literature shows, since the onset of the recession in the early 1990s the demand for emergency relief has risen substantially. In December 1992 the Salvation Army's communications director, Mr John Dalziel, stated that the Christmas of that year was easily the worst in 50 years. He stated that the Salvation Army's 50 distribution points across Australia were giving out more than double the number of food packages required in the previous year. In that same month, the Prahran City Parish Mission in Victoria reported an increased demand for aid of 250 per cent since the beginning of the recession. This agency expressed concern regarding such issues as mothers presenting with health problems as a result of denying themselves food so that their children had enough to eat, and of some people shoplifting in order to survive (*Emergency Relief News Victoria*, 1992, p. 4). In May 1993 a spokesperson for the Society of St Vincent de Paul stated that the demand for assistance so far that year had overtaken the demand recorded in 1992, which had in turn seen a 40 per cent increase over 1991 (Milburn, 1993).

The total federal government emergency relief allocation has increased over the period 1991–4. Importantly, the federal government has decided that future budget allocations for emergency relief will be related to the forecast level of unemployment for that year. This action on the part of the federal government clearly recognizes the structural linkage between the numbers of people unemployed, the numbers of sole-parent pensioners and emergency relief. Nevertheless, in terms of other federal social services outlays, emergency relief remains an extremely small and marginalized budget item, as reflected in the small staff complement allocated to administer it, the absence of any legislative base, its insecure and frequently changing location within the federal bureaucracy and the inadequate allocations provided for training, support and administration at the agency level. Training and support are urgently required since emergency relief distribution is frequently unpleasant, difficult and dangerous work, whilst for recipients, it is often charged with some of the worst stigmatizing aspects of the charity model, which emphasizes merit, gratitude, rationing and control. Progressive NGWOs are changing their approach to emergency relief provision, however, as the following example illustrates.

Lifeline Brisbane is part of a network of nationally accredited semi-autonomous Lifeline Centres which provide 24-hour crisis telephone counselling as their core service. Lifeline Brisbane is largely self-funding and receives approximately 15 per cent of its income from government grants and subsidies.

Brisbane is located in the southern corner of the State of Queensland, a region perceived to offer relatively attractive economic prospects for young families and single people seeking secure employment, and relatively attractive lifestyle prospects for retirees. The region has been identified as the sixth fastest growing large urban area in the developed world. There is in consequence a significant and highly segmented population drift from other states, and a high proportion of newcomers are either unemployed or on low incomes. These demographic trends are written over a political landscape which for many years was highly conservative and isolationist. Despite the election of a 'progressive' state Labour government since 1989 on a platform of political and social reform, 1993 Commonwealth Grants Commission figures show that Queensland still has a per capita expenditure on social and community services just over half that of the national average, and well below that of any other state (QCOSS, 1994, pp. 16–17, 32). Levels of disadvantage remain high. It is estimated that 14.4 per cent of all Queensland income units, as measured against HPL, are living in poverty (Queensland Poverty Research Project, 1994, p. 8). The official unemployment rate is 9 per cent.

In the 1993–4 financial year, Lifeline Brisbane distributed $270 000 (13 per cent of overall expenditure) in financial aid and food. Reimbursement to Lifeline in the form of Emergency Relief Grants for the same period totalled $105 000 (Lifeline Brisbane, 1994, p. 14). Lifeline Brisbane is a large, complex, non-government organization with a mission 'to respond to the needs of people in crisis with acceptance, love and compassion. . . . Lifeline respects individual dignity, builds community, practices social justice and creates opportunities for change' (*ibid.*, p. 2). This mission statement reflects new directions and emphases for the organization, which are well illustrated by changes to emergency relief and food aid as administered by the Lifeline Community Services Unit. Brian Procopis, a senior welfare worker in that Unit, commented on these changes:

Ten years ago, we began to look at the demographics of people seeking emergency relief from Lifeline. We found many people came from the same local community. So we went out there, walked the streets, located the natural leaders and called a public meeting. Out of that initiative came a local Neighbourhood Centre and food co-operative. After a few years, when we had assisted this group to become autonomous and self-funding, Lifeline withdrew. We learnt a lot from that experience and now there's no turning back from a developmental approach to assisting people in poverty.

We now operate an extensive Creative Living Skills Programme (CLASP) which, in addition to providing material aid, trains volunteer 'befrienders' to visit those who approach us regularly for emergency relief in their own communities, to assist them in locating and linking with local, community-based resources. If appropriate local services don't exist, then we encourage people to act together at the local level to agitate for the services and resources they need. We see ourselves nowadays much more as one service amongst many. As a bigger, well-established and relatively well-resourced organization, we see our role as promoting and clarifying the restlessness for change that exists in disadvantaged communities. Our CLASP programme was recently extended to assist Spanish-speaking immigrant families in Brisbane. In conjunction with the Commonwealth Department of Immigration and Ethnic Affairs, we are training Spanish-speaking community workers to provide personal support and assist people to identify service gaps, and advocate with them for appropriate new services. (oral communication)

Hunger in a Regional City: NGWOs Respond

Townsville is a regional city of approximately 120 000 people located on the coast in northern Queensland. The following are two programme examples of how local NGWOs are responding to hunger in that city.

SKIDS
Homelessness describes a lifestyle which includes transiency and insecurity of shelter. It signifies a state of detachment from family and vulnerability to dangers, including physical and sexual abuse. A national inquiry into homeless youth reported in 1989 that there were between 25 000 and 70 000 homeless youth in Australia (Human Rights and Equal Opportunity Commission, 1989, p. 69). Although the report

documented hunger and malnutrition amongst some homeless youth, this and subsequent reports and studies all emphasize the importance of adopting a holistic and preventative approach to service delivery. The reasons why young people are homeless are complex and multifaceted, as are the sets of problems that they experience as a result. SKIDS (an acronym for Street Kids) is a service which aims to reach out to those youth who are homeless, in need of emotional/physical support, suffering from addiction of any kind, at risk of entering crime or prostitution, and who are disadvantaged in any way. A non-sectarian organization, it is operated by a community-based management committee and is self-funded. Staffed largely by volunteers, SKIDS operates a night-time outreach van and foot patrols. Assistance includes on-the-spot hot drinks and sandwiches, emotional support, information and referral. The service is used by several different groups of young people, as the coordinator and youth worker, John Livingston, explained:

We aim to have a high profile on the street by regular van and foot patrols, and by creating an awareness that we exist among young people and in the local network of welfare services. There are at least three groups of young people that we see. There are young people who have a home that they return to at night and who like to congregate on the streets and 'hang-out' together. They often end up in some kind of trouble. Then there are the house-hopping homeless kids who are moving around Townsville, maybe from one relative or friend's house to another. Basically, they do have somewhere to go but their families are in crisis. Then there are the real homeless kids. They are completely different and have their own sub-culture. Mostly they remain hidden away. They don't want to be seen because they are vulnerable. If they commit an offence, it's usually to survive and they don't boast about these things. Really, they are the most vulnerable group in our community as far as sexual or physical abuse or malnutrition goes. They're not violent. They sleep during the day in safe public places to avoid being assaulted and they hide away at night. They either don't know about, or can't access for themselves benefits such as the Youth Homeless Allowance. They are always hungry, and in very poor health. We use food as an icebreaker – to win some trust so that we can be a support or backstop if they want that. The only research done in Townsville on the possible numbers of these kids was some years ago and the estimate was 500. There are at least that many now. It's difficult to get a true estimate, because many of them are transient and because they keep themselves hidden away. (oral communication)

Townsville Community Emergency Support Centre
The Townsville Community Emergency Support Centre is an organization that provides day shelter for disadvantaged people in a non-regimented environment where opportunities for participation in communal activity and decision-making exist. Provision of a light breakfast and midday meal, recreation facilities, shower and clothes washing facilities, accommodation advice, financial counselling, emergency relief, advocacy and referral, and limited employment opportunities are all available to service users without charge.

One of the programmes initiated by the Centre is the Work Co-op. By advertising for lawnmowing and other odd jobs, the Centre provides paid work for those who are unemployed. The Centre also has a contract to assemble roofing screws for a local firm, and this enables those that are not fit enough for outdoor work to obtain some employment. As well as helping people financially, the Co-op aims to restore self-confidence to the long-term unemployed. It teaches new skills to people, thus enabling them to have the chance to gain employment in the mainstream workforce. The Work Co-op purchases and owns its equipment and contributes to the cost of the Centre's two vehicles.

Despite not receiving any real increase in funding for the past four years, the Centre has experienced a substantial increase in demand. Meals served per day have risen from 100 to 130 during that period, for example, and Maureen Hurst, the Centre Coordinator for the past 13 years, has noticed a dramatic change in the characteristics of service users over that time:

> When we began our service-users were mainly Aborigines. Now they are predominantly non-Aboriginal, much younger, and long-term unemployed. We didn't see this group ten years ago. High levels of unemployment have made a big difference to our Centre. Most of our service users are now between 20 and 35 years old and we are seeing many more skilled or semi-skilled people, including people with tertiary level education and tradesmen. Predominantly males, although we are seeing a lot more young single mothers now. Income levels for those on pensions and benefits are way below the poverty line and many people simply run out of money a couple of days before their benefit is due. So they come to us saying that they just need groceries for themselves and the children for two or three

days. They don't just grab at the food here. They only take what they need.

As well as unemployment, de-institutionalization has had a big impact on our Centre. We see many young people with severe psychiatric difficulties who are not being assisted by the mental health services.

Many pressures face the six Centre staff, as Maureen explains:

Because of our increased numbers, our service is less personal and intimate than it used to be. We have more angry people now – angry because they are unemployed and poor, or angry because of psychiatric problems. Many of this latter group are completely isolated and alone in the community, without stable accommodation and very vulnerable to exploitation. We try and provide an environment which is hassle-free, non-intrusive and gives people chances to participate. We work in a non-authoritarian way and try to gain people's trust. We only have two rules – no alcohol or drugs on or near the premises, and no fighting.

Our staff are highly skilled and work under a lot of stress, yet we have no award (nationally determined pay rate) and are paid less than workers in comparable positions in most other states.

Finally, Maureen discusses the Centre's relationships with state and federal governments, which between them largely fund the Centre's programmes:

We are supposedly a first world country and I think that food and shelter should be a right, not a privilege. On any one night in Townsville there are at least 50 people sleeping out because they have nowhere to go. A lot of our service users are unemployable. There is no 'quick-fix' for these people. It's a long slow process, but governments want instant results. The pressure is on us to show that we are being efficient and effective. That's OK but throughput statistics don't really tell the true story in a Centre like this. We've just been working hard with one man recently released from prison. He was very angry to begin with, with a real chip on his shoulder. We've learnt to deal with him so that now he's a regular here and he's stopped making a nuisance of himself around the streets. That's a real success for us but you can't quantify it.

The government says our emergency relief funding is not an income subsidy, but it is! Because pensions and benefits are so low many people just don't have enough income to pay the bills and feed themselves. Especially those on unemployment benefits, because they miss out on any fringe benefits such as transport concessions. We have been lobbying hard with other agencies for better wages and conditions for our staff, increased levels of funding, and some additional support services for the many people with psychiatric difficulties whom we now service as well.

All the time we are asked to absorb costs that are hidden but very real to us. For example, half our time is spent on administering our emergency relief fund yet we get less than $5000 per annum in administration costs. We made a submission to the Industry Commission about wages and conditions. We have to find the time to do that and if we want to send someone down to Brisbane to the public hearings (1400 km south), we have to find the money for that. Governments are always looking to non-government welfare agencies to sponsor and provide new programmes or services, but non-government agencies are also expected to absorb the administrative costs of this into existing budgets. (oral communication)

Flood, Drought and Hunger in a Rural Community

Australia has a land area of about 7.7 million square kilometres and in 1991 had a population of 17.3 million. Settlement away from the southeast coast is sparse. The rural population (about 17 per cent of the total, or three million people) is scattered over 7 million square kilometres whilst 9 million Australians (53 per cent of the population) live in Sydney, Melbourne, Brisbane and Adelaide (Lester, 1994, p. 6). Industrial and commercial activity is concentrated in these densely populated coastal areas. Floods, droughts and bushfires are persistent features of Australian rural life and impact significantly on the well-being of rural families, as the following example illustrates.

Nathalia, a rural town of 1500 people, is located in central northern Victoria, in the heart of Australia's most densely irrigated region. Often referred to as 'the fruit bowl of Australia', the Goulburn Valley region produces a large volume and variety of stone fruits that are distributed Australia-wide. There is also a substantial dairy and crop-growing industry. The region suffered a devastating flood in late 1993, followed by a year of drought.

The Nathalia District Community Association was formed by a group of concerned Nathalia citizens in 1988, to consider the special needs of disadvantaged, elderly and isolated persons in the district, which is 123 000 square hectares and has a population of 3500. The association employs a part-time community development officer, Sue Logie, who spoke about the economic and social hardships experienced by local rural people as a result of natural disaster and inadequate policy responses:

> The floods, which came in October 1993, are now regarded as Australia's fourth largest national disaster in the past 50 years. The floods arrived at the worst possible moment, when the crops were near ripe and ready to strip. The timing of the flood had an enormous impact on the amount of damage, loss of production and income experienced by farmers. In October, crops had not been harvested, dairy cows were in peak production and hay was ready for baling. Then the drought which followed put enormous pressure on local resources. This last Christmas we distributed 35 family food parcels, 20 more than the Christmas before. The men are too embarrassed to come for help, so it's always the women, and usually they come to us for assistance way too late and seriously understate the help they need. It's all to do with pride – and people often express this pride by claiming that there is always 'so-and-so' next door or down the road that's worse off than me! We provide food vouchers and food parcels, and financial assistance. We work in closely with the St Vincent de Paul Society, Red Cross, Rotary and the Lion's Club. The community spirit is very strong and between us we cover all of those families that we know need on-going assistance. The St Vincent de Paul volunteers take food parcels out to certain homes, so that people can avoid the stigma and embarrassment attached to receiving charity in a small community where this assistance is often very visible and personalized. So we do visit discreetly some families that need a lot of support. Over 200 homes received damage in the floods, yet only 30 received emergency or re-establishment grants from the state. And the Victoria Rural Finance Corporation offered loans which were severely means tested, and very difficult to access. Low-cost loans are no use to people who have lost everything and are already in debt. (oral communication)

Don Farrell, outgoing president of the local branch of St Vincent de Paul Society, added:

> At least the floods have taught the various agencies about the need to work co-operatively. Responding to rural hunger here is basically a huge local and largely voluntary effort. We run raffle after raffle. We co-ordinate our activities to ensure that everyone who needs assis-

tance is offered this in a non-judgemental way, and as confidentially as possible in a rural community. Our situation for the future is dependent on largely outside forces, however – on unemployment levels, on assistance to overcome salinity and soil degradation problems, on United States tariff policies and on climate change.

Child Hunger in a Remote Aboriginal Community: Meeting Basic Human Needs[2]

Among Aboriginal people, the interrelationship between education, employment and income is considered to be both the cause and consequence of poverty. Aboriginal people achieve far lower educational levels than those of the non-Aboriginal population. Aboriginal unemployment is five times the national rate, and the Aboriginal employment that does exist is often casual, temporary, seasonal, lower-skilled and lower-paid (Choo, 1990, p. 50). The average income of the Aboriginal people is almost half that of other Australians. The health status of Aborigines has been discussed earlier in this chapter.

As a response to these issues, the federal government instituted in 1989 a National Aboriginal Health Strategy, injecting additional funding into Aboriginal health programmes and transferring administrative responsibility for funding and delivery of services to the Aboriginal and Torres Strait Islander Commission (ATSIC), the peak national representative body for indigenous people. The strategy has, however, failed in any significant way to improve the health status of indigenous Australians and is currently beset by on-going political struggles over control of the health dollar between ATSIC, the federal and state governments and other indigenous peak organizations representing various regional interests. Complex governmental and bureaucratic structures, the fracturing of indigenous interests, the intractability of health problems especially in remote locations, and the inability to deliver health, housing and infrastructure services in a co-ordinated fashion are all contributing to a continual indigenous health crisis.

During 1990, the author worked with Aboriginal people in a remote area of the Kimberley region of Western Australia as a social worker employed in the Fitzroy Crossing District Office of the Western Australian Department for Community Development (DCD). In that capacity, he had a legislatively derived role to undertake child protection work which mandated coercive interventions into Aboriginal family and community life and, paradoxically, a brief to engage with the same Aboriginal people in community development work.

A history of the role that the DCD has played in the lives of Aboriginal families in the Kimberley could probably best be understood as a history of the benign face of colonial rule. Like state welfare agencies across Australia, DCD was directly responsible for the removal of many Aboriginal children from their families, and the enforcement of government policies of protection and assimilation which robbed Aboriginal communities of their children, their land, their economic base and their ability to make independent decisions for themselves and determine their futures. This is *living* history in the Kimberley. Many adults in Fitzroy Crossing today were forcibly removed from their families as children and raised in institutional or substitute 'care'.

Krumba[3] is a community of approximately 50 adults and children located in desert country 150 kilometres from Fitzroy Crossing, which is the closest township. Access to the community is via a sealed road for the first 80 kilometres, then four-wheel drive track. Travelling time is about 4 hours one way. There is no air strip. The community is comprised of two extended family groups who claim a spiritual stewardship of this particular land reaching back hundreds of generations. Their current legal status is tenuous, having been granted a 99-year lease on a pastoral excision. As part of a growing homelands movement in the Kimberley, the people in this community have only recently returned to their traditional land, having earlier this century been 'resettled' in labour camps attached to pastoral leases which covered their land. More recently they have been forced into Fitzroy Crossing as welfare dependants when pastoralists were no longer able to exploit their labour cheaply. These people have returned to their traditional lands determined to re-establish their spiritual stewardship and retain and strengthen their traditional language, law, culture and kinship arrangements.

Conditions are harsh. Town water, sewerage and electricity are not available. There is no radio transmitter, no housing, no store. School-age children must live away from the community to attend school. Water is collected in tanks or brought in by road with other supplies. A generator provides electricity for a small refrigeration unit. Housing consists of caravans, tents and lean-tos artfully constructed out of materials to hand – old car parts, broken furniture, cardboard, plastic, branches, groundsheets, sheets and blankets, tin cans and bottles, and the like. For medical assistance, Krumba relies on a fortnightly visit from the doctor and community nurse based at Fitzroy Crossing. The climatic and physical conditions are forbidding. Temperatures daily climb into the high 40°Cs. Fierce winds whip up dust storms. In the wet, the humidity is oppressive and torrential rains bring flooding and the access road and bush tracks become an impassable bog. Although most of the adults cannot read or write, their culture is complex and they are a politically sophisticated group, aggressively pursuing their rights to the traditional land which is the well-spring of their culture, and to basic services such as water, housing, health, services and communications so as to promote their physical, social and psychological well-being.

Working as the local DCD officer alongside the people of Krumba the inherent paradoxes of the role were brought into sharp relief by the practice issues which emerged around the health status of the seven children aged 0–5 years living there. All seven were clinically listed as failing to thrive ('FTT'), that is, severely retarded in their physical growth and developmental 'milestones'. All seven were at one time or another hospitalized at Fitzroy Crossing, some with life-threatening illness. All were regarded on clinical assessment as malnourished and at grave risk of further life-threatening illness. All were expected to experience moderate to severe developmental delay, serious chronic ear and eye infection and learning difficulties.

The DCD officer had statutory authority to apprehend all these children as being children 'in need of care and protection' as defined by the relevant legislation. However, to do so would have brought about conflict with the entire adult community at Krumba, since it would have meant invoking, yet again, colonial law and administration as a means of removing Aboriginal children from their community. The alternative option and the only viable one, as the social worker, was to apply the principles and strategies of community development, to identify with the community the common problem and common goals and strategies for dealing with the problem. This approach required joining with the doctor and community nurse as a health care team, in adopting a shared approach to working with the community.

Both the community members and the health care team shared common goals, including the goal of building a more viable community at Krumba where children were strong, healthy and well placed to contribute as leaders and providers in the next generation. The paucity of basic resources and the scant attention hitherto paid to people's basic human needs could be highlighted, and members of the health care team were able to identify and undertake appropriate advocacy roles for improving overall living conditions and access to health-related services. Community members were able to identify and act upon deficiencies in their own arrangements for the transport, refrigeration and supply of basic food items, and for linking their children into available health services. Health education needs for primary caregivers and the whole community in relation to the care and developmental needs of infants and young children were identified and addressed with hands-on health education clinics on site. Access to clinical services was improved. Political strategies for securing more adequate infrastructure (especially housing, a clinic, and water and electricity supply) were reviewed and pursued, including direct representations from the community to relevant state and federal politicians.

Food Banks

A food bank is a central food distribution point for both donors and agencies. Food donors, manufacturers, wholesalers and retailers make deposits of surplus and damaged food into the bank where it is stored. Agencies can then make withdrawals and pass this food on to those people who need it. The aim of food banks is to reduce food waste and pass on surplus, salvaged and donated food to people in need. Centralized distribution allows for considerable economies of scale for welfare agencies, as well as providing significant economic benefits for food producers who can then forgo costs associated with food dumping and at the same time attract tax concessions and deductions associated with charitable donations.

The origins of Australia's four existing food banks are somewhat different. The first of these, in Sydney, resulted largely from the vision and efforts of one charismatic social reformer. In Perth, however, the food bank relied on corporate sponsorship and an establishment grant from the State Lotteries Commission to open in October 1994. The Commission initiated the concept and hired an accounting firm to undertake a food bank feasibility study in response to the growing and diverse demands for funds being placed on the Commission by welfare agencies. The cost of operations is funded by a small service charge on agencies to cover direct expenses. Breakeven is expected within two years without any government support, mainly due to a major three-year sponsorship by CRA (one of Australia's largest mining houses) and Rotary International's significant contribution. Whilst other food banks continue to seek state and federal government support directly, Perth Food Bank has not done so, and runs the operation as essentially a business relying on fee for service income and support from the corporate sector. John O'Donnell, the Foundation Chairman of the Perth Food Bank, commented:

Our business planning research showed us that we can only survive in the long term through strong support from the food companies. They told us in no uncertain terms that they would only donate on a consistent basis if we were not controlled by any one sector of the welfare industry; we could demonstrate a 'whole of community' customer base; food was never resold and the operations of the food bank were conducted along commercial food industry lines. We have enshrined those principles into our constitution and operating culture. Without food company support we don't have a food bank. So far it is working. Our Board is made up of a majority of directors from commerce and industry with the balance from the welfare sector. We select directors who we believe can make the maximum contribution to our mission – not because they are the 'elected representatives' of another sector or interest group.

We have not sought support from government for operational funding because we know how changeable this can be – particularly in the welfare arena. We cannot afford to base our 'business' on the unpredictability of bureaucrats and government whims of policy. Too often too much depends on one person in a department and when he/she leaves that person is replaced by another with a 'better idea' and funds dry up because 'you don't meet the criteria of our programs any longer'. So far the corporate world has been fantastic. All our approaches are made on the basis of a business proposal that benefits both parties. We will not be seen, ever I hope, as an organization seeking handouts based on cries for help.

We are working very well with other food banks in developing a national network. It is especially important to us since most of Australia's large volume food manufacturers make their products in Melbourne or Sydney and that is 4000 kilometres from us and we need access to them. (oral communication)

Food Bank Victoria which opened in January 1993 evolved out of a coalition of NGWOs and operates under the auspice of the Council for Homeless Persons of Victoria. It relies on a mixture of corporate and state government support, and attempts to receive funding from the Commonwealth have not yet been successful. An extremely efficient organization, Food Bank Victoria distributed nearly 1.8 million kilograms of food, valued at $7.66 million, during its second full year of operation, with a total staff complement of five employees (only four of whom are full-time) and 20 occasional volunteers. Betti Knott,

Chairperson, Victoria Food Bank Management Committee, discussed aspects of the operation with me:

> We get no financial assistance from the Commonwealth. Why? The reasons are both ideological and political, I believe. Firstly, the thrust of Commonwealth policy is provision of a safety net of income security and services that guarantees a basic yet sufficient minimum. But we know in the welfare agencies that the so-called safety net has gaping holes in it and that people fall through it at an alarming rate. We know that there's a huge difference between the government's notion of a safety net and the realities for many people of trying to live on what the government provides. So the Commonwealth doesn't like food banks because they are pointing out the need and highlighting the inadequacy of existing income security arrangements. We operate on a shoestring budget. Research and evaluation are important as we are aware of their value but who is going to pay for it? We struggle here to employ enough people to move the food in and out and this is our core function – to move the food. We keep statistics. We know how much food we move and how much person power it takes. Beyond that, research is the purview of the wealthy institutions such as universities. Food banks don't mask structural inequalities. Rather, they illustrate them, like the pimple on your nose. As long as there are welfare agencies who feed hungry clients, there will be a need for food banks. Our clients are the agencies, not individuals. We service 225 Victorian welfare agencies who are feeding people, so there is a real need and we are not duplicating services, or intruding on the particular relationships that agencies build with their clients, nor are we involved in issues of deservingness. Food producers will always need outlets to unload stock that they can't sell. Corporations take very readily to the food bank concept. They can understand it, because it is pragmatic, extremely cost-effective from a business point of view, and because they understand the problems associated with waste and production error and disposal of excess product.

I think the future of food banks in Australia is, regrettably, one of continued expansion. Here in Victoria, for example, we are regenerating our service so that soon there will be subsidiary operations in centres both east and west of central Melbourne. The food banks are almost ready now to start acting with one voice on some issues. A national association of food banks may develop and this could bring some advantages in terms of increasing our political leverage at a federal level, generating further sponsorships, sharing our expertise and resources, and giving us better prospects for developing our research, evaluation and advocacy. (oral communication)

The mission of the Brisbane Food Bank is 'to respond to poverty and hunger in the community by establishing a co-operative and co-ordinated redirection of surplus food products' (QCOSS, 1994, p. 1).
Its principles of operation are:

1. Hunger in the community results from structural inequalities and personal crises.
2. Food supplies surplus to requirements of the market can be redistributed equitably and efficiently to food bank member agencies.
3. The experience of the food bank should be used in order to educate, empower, catalyse and advocate in the interests of those most affected by poverty.
4. The food bank will be an accessible resource, based on the co-operative and mutually supportive efforts of its member agencies (QCOSS, 1994, p. 1).

Wayne Sanderson, Director of Lifeline Brisbane, and Chair of the Brisbane Food Bank Interim Management Committee, talked with me about some of the tensions and contradictions inherent in the food bank concept:

The food bank has substantial corporate support in this town. We have had large private donations in cash and kind, substantial support from the former and present Lord Mayor of the City, and also from the major food industry leaders. The food bank does represent a significant new body of resource for all the local welfare agencies, and especially for the many smaller community-based agencies that operate with very little government support and limited resources.

I agree with the critics of the food bank who claim that they let governments off the hook by helping them to evade responsibility for dealing with hunger and by masking the structural causes of poverty and hunger, especially unemployment, low wages and high costs of housing.

But I'm also a pragmatist. People do die of hunger in Australia. Some of these are alienated homeless youth in the inner cities. Some are socially isolated alcoholic men in rural or urban settings. Some are deinstitutionalized clients of psychiatric services. So the question for me is one of how pure you want to be and how long it's going to take to ensure everyone's right to adequate food and shelter. These are real needs now that people have for food, shelter. So there is a moral responsibility to respond to that need and be able to live with the ambiguities that this entails.

Commitment by NGWOs in Queensland to the food bank concept has grown out of a commitment to a community development model of service delivery and in the context of a state government with a long history of defaulting on its responsibility for providing adequate social welfare infrastructure. This food bank is auspiced by the Queensland Council of Social Service and is a company limited by guarantee, and operated by a board, chaired by a former Lord Mayor of Brisbane. It has 70 affiliated members who give food aid free of charge as part of their regular service to a defined locality or community.

Although without any formal recognition or legislative or financial support from the federal government, food banks are a significant and rapidly emerging state-level response by NGWOs to the problem of hunger in Australia. Their pragmatics and economies make them an attractive proposition for food producers and welfare agencies alike. They are here to stay. It is likely that they will increasingly act together as a loose national coalition to lobby for federal recognition and support, develop cross-state standards for best practice and ensure the most effective use of their limited resources.

CONCLUSION: A 'RAFFLE AFTER RAFFLE' WELFARE STATE?

In the Lucky Country, where the existence of hunger is officially denied, this decade has already seen two nationwide food collection and emergency relief drives, initiated not by governments but by NGWOs in co-operation with the private sector and the media. The first, Food for All, was a community-inspired response to increasing poverty in the wake of the 1990–2 recession. The second, Farmhand, is a current response to the plight of Australia's rural communities experiencing one of the worst droughts in the nation's history. In two months from August to October 1994 over 15 million dollars was distributed by Farmhand throughout rural Australia.

Australia's Aborigines experience the severest poverty and hunger, and whilst the myth of the Lucky Country has never held true for them, at least their hunger is visible and targeted. Such a situation, whilst appalling in the extreme and reinforcing much of the stigma and many of the racist stereotypes associated with Aborigines, at least permits a modicum of political debate and pressure for reform. The hunger of other Australians, however, remains relatively invisible. In either case hunger cannot be 'treated' in isolation from the deeper forces from which it arises. All of the programme examples described above illustrate the absolute necessity of tackling hunger in the broader contexts of poverty, powerlessness and exclusion, as well as illustrating the difficulties NGWOs face in delivering programmes on shoe-string budgets that are costed and reimbursed by governments for little beyond direct service exchanges or 'throughput'.

As Australia continues to move into the brave new world of internationalized unprotected markets and a deregulated labour force, whilst remaining firmly committed to 'trickle-down' economic models of growth and wealth-creation, poverty and the consequent hunger that accompanies it are likely to increase further. Food banks and other responses by NGWOs to the problems of poverty and hunger will not significantly impact on the extent or dimensions of these problems. This is not to argue that such responses are either unnecessary or ineffectual. Clearly, such responses are both important in their impact on the real daily lives of many tens of thousands of Australians as well as their illustrative and reforming potential since they can continuously alert governments and the public to the need for broader social reform in Australia. Currently, it is clear that our 'safety net' approach to the welfare state is insufficient: indeed, adopting Don Farrell's words from earlier on in this chapter, it could perhaps be more accurately described as 'the raffle after raffle' welfare state.

The 1994 White Paper on Employment and Growth, titled *Working Nation*, makes an instructive comparison with the 1945 White Paper on Employment, as Stilwell (1996) explains:

Certainly the policy innovations in Working Nation are modest. Dominant reliance is placed on economic growth in the private sector of the economy as the best way of generating new and worthwhile jobs to meet the needs of an expanding workforce and make inroads into unemployment. But no substantial new policies are proposed to generate the faster growth. There is no reaffirmation of the 1945 White Paper's commitment to the leading role for government, and the full employment goal is replaced by a more modest 5 per cent unemployment target [for the year 2000].

The changing relationship between output growth and employment growth is side-stepped, although the 'jobless growth' phenomenon is now well in evidence. Environmental concerns about the limits on a 'go for growth' strategy are set aside. The faith in international economic integration, linked to the economic rationalist' policies of the 1980s remains apparently unshaken.

In Australia, even the rhetoric of the Conservative and Labour political forces has merged so that both essentially portray the welfare state as a corrective adjunct to capitalism, and envisage the scope of the welfare state as contingent on economic growth (Smith, 1994).

By international standards, Australia's public sector and social expenditure are well below the levels existing in most other industrialized countries (Jamrozik, 1991). We can do much better. In 1993, Australia was the lowest taxed country of all the countries in the Organization for Economic Co-operation and Development (OECD). In 1993–4, federal government budget revenue was 23.4 per cent of Gross Domestic Product (GDP), its lowest level as a proportion of GDP for almost 20 years (Brotherhood of St Laurence, 1994b, p. 2).

This level of social welfare outlays exists against an environment in which there were, in October 1994, almost 755 000 people registered as unemployed and 280 000 of these had been unemployed for a year or more; 280 000 families with children under 15 had no family member employed and 50 per cent of unemployed people would have been the family breadwinner if they were not unemployed. There were 16 people seeking work for every job vacancy. Yet *Working Nation* failed to spell out proposals to accelerate the rate of job growth in Australia and unemployment (currently at about 9 per cent) is unlikely to fall below 7 per cent by the year 2000, even if existing high rates of economic growth continue (Brotherhood of St Laurence, 1994b, p. 9).

The way forward, however, is not clear. Even mildly reforming proposals such as those advocated by Longmore and Quiggan (1994), which call for a serious recommitment by the state to full employment through more expansionary fiscal policy, a greater role for the public sector and labour market programmes, are regarded as radical by many in an environment so dominated by economic rationalist ideologies. Yet such proposals are essentially Keynsian in their regulatory and targeted approach. What is required in the first instance is a widening of the debate so that a diverse array of options can emerge as against the increasingly narrow parameters of the current debate. As this chapter has illustrated, poverty and the associated problem of hunger is a reality for many thousands of Australians, and current policies and programmes are not offering an adequate response to these problems in Australia today.

NOTES

1. The considerable assistance of Mary and Gordon Wilson in the preparation of this section is acknowledged.
2. This is a revised version of J. Wilson, 'Social Work Practice and Indigenous Australians', in P. Swain (ed.), *In The Shadow of the Law* (Federation Press, 1995).
3. Pseudonym used.

3 Hunger in Canada: Abandoning the Right to Food
Graham Riches

INTRODUCTION

The problem of hunger in Canada in the 1990s is persistent and see-mingly intractable. Food banks brought the issue to public attention in the early 1980s. Yet a decade earlier poverty had been rediscovered in Canada (Senate, 1971) and in 1977 the People's Food Commission was formed in response to escalating food prices and the suffering and mis-ery of low-income Canadians. Yet despite all that has been written and said in the intervening years about unemployment, child poverty and welfare reform, hunger continues to grow. Indeed, to the extent that charity has attempted to meet the needs of hungry people, hunger has been depoliticized and ignored by the state. Federal and provincial governments have deliberately turned a blind eye.

This chapter argues that previously established rights to adequate welfare benefits and to food security are today being abandoned by the Canadian state and that the issue of what to do about hunger demands national attention. This analysis first considers the evidence of hunger in Canada which, in 1994, was ranked highest in the world by the United Nations Human Development Index (UNDP, 1994, p. 129) and seeks to explain this apparent contradiction, exploring both the causes and consequences of hunger in a country which is also a major produ-cer of food. It then reviews the responses to the hunger problem of the food bank movement, governments and NGOs, including those on the receiving end of charity, before analysing current proposals for so-cial security reform. It then discusses specific policies advanced by food banks, anti-poverty and welfare rights organizations, as well as the nutrition, food policy and community health sector directed to-wards establishing rights to income adequacy and to food security in Canada. Finally, a range of local, national and international strategies and the public action necessary to implement these rights will be assessed.

This analysis is informed by the view that hunger is, at root, a political issue which, if it is to be eradicated, must first be acknowledged and then addressed by both the community and the state as a fundamental matter of human rights. In fact, it has been the failure of successive federal governments in Canada to assert the legitimate rights of social assistance claimants under the provisions of the Canada Assistance Plan (CAP, 1966) to obtain adequate relief to meet basic requirements (for example, food, shelter, clothing), which initially triggered the collapse of the social safety net in the early 1980s and led to the rise of the food banks (Riches, 1986). To make matters worse, these provisions, although never effectively enforced, are currently being abandoned by the federal government as part of its welfare reform strategy. Perhaps the key question to be asked about hunger in Canada today is how is it that Canadians proclaim their right to health care, indeed see it as a distinguishing hallmark of Canadian identity, when basic human needs are left unmet and rights to food security, adequate incomes and freely chosen work are not addressed?

In the discussion that follows, it should be recognized that Canada is a federal state and that health, education and welfare constitutionally are matters which fall within provincial jurisdiction. This, therefore, means that any discussion about poverty and what to do about it necessitates consideration of the competing jurisdictional claims and respective roles of the federal and provincial governments. Indeed in some provinces, the municipalities continue to play an important role in relation to welfare relief. In terms of hunger, the crucial question is which level of government both has, and should have, the primary constitutional responsibility for ensuring that basic needs are met. In the broader context of the development of Canada's welfare state, the federal government uses both its constitutional amending powers (for example, unemployment insurance) and its taxation and spending powers to gain the compliance of the provinces to support national legislation.

DIMENSIONS OF HUNGER AND FOOD SECURITY

Hunger, according to the Bread for the World Institute (BWI), is 'a condition in which people lack the basic food intake to provide them with the energy and nutrients for fully productive, active and healthy lives' (BWI, 1995, p. 124). As pointed out in Chapter 1, definitions of hunger are open to a variety of interpretations and distinctions must be made between the meaning of hunger in developing countries and in the first

world, and understanding it as a physiological, social and psychological term (Davis and Tarasuk, 1994, p. 51). There are important differences between the starvation and malnutrition to be found, for
example, in sub-Saharan Africa (BWI, 1995, p. 48) and the undernutrition, and indeed overnutrition, of significant sections of the population
in advanced industrial societies

Unfortunately, there is a wide range of evidence testifying to the fact
that from the early 1980s continuing to the present day, too many Canadians have been suffering from hunger because of their 'inability to obtain sufficient, nutritious, personally acceptable food through normal
food channels or the uncertainty that one will be able to do so' (Davis
and Tarasuk, 1994, p. 51). This emphasis on lack of access to assured
food sources, or food insecurity, informs the description and analysis
of hunger presented in this chapter. However, the larger question of
food security in terms of 'food availability and food quality at a societal
level' (*ibid.*, p. 51) must also be addressed if hunger is to be eliminated
in Canada. According to the Ontario Public Health Association
(OPHA), 'People have food security when they can get enough to eat
that is safe, that they like to eat and that helps them to be healthy. They
must be able to get this food in ways that make then feel good about
themselves and their families' (OPHA, 1995, p. 2).

Yet the definition of hunger and its prevalence remain problematic.
It has correctly been suggested that it is important to distinguish
between direct and indirect indicators of hunger, the latter being the
more common yet less precise (Radimer *et al.*, 1990, pp. 1544–5). Indirect measures in Canada include: the emergence of food banks as a residual extension of the Canadian welfare system, widespread food bank
usage, sub-poverty line welfare benefits, the increasing use of school
meal programmes, as well as the perception, according to Gallup polls,
of a majority of Canadians, that hunger remains a serious issue in the
1990s. This is to say nothing of begging on the streets of Canada's urban centres nor of the plight of rural and northern Canadians and the
conditions on many First Nations reserves where unemployment rates
of 90 per cent are widespread. Direct indicators of hunger are less
common, but are found in hunger surveys such as the one conducted
in 1990 by the Edmonton Food Policy Council (Olson, 1992).

Indirect Indicators

In important respects, the story of hunger in late twentieth-century
Canada is directly related to the rise of charitable food banks as the

Table 3.1 Food Banks in Canada, 1981–95

	1981	1984	1988	1991	1994	1995
Newfoundland			1	17	24	20
Prince Edward Island			2	3	5	5
Nova Scotia		2	8	27	32	31
New Brunswick		2	27	40	40	44
Quebec*		2	5	11	8	8
Ontario		4	19	88	175	174
Manitoba		1	1	4	14	14
Saskatchewan		5	5	11	19	19
Alberta	1	12	16	40	63	61
British Columbia		47	42	51	73	76
NWT					2	2
Yukon					2	2
CANADA	1	75	126	292	457	456

* Food banks in Quebec are regionally organized.
Source: Riches (1986); Oderkirk (1992); CAFB (1995).

primary institutions providing emergency food assistance to those in need. As Table 3.1 shows, the first food bank was established in Edmonton in 1981. Three years later 75 food banks were operating in eight of the ten Canadian provinces, but by October 1991, as the economy underwent another recession, this number rose to 292 with the Canadian Association of Food Banks (CAFB) network operating or supplying over 1200 grocery programmes and 580 meal programmes in more than 300 communities across the country (Oderkirk, 1992, p. 7). Food banks outnumbered McDonald's franchises by a ratio of three to one (Webber, 1992, p. 14). By 1995 the number of food banks had jumped to 480 (*Vancouver Sun*, 3 June 1995) an increase of 64 per cent.

In 1992, Statistics Canada reported that 'two million individuals, 7.5 per cent of the population, including 700 000 children under age 18, are expected to receive food assistance at least once in 1991' (Oderkirk, 1992, p. 7). By 1994 this figure had jumped to 2.5 million food bank users (CAFB, 1994, p. 1). It was also noted that the province of Ontario showed the highest food bank usage with Quebec having the fastest rate of increase (*ibid.*, p. 7). In 1994 Gerrard Kennedy, the Director of Toronto's Daily Bread Food Bank, the largest in the country, reported that '418 000 persons in the Greater Toronto Area received emergency food assistance at least once, and on average 4.3 times. This represents 12 per cent of the population' (*ibid.*, p. 6).

Food banks in other parts of the country show similar trends. In Regina, in the heart of the wheat belt, food bank requests more than quadrupled to 31 935 per annum in the ten-year period to 1994, representing 49 176 adults and 38 711 children (Regina and District Food Bank, 1994). In Halifax, Nova Scotia, the Metro Food Bank was responsible for 821 324 food bank shipments to member agencies in 1994 and in 1995 in Edmonton, capital of the oil-rich province of Alberta, the food bank reported an explosion of demand. In 1995, 17 909 adults and children received hampers, a 30 per cent increase in one year (Edmonton Food Bank, April 1995).

Of course, it can be argued that food bank data are not reliable, that their figures include double counting and that they overestimate the numbers who turn to them for support. Yet it has also been pointed out that whilst 'receipt of charitable food assistance strongly suggests an inability to satisfy one's food needs through normal channels', nevertheless this 'is an insensitive measure of hunger believed to underestimate the true prevalence of the problem' (Radimer *et al.*, 1990 quoted in Davis and Tarasuk, 1994, p. 51). As the authors suggest, people can still be hungry even if they do not seek emergency food assistance and there is no particular reason to assume that their hunger has been satisfied simply because they have patronized a food bank. Nevertheless, studies conducted by food banks, research undertaken by municipalities, social planning councils, health and nutrition agencies and food policy councils demonstrate that food bank data are a reasonable yardstick by which to measure food insecurity in Canada (see Regina and District Food Bank 1986, 1994; SPARC, 1986; Metro Food Bank Society, Halifax 1993; Daily Bread Food Bank, Toronto since 1987; Winnipeg Harvest 1989; City of Regina, 1989).

The profile of hungry people which emerges from these studies and which remains reasonably consistent when compared to the findings of the mid-1980s (Riches, 1986) is confirmed by research conducted by the Edmonton Food Policy Council in 1990. It found that those people in the city of Edmonton who are having the most difficulty with food security are people living on social assistance, families with children (including single parents) and working poor families (Olson, 1992, p. 2). These findings are generally applicable across the country with other studies pointing to the over-representation of children (Oderkirk, 1992), the high incidence of women with family responsibilities, single men, those with disabilities and refugees (SPARC, 1986; SP Research Associates, 1989; Metro Food Bank 1993; Kennedy, 1995). Mothers with babies and small children are a particular concern and Black

Canadians and those of First Nations and Latin American ancestry are over-represented among food bank users (Kennedy, 1995, pp. 6–8). Students, the elderly and the new poor are also amongst the ranks of those turning to food banks (Webber, 1992, pp. 41–4). Indeed, the *Globe and Mail*, Canada's only national newspaper, recently reported the establishment of the first food bank for veterans by the Royal Canadian Legion in Calgary, Alberta (12 April 1995). Three notable characteristics of the hungry are that they are unemployed, dependent on welfare incomes and live in rental accommodation.

The increasing use of school meal programmes in Canada in recent years provides further evidence of the existence of child hunger and undernutrition. A study by the Toronto Board of Education (TBE) reported that a national survey of school boards across Canada, conducted in 1989 by the Canadian Education Association, revealed that: 'twenty-six per cent of the responding boards provide free or subsidized milk or snacks; 21 per cent provide free meals, either breakfast or lunch; and several others offer subsidized meals. Usually, recipients are in schools targeted as "inner city" or in neighbourhoods otherwise described as economically disadvantaged' (TBE, 1991, p. 1). It is difficult, given the available data, to say with any precision how many children are being fed in this way, but the study suggests that the numbers are significant and that many thousands of Canadian children are utilizing school meal programmes. In Edmonton 4000 children in 20 low-income schools were being provided with snacks (*ibid.*, p. 1); in Vancouver, in 1990, 8500 children in 40 low-income elementary schools were benefiting from an expanded lunch programme (*ibid.*, p. 1); in Montreal, where the most comprehensive food and nutrition programme is reported, 26 000 students in 56 elementary and nine secondary schools are served and in Toronto, almost half the Toronto Board of Education's 113 elementary schools provided some form of food assistance (TBE, 1991, pp. 1–2).

Again, the question arises as to whether the provision of school meal programmes provides hard evidence of the existence of hunger or undernutrition. The Toronto Board of Education's study quotes research which reveals that a high percentage of Canadian children have unbalanced diets (King, Robertson and Warren, 1985) and that their diets are too high in sugar, salt and fats (Avard and Hanvey, 1989, p. 65). The study goes on to say that almost 10 per cent of children in a national sample of Grade 7 students were found to be distinctly underweight, and 30 per cent slightly underweight. However, these numbers were considerably lower for the Grade 10 population, falling to 2.5 per cent and 20 per cent, respectively' (King, Robertson and Warren, 1985). Yet its main conclusion is that poor children in Canada 'are likely to be less well nourished than others', quoting a 1990 Public Health survey of Toronto principals of whom more than a quarter identified hunger as a common problem in their schools (TBE, 1991, p. 3).

Direct Indicators

Perhaps the most significant study of food security in Canada to date has been the community food needs assessment conducted by the Edmonton Food Policy Council in 1990. It undertook to measure the prevalence of hunger through a survey of 460 low-income households from all parts of the city of Edmonton and included random telephone interviews and face-to-face interviews (Olson, 1992, p. 7). Hunger was defined on the basis of answers to a five-question scale based on how well people were meeting their food needs. There was both an adult

Chart 3.1 Edmonton Hunger Scales

Questions in the Adult Hunger Scale	Questions in the Child Hunger Scale
Worry, Anxiety 'I worry whether my food will run out before I get money to buy more.'	*Quality of Food* 'I can afford to feed my child good quality food.'
Lack of Income to Buy Food 'Does your household ever run out of money to buy food?'	*Variety of Food* 'I can afford to give my child many different kinds of food.'
Food Insufficiency – Quantity 'Do you ever eat less than you feel you should because there is not enough money for food?'	*Food Insufficiency – Quantity* 'Do you ever have to cut the size of your child's meals because there is not enough money for food?'
Diet-Inadequacy – Quality 'Do you ever cut back to eating just a few kinds of cheaper food because of not enough money?'	*Reported Hunger* 'Is your child ever hungry because there is not enough food in the house and there is no money to buy more?'
More Severe Food Insufficiency 'Have you ever gone without food for a day or more because there wasn't enough money to buy food?'	*Severe Food Insufficiency* 'Has your child ever gone without food for a day or more because there wasn't enough money to buy food?'

Source: Olson (1992, pp. 7, 50).

and a child hunger scale. The scales were adapted from the instrument used by the Washington-based Food Research and Action Center in their Community Childhood Hunger Identification Project (CCHIP, 1991) in the United States, which at that time had been used to document hunger in seven states and in New York City (*ibid.*, p. 50).

As Chart 3.1 shows, people were ranked as not hungry, at risk, hungry or very hungry. Adults who answered 'yes' to all five questions were considered 'very hungry', 'yes' to 3 or 4 questions 'hungry', 'yes' to 1 or 2 questions 'at risk', and 'no' to all questions as 'not hungry'. On the child hunger scale a 'no' answer to the first two questions and a 'yes' to the last three meant that the child was 'very hungry'.

The survey revealed that three-quarters of the low-income people interviewed 'were having trouble getting healthy food on a regular basis' (*Ibid.*, p. 8). Other findings were that families with children, and particularly single-parent families, had real difficulty meeting their food needs; single people also faced difficulties while those receiving social assistance were twice as likely to be hungry or very hungry compared to those not on welfare. Working poor households were also found to be hungry. The study showed that 28 per cent of low-income Edmonton households were 'hungry' or 'very hungry' (19 000 adults and 18 000 children) and 34 per cent were 'at risk' of hunger (25 000 adults and 15 000 children). In total, the survey found that 77 000 people in the city, or 12.5 per cent of Edmontonians, were having some trouble meeting their food needs (*ibid.*, pp. 2–10, 56). This proportion is comparable to the 12 per cent reported to be seeking emergency food assistance in the Greater Toronto area in 1994. It suggests that the figure of 2.5 million Canadians resorting to food banks, that is 8.6 per cent of the population in 1994, is not an overestimate.

Thus, direct and indirect indicators of hunger point to a considerable degree of food insecurity in Canada. This is reflected in Gallup public opinion polls conducted annually since 1989. In 1995, 61 per cent of Canadians believed that hunger was very serious (20 per cent) or quite serious (41 per cent) compared to 65 per cent who held similar beliefs six years earlier. Only 10 per cent of Canadians in 1995 believed that hunger was not a serious problem at all (Gallup, 1995, p. 2; 1989, p. 1).

THE CAUSES OF HUNGER

The roots of hunger in Canada today are to be found in the structural preconditions of poverty, inequality and powerlessness, all of which are increasing. Hunger is not caused by the lack of food within Canada even though, as the Toronto Food Policy Council (TFPC) points out, 'when the grain trade is removed from calculations Canada is a net importer of agricultural products' (TFPC, 1994a, p. 22). Rather, as Warnock has observed, the major reasons for continuing poverty (and thus hunger) in Canada, are the existence of gross inequalities in income, the even more unequal distribution of wealth and the fact that the persistence of inequality of income and wealth is assisted by government policy (Warnock, 1987, pp. 21–2). A society of three nations is being created: the 'haves', the 'also rans' and the 'have nots', whose social and economic rights are being steadily eroded by the economic and social policies of the federal and provincial governments.

Economic and labour market restructuring precipitated by the demands of economic globalization (Johnson *et al.*, 1994, pp. 5–6), and spurred on by the federal government's neo-conservative agenda of deficit reduction, free trade, increased international competitiveness, high interest rates and faith in trickle-down economics, has resulted in jobless growth, persistently high unemployment rates, significant underemployment and the emergence of insecure and low-wage employment, largely at the expense of women (Ternowetsky and Riches, 1992, p. 9). 'Good' jobs have certainly resulted for some, but 'bad' jobs and increasing labour market vulnerability and insecurity have been the price for millions of Canadians. Not only have these conditions placed enormous strain on the country's social safety net of unemployment insurance and social assistance programmes but governments, in blaming deficits on social spending and not macroeconomic policy (Bradfield, 1994), and in their quest for minimal government, have deliberately targeted the poor. They have cut public sector jobs, eliminated social programmes, tightened eligibility and reduced benefits. In essence they have privatized welfare by increasing dependence on voluntary activity and, in the case of hunger, on charitable food banks. Selectivity has replaced universality as a distinguishing principle of Canadian social policy and even Medicare, Canada's pre-eminent social programme, is under threat.

Given that hunger is a function of poverty and inequality, it is important to note that poverty rates in Canada have remained high since the early 1980s. Although Canada has no official poverty lines, it is the accepted convention that Statistics Canada low-income cut-offs (LICOs) are regarded as the official benchmarks of poverty. The National Council of Welfare (NCW), an advisory body to the federal government, produces an annual survey of poverty in Canada in which it compares the results of the yearly Statistics Canada household survey of consumer finances and expenditures with the LICOs. As the 1995 report indicate:

> The cut-offs represent levels of gross income where people spend disproportionate amounts of money for food, shelter and clothing. The bureau (Statistics Canada) has decided over the years – somewhat arbitrarily – that 20 percentage points is a reasonable measure of the additional burden. The average Canadian family spent 36.2 per cent of gross income on food, shelter and clothing according to 1986 data on spending patterns, so it was assumed that low income Canadians spent 56.2 percent on the necessities of life. (NCW, 1995, p. 2)

The cut-offs vary by family size and the population of the area of residence thereby producing 35 different 'poverty lines'. For example, the poverty line for a single person living in Toronto or Vancouver in 1993 was $15 452 and for the same person living in a rural area was $10 520. A single parent with two children would need an income of more than $26 624 to climb out of poverty in Toronto or Vancouver and would need more than $18 216 in rural Canada (*ibid.*, p. 3).

Bearing in mind that other Canadian welfare organizations such as the Canadian Council on Social Development (CCSD) and the Social Planning Council of Metropolitan Toronto produce more relative and thereby more generous poverty lines, the NCW nevertheless reported that 1993, the latest year for which its data are available, was a sombre year for poor people (*ibid.*, p. 6). In 1981, the year the first food bank was established, 3.6 million Canadians, or 15.3 per cent of the population, were judged to be in poverty. By 1993 4.7 million people were poor and the rate had climbed to 17.4 per cent (*ibid.*, p. 7). Family and child poverty remain significant problems. In 1993, one in six Canadians, and one in five children, were living in poverty. There were over a million poor families and more than 1.4 million poor children (*ibid.*, p. 8) and the poverty rate for female-headed single-parent families with children was an astonishing 59.8 per cent (NCW, 1995, p. 31).

The poverty rate closely reflected changes in the country's official unemployment rate. Indeed, the first indications of hunger and the initial impetus for the start of food banks has been traced to the harsh economic recession of the early 1980s (Riches, 1986). From a low of 7.5 per cent in 1981 unemployment rose to 11.8 per cent in 1983 declining again to 7. 5 per cent by 1989 and then returning to 11.2 per cent in 1993 (NCW, 1995, p. 9). In early 1995, 1.4 million Canadians were officially registered as jobless and the unemployment rate stood at 9.6 per cent.

Again, the rate disguises significant provincial regional differences varying from a high of 19 per cent in Newfoundland to a low of 6.5 per cent in Saskatchewan (Statistics Canada, 1995). Women, children, First Nation peoples, those with disabilities and older men suffered disproportionately. Long-term unemployment remains a serious issue.

In light of these depressed conditions and the failure of the Canadian economy to generate sufficient well-paying jobs, it is of no surprise that more than 3 million people were dependent on unemployment insurance (UI) benefits in 1994 (*ibid.*, p. 35), and more than 3.1 million were dependent on provincial social assistance. Whilst UI beneficiaries are now falling as a result of tightening eligibility, the numbers on social assistance have been increasing annually since 1988 (*ibid.*, p. 35).

The adequacy of welfare income and the capacity of people dependent on such benefits to be able to feed themselves and their families, is significant in that the majority of food bank users are social assistance claimants. In general, social assistance benefits fall well below Statistics Canada poverty lines. In 1986 welfare income for a couple with two children, which included social assistance, family allowance, child tax credit and in some cases provincial tax credit varied between a low of 46 per cent of the poverty line in New Brunswick to a high of 83 per cent in Prince Edward Island (NCW, 1987, pp. 66–7). In 1993, the National Welfare Council reported that the adequacy of provincial benefits had shown no significant improvement since 1986 (NCW, 1995, p. 25). In that period Quebec, Ontario, Manitoba (with the exception of single parents), British Columbia and the Yukon saw real rate increases. Yet in Newfoundland, Prince Edward Island, Nova Scotia, New Brunswick and Saskatchewan the rates marginally declined.

In Alberta the rates were actually cut by the provincial government in October 1993, leading to a 73 per cent increase in demand at the Edmonton food bank. This prompted Marjorie Bencze, the food bank director, to comment that the government 'have turned their back on people, needy people... social welfare policy has become very punitive' (*Edmonton Journal*, 14 April 1994). In Alberta, the value of benefits was reduced by 10.6 per cent for families, 14.7 per cent for single parent families and 31.5 per cent for single employable persons (NCW, 1993, pp. 34–6). In July 1995, Ontario followed Alberta's example and cut its welfare benefits by 21.6 per cent (*Globe and Mail*, 22 July 1995, A4). Only in Quebec, for certain welfare recipients, are provincial social assistance rates indexed to the cost of living.

In 1995, the Poverty Action Group in Regina released a study entitled 'Please, Mr. Minister, I Need Some More!' which is illustrative of the problem of inadequate welfare benefits across the country. The report concerns welfare issues in Saskatchewan, a province which at least since the election of the New Democratic Party government in 1991 has seen itself as being sympathetic to the problems of hungry people. In Saskatchewan the amounts allocated for food, rent, utilities, clothing and personal needs fall well below Statistics Canada basic allowances and in the case of single parent families are only 67.13 per cent of what is required to meet a poverty level income. Food allowances are 78.5 per cent of what is required and rents for a two bedroom apartment fall nearly 20 per cent below actual rates. As the report states: 'Many families face hunger because the only expendable income they have is in their food and clothing allowances thus leaving them little leeway to adjust to unforeseen expenses or, indeed, to accommodate ongoing needs' (PAP, 1995, pp. 4–5). Such findings reflect those of nutritionists, who show that the amounts of welfare income allocated for food allowances are insufficient to meet Agriculture Canada's nutritious and thrifty food basket costs (Davis *et al.*, 1991, p. 143). Lack of affordable housing is also a primary cause of hunger and supports the claim of Toronto's Daily Bread Food Bank that 'the pattern of need had a single core characteristic. These people had to pay their rent first, then scramble for their other needs' (Kennedy, 1995, p. 2).

A recent study of the Canadian Council on Social Development has observed that provincial assistance rates are based on absolute rather than relative definitions of poverty (Ross, Shillington and Lochhead, 1994, p. 33), but this seems a generous interpretation when such allowances do not permit welfare recipients to put food on the table. People are not going hungry in Canada because there is no food, but rather because they lack the necessary income to access it through normal channels such as supermarkets and food stores. Food is not equally available to all. Only wasted or unwanted food, much of dubious nutritional value, is handed out to the poor. Hunger is primarily a political issue and a matter of distributive justice.

CONSEQUENCES

The consequences of hunger are far-reaching. Whilst there has been no national survey into hunger in Canada, its impact can be assessed from a range of local studies. The Ontario Public Health Association (OPHA) has recently drawn attention to the problems facing people whom it describes as nutritionally vulnerable: those living in poverty, growing children, women of reproductive age, people with disabilities or chronic illness, the elderly, Aboriginal populations, refugees and the homeless (OPHA, 1995, pp. 14–16). It is these people who are among the major users of food banks. The study makes a number of specific points: the Ontario Health Survey (1990) reports that a quarter of Ontarians living on low incomes reported three or more health problems, compared to 16 per cent of people in mid to high income brackets; low birth weight (LBW) infants are born more frequently to women living in poverty, with physical and mental development in these infants being more likely to be delayed and the resulting mental, psychological and educational disabilities not being completely reversible; children living in poverty and experiencing inadequate nourishment are also vulnerable to health problems, with research showing that not only do they suffer material and cultural deprivation but also they are more likely than other children to die in infancy, experience physical and mental health problems, eat less nutritious foods, be at greater risk of developing iron deficiency anaemia and to face discrimination; children who are poorly nourished are more likely to experience school performance problems; Aboriginal children have higher morbidity and mortality rates than Canadians in general, are much more likely to be impoverished and are more susceptible to infectious diseases such as pneumonia, tuberculosis and gastroenteritis (*Ibid.*, pp. 14–16). Given that one in five Canadian children live in poverty these are critical issues.

Concerns have also been expressed recently about Canada's infant mortality rate, a prime indicator of health in society and of women and children in particular. Whilst the rate declined markedly between 1971 and 1986, in 1986 the rate was 1.7 per cent higher in the poorest quintile than in the highest (Aitken and Mitchell 1995, p. 25). The *Globe and Mail* gave prominence to a Statistics Canada report concerning the first rise in 31 years in the infant mortality rate from 6.1 deaths for every 1000 live births in 1992 to 6.3 deaths in 1993. The causes have yet to be analysed but possible explanations presented included environmental factors, problems in the delivery of health and social programmes, poor nutrition of would-be mothers and the link between unwanted unemployment and poor health (*Globe and Mail*, 2 June 1995, p. A4). As Aitken and Mitchell observe, 'the long-term impact of poverty on child health and well-being is undeniable' and 'the level of child poverty in this affluent country is shortsighted and will ultimately thwart Canada's economic well being' (Aitken and Mitchell, 1995, p. 30). Despite an all-party declaration in the House of Commons in 1989 that child poverty was to be abolished by the year 2000, nearly half a million more children now live in poverty (Caledon Institute of Social Policy, 1995, p. 1).

Why is it that in the final years of the twentieth century, as in the early 1900s, Canada is still struggling with absolute poverty? Despite being one of the world's richest countries and a member of the exclusive G-7 club, and despite having developed a strong social safety net which included the right of people to have their basic needs met, hunger remains a critical issue. How have Canadians responded to the issue of hunger and with what effect?

RESPONDING TO HUNGER

This review of Canadian responses to the problem of hunger since the early 1980s considers the respective roles played by food banks, governments, NGOs, anti-poverty groups and the community health sector, as well as the courts and the media. For those concerned to establish a right to food security in Canada, it makes for depressing reading. Essentially, it is a story of failure on the part of the food banks, NGOs and lobby groups in their attempts to require governments to accept their legislated and moral responsibilities to recognize and address the rights of low-income Canadians to food security; and a story of success for governments wishing to avoid their obligations to ensure that people on welfare are in receipt of adequate benefits as expressed in domestic legislation and as ratified in international law.

Social Security and the Right to Food

Until the changes introduced by the Progressive Conservative government of Prime Minister Mulroney in the 1980s, it could be argued that the development of Canada's welfare state was based upon a commitment to economic growth and high employment, universality and a guaranteed social minimum, including a right to food. The foundations of its modern social security system can be traced to the unemployment, social disintegration and despair brought about by the Great Depression of the 1930s and to the period of social reconstruction generated by World War II (Guest, 1985). Its specific development can be seen in the introduction of unemployment insurance in 1940 and the publication of the Marsh Report on Social Security for Canada in 1943. By 1966, the major building blocks of the post-World

War II welfare state were in place, including workers compensation, minimum wage legislation, unemployment insurance, family allowances, hospital and medical care, old age security and occupational pensions, social assistance and a range of personal social services (see Davis and Tarasuk, 1994, p. 52). Universality, social insurance and selectivity in terms of cash benefits and social services became established as the key organizing principles of Canadian social programmes, and universal health care became an important symbol of national identity, particularly in terms of contrasting the more collectivist values of Canadian society with that of the individualism of its southern neighbour.

Today, the welfare state is being dismantled as the principle of universality is rolled back: unemployment insurance is being restricted, family allowances have given way to child tax credits, and old age security and medicare are under review. Indexation of benefits is at best partial and universal day care is a forgotten hope. Canada's commitment to a guaranteed social minimum, the last line of defence against hunger and poverty, has been undermined. In 1996, as part of an extensive review of social security, the federal government has repealed the Canada Assistance Plan Act (CAP) of 1966, thereby fundamentally altering the way in which provincial social assistance programmes are supported.

CAP merits particular attention as it is *the* public welfare programme of last resort for destitute Canadians including unemployment beneficiaries, who must turn to it when their benefits are exhausted. Until its demise was announced in the 1995 federal budget, CAP had been a significant instrument in the struggle against hunger and poverty. When it was introduced in 1966 it reflected a period of co-operation between the provinces and the federal government in terms of developing and ensuring a guaranteed social minimum. The preamble to the CAP legislation recognized that 'the provision of adequate assistance to and in respect of persons in need and the prevention and removal of the causes of poverty and dependence on public assistance are the concerns of all Canadians' (CAP, 1966, C-1, p. 711). CAP was developed as a conditional and open-ended cost-shared programme in which the federal government agreed to pay half the costs of provincial social assistance and welfare programmes. In exchange for federal dollars, the provinces were required to meet a set of national standards in relation to the provision of social assistance benefits and social programmes. These included: the right to income when a person is in need; the right to an amount of income that takes into account budgetary requirements including food, clothing and shelter; the right to appeal; the right not to have to work for welfare and the right to assistance regardless of the province the person is from (NAPO, March 1995).

These human rights were seemingly given the imprimatur of international inviolability when, in 1976, the federal government, after reaching agreement with the provinces, ratified the United Nations' *International Covenant on Economic, Social and Cultural Rights* (1966). Article 11 of this Covenant reads, 'The States Parties to the present Covenant recognize the right of everyone to an adequate standard of living for himself and his family, including adequate food, clothing, and housing, and to continuous improvements of his living conditions' (UN, 1966; Riches, 1986, pp. 99–100). Again in 1992, the Canadian government appeared to confirm its commitment to income adequacy, when it ratified the 1989 United Nations' *Convention on the Rights of the Child*. Article 26 obliges ratifying countries to recognize the right of every child to benefit from social security, including social insurance, and to take the necessary measures to achieve the full realization of this right in accordance with their national law (UN, Article 26, p. 1). In addition, the Convention stipulates that every child has a right to an adequate standard of living and that whilst parents are primarily responsible for securing these rights, within their abilities and financial capacities, government should take appropriate measures to ensure these rights are met, specifically in terms of nutrition, clothing and housing (UN, Article 27, pp. 1–3). Significantly UN conventions become international law after they have been ratified by 20 or more countries. Moreover in 1992, Canada signed the *World Declaration of Nutrition* which affirms that 'access to nutritionally adequate and safe food is a right of each individual' and committed itself to developing a national plan of action (FAO, 1992).

In terms of meeting basic needs Canada's stated domestic and international welfare obligations and commitments to food security are to be applauded. Historically, poverty and hunger have not been neglected by the state, and social and economic rights to income adequacy and food security have slowly been advanced. Since 1966 a social safety net has been in place. Yet, despite such developments cumulative evidence from the early 1980s makes clear these rights are steadily being revoked. The rise of charitable food banks, as an extensive system of emergency and substitute relief, provides concrete evidence that the social safety net has collapsed (Riches, 1986, p. 59). Why has this been allowed to happen?

Food Banks and the Depoliticization of Hunger

Confronting the practical, moral and political dilemmas raised by food banks is critical to any analysis which hopes to get to the roots of the massive incidence of hunger and food insecurity which exists in Canada today. As a result of the failure of governments to recognize and address the legislated rights of their country's poorest citizens to be able to put bread on their table, charitable food banks emerged to address the problem of growing hunger in the community. What has developed since 1981 is a vast institutionalized network of food banks, pantries and emergency food outlets. The CAFB now recognizes as many as 456 food banks across the country. Canadian food banks have their origins in church-based organizations, labour unions, the voluntary sector and the ideas and practices of food banks in the United States. Indeed, it can be argued that Canada's food banks are evidence of the increasing Americanization of the Canadian welfare system.

The contradictions and dilemmas are acute. On the one hand, food banks enjoy significant community legitimacy. They touch deep wells of community altruism and permit individuals and communities to express their feelings of common concern for their fellow human beings in very practical ways. Indeed Michael Walker, the head of the right-wing Fraser Institute in Vancouver, in pointing to the 'stupendously effective' service provided by food banks, suggested 'that Canadians are not enthused by the prospect of the further extension of public welfare services, and are more inclined toward what are the increasingly successful operations of private charity' (cited in Jack, 1991, p. 9). Food banks, ironically, are supported by those who have grave concerns about the services they provide, in that many board members and staff believe their agencies should not exist. The fact is that food banks do provide emergency and supplementary relief to hungry people. In that sense they make an immediate and practical difference at a point in people's lives when material assistance is most needed. From a conservationist standpoint, they ensure that wasted and unwanted food can be recycled and put to humanitarian use. At the same time food banks by their existence and public statements have contributed to the debate about hunger in Canada.

On the other hand, food banks have served to depoliticize the issue of hunger in Canada by undermining governments' legislated obligations to guarantee adequate welfare benefits and by obviating the need for responsible public action (Jack, 1991; Webber, 1992; Riches,

1994). Food banks allow us to believe that hunger is being solved. Yet this is not so. Despite the massive amounts of food they give away, they run out of food, cannot guarantee nutritious food and have had to develop systems of rationing and eligibility to protect their food supplies. A common complaint among food bank organizers is that of donor fatigue, a serious issue when the service largely depends on the free supply of goods. Furthermore, the large volunteer army necessary to maintain food bank operations plays into the hands of governments wishing to cut payrolls and services and to privatize social welfare.

The moral and political dilemmas of food banking are acute. In 1989 the Metro Food Bank in Halifax decided to close its doors by 1994. Its central argument was that it had lost sight of its original purpose 'to be an emergency response to the local hunger situation. In essence we were becoming a regular supplement to the inadequate incomes of people on social assistance and the working poor' (Henderson, 1989, p. 9). A challenge was issued to government, business and the community saying it was their responsibility, not the food banks', to solve the hunger problem. Six years later the Metro Food Bank remains open and the decision to remain open was not controversial given the demand and the moral imperative that the hungry must be fed.

Yet continued food bank activity essentially depoliticizes the issue of hunger in society by legitimizing it as a matter for charitable concern rather than of social justice. End Legislated Poverty (ELP), a Vancouver-based advocacy group, has challenged food banks and the public to rethink the role of charity as an effective response to hunger. In a study conducted by food bank participants, they acknowledged their need to use food banks but, through personal testimony, were extremely critical of how they were treated, of the quality and quantity of the food, and of having to wait for food (Hobbs *et al.*, 1993, pp. 94–104). The most telling criticism had to do with the nature of giving. As one food bank user expressed it:

> I thought that giving was supposed to be a pleasure... why are the people receiving made to feel so humble? Why are we made to feel humiliated because we're receiving?...We are not supposed to be arrogant, but why does the giver get to be arrogant? (*ibid.*, p. 99)

Certainly, many food banks have committed themselves to public education and advocacy, yet hunger continues to grow and food banks are now institutionalized as private extensions of the public welfare system, despite the sunset clause in the CAFB constitution which requires it to review its mandate every three years. In fact, many government social assistance staff themselves refer their clients to food banks and even the former New Democratic Party government in Ontario funded food banks. The irony is that 'food banks are stepping in where government social services already exist' (Jack, 1992, p. 9) and governments no longer accept even a residual responsibility to meet the needs of those most at risk.

The way food banks are publicly legitimized plays a crucial role in the social construction of hunger and poverty as private troubles not public issues (Mills, 1959, p. 8). Three interrelated forces are at work: the dependency of many food banks on the corporate food industry, the sponsorship of community food drives and the role played by the media in presenting food banks and the hunger issue to the public. To the extent that food banks require the support of the food industry to supply them with their surplus food, few questions are asked about the financial benefits which accrue to the food industry when food which otherwise would be dumped is instead given to the poor. The cost of such wasted food has undoubtedly been included in the mark-up of food prices in general so that the community has already absorbed the cost of the wasted food, yet it can be regarded as a well-meaning corporate donation. Who, then, is really benefiting from the corporate donation? Food drives also present problems. Karen Shaver, who worked with Parents Against Poverty in Toronto, has commented: 'We encourage a banking institution to have a food drive... but we put absolutely no pressure on that financial institution to look at its own practices and ask itself, "What are we doing that in fact reduces the economic power of low-income people?"' (Jack, 1992, p. 8).

The media role in reporting food bank activities is also highly problematic. It is true that both the print and electronic media occasionally engage the political debate about hunger, but more often than not local television and radio stations, including the publicly financed Canadian Broadcasting Corporation, participate in food drives, perhaps out of community concern but certainly as a way to boost their ratings. Such activities only serve to present hunger and food bank activity as yet another worthy charitable cause and not as a deeply rooted political issue, which engages the fundamental social rights of citizenship. When the media support food banks, they reinforce the view that hunger is a charitable and not a political issue. In this way governments are encouraged to look the other way.

PUBLIC WELFARE AND THE EROSION OF SOCIAL RIGHTS

If, as it is argued in this chapter, hunger is essentially a political question and fundamentally a matter of economic and social rights recognized in both domestic and international law by Canada, we must ask why it is that government policy has permitted hunger to re-emerge as one of the country's significant social problems. Why is it that since the early 1980s Canadian governments of all ideological stripes turned a blind eye to the adequacy of welfare benefits, promoted punitive welfare reform proposals that exacerbated hardship, and in the mid-1990s deliberately abandoned their legislated responsibility for ensuring that the basic needs of the poorest of Canadian citizens are met?

The answers are structural and ideological and have to do with how social and economic rights are understood in liberal market economies. They are structural in the sense that the social safety net was overwhelmed by the dramatic increases in the caseloads of unemployment insurance and social assistance brought on initially by the recession of the early 1980s and the economic restructuring generated by the forces of market globalization. They are ideological in that neo-conservatism favouring deficit reduction, high interest rates, international competitiveness, private market-led economic growth, minimal government and social spending cutbacks became established as political orthodoxy in federal and provincial cabinets alike. In this climate, arguments favouring adequate welfare benefits held no truck, particularly when food banks were seen as significant contributions by those in power.

Canada's neglect of its welfare obligations was brought to international attention in 1993 by a report of the UN Committee on Economic, Social and Cultural Rights established to review the progress of governments which have ratified the 1966 *Covenant*. In addition to receiving the report of the Government of Canada, the Committee also heard from a delegation of representatives of NGOs led by the Charter Committee on Poverty Issues (CCPI). While recognizing 'the general strengthening of the protection of human rights in Canada under the *Canadian Charter of Rights and Freedoms*' (adopted in 1982), the Committee was highly critical of the Canadian government in a number of areas: Canada's failure to achieve any measurable progress in alleviating poverty over the last decade; the high rate of single mothers and of children living in poverty; the lack of any planned measures to alleviate the situation; and the reduction in the ratio of funding allocated to certain provinces (Ontario, Alberta and British Columbia) as part of a freeze of welfare transfer payments under CAP. Concerns were also expressed about the state of homelessness in Canada and the lack of effective policies; the fact that 'in some recent court decisions and constitutional discussions, social and economic rights have been discussed as mere "policy objectives" of governments rather than as fundamental human rights'; and 'that there seems to exist no procedure to ensure that those who must depend entirely on welfare payments do not thereby derive an income which is at or above the poverty line' (UNESC, 1993, pp. 2–5).

Clearly the Mulroney government was being held to account for its neglect of the poor, yet it dismissed the report as 'flimsy' and 'poorly researched'. The Opposition Liberals claimed that 'The UN report is simply confirming things that Canadians see every day with their own eyes. They see the increase in homelessness. They see the increasing recourse to food banks. They see the poverty of single parents.' The report was believed to be the harshest criticism ever levelled by the UN Committee against a major industrialized country (*Globe and Mail*, 1 June 1993).

Later in 1993 the Liberals won federal power with a landslide victory and gave priority to social security reform. However its welfare reform policies have pursued even more diligently the New Right agenda of its predecessor. Obsessed by deficit cutting and in response to persistently high unemployment and climbing welfare caseloads, the federal government has endorsed the 'active society' principle, which sees the social security system not as a passive safety net (where people allegedly are paid for doing nothing) but as a springboard back into the labour market. Making work more beneficial than welfare, easing the transition to part-time and low-wage work, supporting voluntary activity and partnerships with the community are presented, as in other OECD countries, as the way of the future (Canada, HRD, 1994). Specifically, unemployment insurance criteria have been tightened, work and training tests have been more harshly imposed as a condition for the receipt of social assistance and in some provinces, welfare benefits have been held down. In Alberta and Ontario benefits have actually been cut. Workfare, following the repeal of CAP, is likely to become the norm in Canada. It was heavily supported in the 1995 Ontario provincial election and is being introduced by the newly elected Progressive Conservative government. Canadian governments have blindly followed this path despite the fact that the economy has not been creating sufficient jobs, of the right type and with adequate wages, to absorb the available labour. The false promises of welfare reform and workfare have been revealed in a number of studies (Lightman, 1995; Mullaly,

1995), but there is every indication that such policies, which are little more than cynical attempts to manage massive unemployment and exert downwards pressure on wages, will continue.

The clearest evidence for this lies in the 1995 federal budget. Swayed by the argument that deficit reduction is to be Ottawa's salvation and buoyed just prior to the annoucement of the budget, by Moody's Investor Services of New York, that Canada's international credit rating was in jeopardy, Paul Martin, the Finance Minister, announced a major attack on government and social spending. This included the cutting of 45 000 federal civil servants, cutbacks of \$7 billion (15 per cent over three years) to the provinces for health, education and welfare and, with the introduction of Bill C-76, the termination of the Canada Assistance Plan. CAP is being replaced by a new funding mechanism called the Canada Health and Social Transfer (CHST) which is based on a block funding and not conditional cost-shared formula. The effect of this is that the federal government will no longer have to match provincial welfare spending on a shared-cost basis and the provinces will no longer have to meet national standards as a condition for the receipt of the federal transfer payments. Indeed, by the year 2009, federal grants under Established Programs Financing for health care, post-secondary education and welfare will cease (Canadian Centre for Policy Alternatives, 1995, p. 2). The federal government is offloading its spending responsibilities to the provinces and municipalities and, as Graham observes, is reversing 'the uploading process resulting from the 1930s' when municipal and provincial governments found themselves fiscally unable to shoulder the costs of welfare relief (Graham, 1995, p. 11).

The CCSD, NAPO and Lawyers for Just Reform in a joint press release commented that the termination of CAP amounts to the dismantling of the national welfare standards which the Liberals themselves had established 30 years previously. As Lynne Toupin, executive director of NAPO, expressed it:

> The federal government's focus on spending cuts and the deficit seem to have blinded them to the consequences of moving to a block-funding arrangement. Given the fact that the provinces have their own deficits to deal with, and given the contention that fewer dollars will now be transferred to the provinces for social programs, there is little to compel them to maintain, much less increase, their welfare rates (all of which are well below the poverty line). The results will be real human hardship for those most affected by cuts to this safety net of last resort. Without national enforceable standards, it is

conceivable that provinces could cut off welfare entirely for some categories of people such as single employables. (CCSD, 7 February
1995, p. 2)

Once again, three of the country's leading advocacy groups appealed
to the UN Committee on Economic, Social and Cultural Rights to in-
tervene. In their brief, NAPO, CCPI and the National Action Committee on the Status of Women made a number of telling points: that in
repealing CAP, the federal government is not only abolishing 'the only
federal legislation which protects the right to an adequate income in
Canada', but 'CAP has been referred to by the Government of Canada
in each of its reports to the Committee as an essential element of its
compliance with the Covenant'. They reported that no progress, with
minor exceptions, has been made by the federal government with respect to the 1993 recommendations of the Committee and that 'Bill C-
76 is a "deliberately retrogressive measure" in terms of the realisation
of social and economic rights in Canada' (CCPI, 25 April 1995). The
UN Committee was requested to invite the Government of Canada to
report immediately to it on the question of how Bill C-76 can be recon-
ciled with Canada's obligations under the Covenant (*ibid.*, 1995). The
Committee responded by inviting the government to comment on how
the new legislation would conform with the provisions of the Covenant
(UNCHR, 4 May 1995).

What had enabled both the Mulroney and Chretien governments to
slide away from their domestic and international human rights obligations? Echenberg and Porter (1990, p. 2) offer an important explanation. They argue that in industrial countries social and economic
rights (for example, to adequate incomes, health care and food security)
are held to be positive rights only obliging governments to 'provide' services, protect the needy and redistribute wealth 'with the least possible
interference with the market place'. Such rights were not included in
the 1948 *Universal Declaration of Human Rights* as the UK, the USA
and other western bloc countries 'argued vociferously that social and
economic rights lacked the judicial or constitutional status of civil and
political rights in the industrial democracies and are therefore unenforceable' (*ibid.*, p. 2). The compromise was the creation of two separate
covenants, the *International Covenant on Civil and Political Rights* and
the *International Covenant on Economic, Social and Cultural Rights*. In
other words, the right to adequate incomes and food security are held
to be subject to the political process and are not in fact inalienable. Yet
civil and political rights which are viewed as 'negative rights' are

'viewed as inherent, universal and justiciable, while social and economic rights are viewed as evolving gradually in the political sphere, more a matter of social policy than of fundamental justice' (*ibid.*, pp. 2–3). It is not therefore surprising that the *Canadian Charter on Rights and Freedom* (1982) sought to exclude social and economic rights from its provisions.

Echenberg and Porter contest these distinctions, correctly observing that

> the requirement of food, clothing, housing, education and medical care is surely no less universal or inherent to a life of freedom of choice and autonomy than the requisite civil and political rights. Safeguarding social and economic rights also requires putting a 'check' on the power and tendency of the state to marginalize particular groups, and to limit the extent to which these groups share the collective wealth. (*ibid.*, p. 3)

Indeed, in the context of developing effective anti-hunger policies it must be stressed that the protection of 'positive rights' requires a strong collectivist, interventionist and redistributive stance by governments, whereas 'negative rights' and freedoms (although allegedly unobtainable) are largely rhetorical and unenforceable. Significantly, right-wing governments favouring this configuration of negative rights are not in the business of serious redistribution.

TRANSFORMING THE POLITICS OF HUNGER[1]

The period 1981–95 teaches a number of lessons about the politics of hunger and food security in Canada. First, food banks have tried but failed to stem the growth of hunger. As the Toronto Food Policy Council rightly argues, the food charity system has failed because it 'does not have the capacity to address any of the deeper structural issues that have created the conditions of poverty and hunger' (TFPC, 1994a, p. 7). The provision of emergency food assistance is not by itself sufficient. In its view community action and public policy must instead be focused on policies to bring about local food security if hunger is to be eliminated. Second, it is clear that governments, for the time being at any rate, have decided to abandon any commitment to the idea that people have a right to adequate welfare incomes and thereby to the chance of achieving food security. Structural adjustment and welfare reform policies have been wholeheartedly embraced by governments and they have chosen to take aim at the poor and unemployed, with tragic human consequences. Third, despite the view that the majority of Canadians believe that hunger should be addressed by government, the evidence suggests that hunger has been depoliticized as a public policy issue. Today, Canadian federal and provincial social policy is about minimal government, dismantling the welfare state and reimposing the charitable model. In other words, if the right to food security is to achieve the priority attention of governments a difficult task lies ahead. To use the language of the Bread for the World Institute, the politics of hunger must be transformed (BWI, 1994).

Yet the current political climate does not bode well, despite the fact that Canadian public opinion when compared to that of elite decision-makers ranks government intervention and collective rights more highly (Ekos, Research Associates, 1995). Progressive alternatives have few voices in Canada's legislative assemblies and the country could be said to be facing political malaise and a democratic crisis in terms of electoral representation. There is no effective progressive parliamentary opposition at either federal or provincial government levels to the welfare reform proposals that are being currently enacted. In Ottawa, the Reform Party is well to the right of even the right-wing Liberal government and the official opposition, the Bloc Québecois, whilst held to be somewhat progressive on matters of social policy, has another agenda in mind, the independence of Quebec and the breakup of Canada. The possible exceptions are Saskatchewan and British Columbia, where NDP governments, at the time of writing, are in power but the NDP has itself followed fiscally conservative economic policy and restrictive welfare reform. Moreover, given the first-past-the-post electoral system that applies in Canada parties continue to achieve power with less than a majority of the popular vote. For example, Mulroney's election win in 1988 which resulted in free trade with the United States and later the Goods and Services Tax, both policies which were strongly opposed by the Canadian public, represented a minority of the popular vote as did the 1995 anti-welfare election victory in Ontario of the Progressive Conservatives.

The voice of dissent is being silenced in other ways. As the CCSD has noted, the federal government in the 1994 *Social Security Review* failed to indicate its intention to repeal CAP and to introduce CHST, thereby depriving the public of an open debate (CCSD, 1995, p. 11). NGO leaders are being told to curb their advocacy if they wish to continue to receive public funds. The World Food Day Association, the NGO responsible for development education on issues of food security, had its funding eliminated by the federal government. In Alberta, government social service staff and union officials have been disciplined by the Minister of Social Services for speaking out against welfare cutbacks (*Edmonton Journal*, 25 January 1994).

Yet despite these setbacks progressive ideas and actions needed to inform the struggle against hunger and poverty are being debated and to some extent acted upon. Three themes merit consideration: community-based ideas advocating the right to food security; strategies for community and public action aimed at securing such rights; and the need for a coherent and progressive agenda and solidarity within the popular sector by those organizations which voice their criticisms but who, to date, have failed to present a united front.

Establishing the Right to Food Security

In Canada a debate is currently taking place within the activist food community about policy goals and directions. The outcome of the debate has significant implications for resolving the hunger issue. Some within the food bank movement see the challenge as rekindling the charitable and voluntary ethos and continuing to hand out wasted food. The moral imperative informing this approach is difficult to resist given the practical consideration that hungry people require immediate material assistance. Its proponents have the support of governments and enjoy public legitimacy. Yet this approach has failed to stem the growth of hunger.

There is however, within the food bank movement, another set of ideas which is about fighting to prevent the institutionalization of food banks and making the case that effective employment policies, adequate incomes and welfare benefits and affordable housing are crucial to solving the problem of hunger. Public education and advocacy remains the policy of the national CAFB, particularly in regard to securing the rights of those on social assistance to adequate allowances. Such policies support the work of NAPO and the CCPI in their national and international welfare advocacy. This has proved a difficult road to follow in that the Canadian courts have shown only a lukewarm interest in recognizing such rights (Young, 1994, pp. 31–5). Whilst the *Canadian Charter of Rights and Freedoms* has been interpreted by the Supreme Court of Canada to support social welfare rights, lower courts have tended to deny them (see Jackman, 1994, pp. 65–94). Nevertheless this advocacy is strengthened by the resolve of anti-poverty organizations such as End Legislated Poverty in Vancouver and the

Charter Committee on Poverty Issues, which insist that the voice of the poor themselves is heard in the debate.

Importantly, the Canadian Hunger Foundation (CHF), at the request of Agriculture Canada, invited representatives of international aid organizations, domestic food agencies and welfare organizations to help draft the Canadian government statement to be submitted to the Global Assembly on Food Security, held in Quebec City in 1995 to mark the 50th anniversary of the founding of the UN Food and Agricultural Organization. Empowerment and community-based strategies are key elements of the CHF's draft statement as well as the development of a Canadian anti-hunger movement. Similarly, Health Canada in response to the FAO for a global plan of action focused on nutrition, has released a draft of its plan 'Nutrition for Health – An Action Plan for Canada'. It identifies three key challenges: improvement in food choices and practice; increased support for nutritionally vulnerable Canadians and greater emphasis on nutrition in food policies. It sets as one of its targets the two-thirds reduction of the numbers of people using food banks, though it must be observed that this objective seems far removed from the reality of increased hunger caused by federal social security reforms. It is also significant that the Canadian Dietetic Association, the organization of professional nutritionists, is being urged to take up the issue of food security (Campbell, 1991; Davis *et al.*, 1991).

Interestingly, the community health movement and food policy councils in Ontario and British Columbia reflect the ideas of the earlier Peoples Food Commission and articulate a broader critique. They argue that the real goal is local food security. This necessitates going beyond issues of social security reform and requires developing a comprehensive set of policies, focused on rethinking full employment, supporting green economic renewal and industrial strategy, developing food self-reliance and understanding food policy as health promotion. It requires participatory, 'bottom-up' development informed by the principles and practices of community development with local food security as the primary objective (TFPC, 1994a, 1994b; Kalina, 1993).

The OPHA has developed a more specific food and nutrition strategy for Ontario built around the policy objectives of equal access to food (that is, all residents of Ontario having the means to access affordable, nutritious and personally acceptable foods); a sustainable food supply (that is, ensuring a long-term safe, high quality food supply) and food for health (that is, promoting food consumption patterns that maximize health and minimize disease in Canada) (OPHA, 1995).

Equal access to food necessitates: addressing societal inequities; ensuring an affordable, nutritious food supply including creating greater access to farmers markets and community gardens, community kitchens and food co-operatives (rather than food banks); supporting diet and nutritional counselling and services for nutritionally vulnerable people; promoting people's ability to prepare nutritious foods; supporting but rethinking full employment; raising minimum wage and social assistance to levels that cover basic living costs and monitoring these levels; ensuring adequate, affordable housing; raising levels of secondary education and reducing illiteracy (*ibid.*, pp. 49–57).

Long-term policies to support a sustainable food supply require financial incentives to decrease pesticide use, support for farmers in the transition to sustainable agriculture and the development of a full information system for consumers (*ibid.*, p. 58). Food health promotion means enforcing nutrition standards in mass catering settings (e.g. day care centres and school meal programmes) and increasing the opportunities for food preparation skill development (*ibid.*, p. 59).

Essentially what is being argued by progressive food policy experts is that too many people are no longer in control of what they eat, whether or not they have sufficient income. Local control of the production and distribution of nutritious food has been taken over by the giants of the transnational corporate agriculture and food industry where the bottom line is food for profit not nutritional value and the health of the community. Kneen refers to the development of this global food system as a process of 'distancing: separating people from the sources of their food and nutrition with as many interventions as possible' (Kneen, 1993, p. 7). The result is that individuals, families and communities have become disempowered and deskilled in terms of their capacity to produce their own food, make sound choices when they purchase food and feed themselves nutritional and well-balanced diets. Food banks are fundamentally reactive in that they merely pass on the wasted leftovers of a capitalist food system that is organized against the interests of the poor. They also fail to provide the hungry with an effective voice in challenging the system which is making them dependent. Government, by failing to promote integrated agricultural, food, health and nutrition polices focused on establishing food security as a right for all, acts in the final analysis to support profit maximization in the food industry. One obvious conclusion is that those working in these respective fields along with those on the receiving end of their services must join forces in the struggle for local food security.

Action Strategies

Establishing food security as an economic and social right in Canada requires public action in the domestic as well as global arena. Internationally the work of NAPO, the CCPI and others in contesting the repeal of the Canada Assistance Plan to the United Nations is significant. Such actions focus an unwelcome spotlight of attention on Canada particularly given Canadians' perception that they live in a fair-minded and compassionate society buttressed by the *Charter of Rights and Freedoms*. Yet the country's continuing high rates of unemployment and child poverty and its mean-spirited and increasingly punitive welfare policies stand in stark contrast. In this context the UN *Covenant on Economic, Social and Cultural Rights*, the *Convention on the Rights of the Child* and Canada's signing of the *World Declaration on Nutrition* provide important international tools and mechanisms for advocacy and citizens' groups to criticize domestic injustice. International law could become an important point of reference for Canadian courts as and when questions of welfare adequacy or food insecurity are brought to their attention.

A further opportunity is afforded at the international level by the 1995 World Social Summit to stimulate debate about policies designed to eliminate hunger. The *Copenhagen Declaration on Social Development* which was signed by heads of states and governments was the first such international declaration committing itself to the eradication of world poverty and the establishment of a programme of action. In significant ways the declaration fell short of the expectations of Canadian NGOs. Concern was expressed that Prime Minister Chretien failed to attend the Summit indicating the Government of Canada's low priority for the proceedings. The point was well made. The federal government was just at that time cutting social spending and repealing the Canada Assistance Plan, thereby significantly increasing the prospects of even higher rates of poverty. Heavily criticized was the 'reliance on the market economy as the means to achieve social development, when there is broad recognition by NGOs that it is these same market forces which are at the root of rising poverty and unemployment. This contradiction threatens the realization of the goals of the Social Summit' (Shookner and Pfrimmer, 10 March 1995). Yet despite the document's shortcomings it remains an important tool for promoting domestic strategies directed at the elimination of hunger and poverty in Canada.

The declaration includes national-level commitments by states to prepare time-bound strategies to end poverty; it recognizes the central role of women in political, civil and economic, social and cultural life and development and considers their role as a key precondition for social development; it articulates freely chosen full employment as a basic priority of economic and social policies; it affirms that human rights and social development form part of the same continuum and it recognizes that structural adjustment policies and the need to balance budgets should not be at the expense of destabilizing society and of the poor; and it recognizes that the empowerment of civil society is a *sine qua non* for sound social development policy. It also declares the first UN decade for the eradication of poverty to begin in 1997 (World Summit for Social Development, 1995, p. 2).

At the federal level given the government's offloading of its welfare responsibilities to the provinces, a task now made easier by the election of an anti-welfare government in Ontario, the largest and most influential of the provinces, it will be more difficult for the debate about economic and social rights to be addressed. Whilst the federal social security reform agenda continues its real purpose has been confirmed by the 1995 national budget including the repeal of CAP, the move to block funding, the cuts to transfer payments and the eventual elimination of direct health, post-secondary education and welfare funding to the provinces. National standards, it is said, will be replaced by national policy objectives, but unless federal transfer payments under the new CHST are tied to specific conditions, it is unlikely the provinces will comply. The social and economic rights of Canadian citizenship are on the chopping block. Reforms to unemployment insurance have resulted in stricter eligibility criteria and further benefit cuts. Moreover the continuing debate over Quebec independence, although quietened by defeat in the 1995 referendum, will weaken any attempts by those wishing to see national standards retained in the long run. Quebec will reject any idea that its social policies should be required to conform to federal norms established in Ottawa, preferring to have the dollars in their own hands to spend as they please, an attractive proposition for other provinces. In this climate, with a hostile media and with no parliamentary opposition to support them, advocacy for progressive ideas at the federal level will be difficult to sustain.

However, as a result of federal offloading the focus for public action about hunger and food security in the foreseeable future is likely to shift to the provincial and municipal levels. Indeed it is probably essential that it does. If provincial governments act on their constitutional mandates and pursue welfare reform with the same harshness as Alberta and Ontario, where Professor Lightman has warned that the politics of punishment is now being waged, the poor and unemployed will face workfare, reduced benefits and increasing hunger. Food banks will face a growing demand, but the focus of political struggle is likely to be directed at provincial governments. Evidence of this is already apparent in light of the Bread and Roses March on the Quebec National Assembly organized by the women's movement in early June 1995 and mass demonstrations against the Ontario government. Indeed, if the debate and strategizing at the national and international levels are to be sustained, and it is crucial that they are, local advocacy groups will need to hold provincial governments accountable for the Government of Canada's commitments under international law and its signing of the *World Declaration on Nutrition* the *Declaration and Programme of Action of the World Social Summit*, particularly their pledges to develop national action plans to advance nutrition and eliminate poverty. The significance of such a strategy lies in the fact that prior to the federal government's ratifying international convenants it must constitutionally have the prior approval of the provinces. This suggests that provincial governments are a primary focus for advocacy and organizing. Slowly it might then prove possible to articulate and reclaim the right to adequate welfare benefits and then assert and establish the right to food security and all that it implies.

In conclusion, what are the minimum requirements for the eradication of hunger in Canada? From the standpoint of political strategy, the progressive revival of the social sector in Canada is essential. It will need to overcome the politics of difference which currently fragments it and which enables neo-conservative ideas to claim the public agenda because progressive forces are themselves unfocused. It will need to bring together those working in charitable food banks with those in anti-poverty organizations as well as effecting strategic coalitions between the health, welfare, education, nutrition, and food policy and agricultural sectors. A Canadian anti-hunger movement is required. It will need to engage labour, the women's movement and environmentalists. As Leonard has argued, there is a need for a reforged sense of solidarity and emancipatory politics committed to economic and social justice. As he suggests, it 'requires rejecting market dependency... and empowering those who experience the state and the economy as repressive' (Leonard, 1994, pp. 62–3). If hunger is to be beaten, it must first be recognized as a universal need and food security accepted as a basic human right. Only in this way will a new social vision for Canada be developed and one which can transform the politics of hunger and ensure that food security is a fact of life for all.

NOTE

1. This heading is taken from the 1994 Report of the Bread for the World Institute, *Transforming the Politics of Hunger.*

4 Hunger in New Zealand: A Question of Rights?

Stephen Uttley

INTRODUCTION

A. H. Boerma, a past head of the Food and Agriculture Organization of the United Nations, in introducing a collection of his speeches which he made in 1974 on questions of food, hunger and development, stated, 'If human beings have a right to life at all, they have a right to food' (Boerma, 1976). Whilst this may seem a self-evident assertion to which everyone could subscribe, during the 1990s New Zealand has seen a vigorous debate about such a proposition and its implications for both individual responsibility and government social policy. In a food producing and exporting country such as New Zealand, little attention has been paid to questions of hunger, or indeed poverty, since the economic depression of the 1920s and early 1930s. It is only recently that issues of hunger, lack of access to food and a broader concern about poverty in general have entered into the public arena for discussion. This concern has paralleled a rapid growth in both the numbers of food banks and foodbank users since about 1990.

Unlike many other countries such as the UK, USA and Canada there was no 'rediscovery' of poverty in New Zealand during the 1960s and 1970s. In essence poverty has been seen as part of the history of European colonization and was eliminated to all intent and purposes in the wake of the Great Depression. Since that time poverty has been regarded as a minor and unwelcome adjunct to economic growth and development through which small groups of people are at least partially excluded from the benefits of rising material expectations and standards of living. The Royal Commission on Social Security, which reported in 1972, played a key role in consolidating a social security system which had been set up in 1938 to respond to the needs of such groups. They explicitly considered the question of poverty and its measurement and concluded that New Zealand was indeed fortunate that poverty was not an obvious social problem. The Commission did link future economic growth and development with the risk of increasing poverty but it was couched in terms of poverty amidst plenty and the need to commit part of these extra resources to assist those who found themselves in poverty because of structural or personal reasons (Royal Commission on Social Security, 1972, p. 106). This general approach to poverty was mirrored throughout the 1970s by a series of reports from government advisory bodies, which expressed concern about the impact of changing economic circumstances on family incomes but which presented this as being caused by a small group of families falling a little behind as the standard of living and related expectations rose (New Zealand Council of Social Services (NZCSS), 1976, p. 1; New Zealand Social Development Council (NZSDC), 1977, p. 5)

New Zealand still has no official system of measuring poverty and changes to the nature and extent of hardship. Although the 1972 Royal Commission did urge the development of better social statistics to monitor household income and expenditure the only tangible result of this has been a household income and expenditure survey. This survey has not, however, been used to develop specific measures of poverty. New Zealand academics have paid little attention to poverty with the exception of economist Brian Easton, who has attempted to measure and monitor poverty rates since the early 1970s.

Concerns about poverty have been voiced for some time by a variety of community social agencies. In the mid-1970s a Citizen's Advice Bureau (CAB) in a suburb of Auckland sought to identify detailed family expenditure patterns in order to understand better a perceived increase in poverty (Glen Innes CAB, 1975). A budget advice service in Christchurch found that families in financial difficulty usually had little or no discretionary income once they had met their basic household costs. These families frequently had to cut spending on several fronts in order to balance their budgets, and reducing food costs was at the forefront in these economies. As a result families often dropped below a baseline food allowance which had been defined by the advice service (Crean, 1982, pp. 12–15). This picture of families cutting back on food expenditure, heating costs and postponing visits to doctors was confirmed in an opinion poll conducted by the Heylen organization in 1984 (Waldegrave and Coventry, 1987, pp. 35–7). As part of a review of administrative compliance, the Department of Social Welfare[1] (DSW), the government agency responsible for administering the social security system, looked at the financial position of those receiving unemployment benefit (UB) and the domestic purposes benefit (DPB) (usually a payment to sole parents caring for children) in 1985. This research indicated problems in meeting health, housing, clothing and food costs and was regarded as likely to have significantly underestimated financial deprivation and hardship (Rochford, 1987).

By the 1990s hunger and access to food had become firmly established on the political agenda. An advisory group looking at diet and nutrition argued that there were strong links between food and health with good access to food promoting physical and mental well-being and poor access leading to illness and premature death (Nutrition Taskforce, 1991, p. ix). The Public Health Commission (PHC), which was responsible for promoting public health, in a wide-ranging review of the health status of New Zealanders argued strongly for the adoption of the UN's definition of food security: 'A household is food secure when it has access to food needed for healthy life for its members (adequate in terms of quality, quantity, safety and cultural acceptability) and when it is not at undue risk of losing such access' (PHC, 1993, p. 80). The Commission went on to observe that in a modern industrial economy food security depends on the purchasing power of households because the options available under subsistence agriculture have been largely removed. Any measures which endanger purchasing power may in turn endanger food security for households. Groups committed to challenging government policies were indeed claiming that many New Zealanders no longer had basic food security as defined by the United Nations. A member of the People's Select Committee, a group of public figures invited by community groups to run a public inquiry like a government commission of inquiry, said of her experiences of listening to people's 'evidence' to the group: 'I found the evidence of widespread hunger, the anguish of mothers unable to feed their hungry teenagers, particularly gruelling, knowing in a land rich in food resources this is a man-made need' (People's Select Committee, 1992, p. iii).

FOOD BANKS: A RESPONSE TO HARDSHIP

The rapid rise of food security to the status of a major public concern in New Zealand has been closely linked to the emergence and dramatic growth in food banks. Food banks in New Zealand act as both the central points for collection and storage of food aid as well as being the point of distribution to those seeking help. The first food bank is thought to have started in Auckland which is by far New Zealand's biggest centre of population during 1980. There were further food banks developed during the 1980s although the number of food banks was still quite small, even by the end of the decade (Social Policy Agency

(SPA), 1994, p. 2). At the same time the more traditional channels of providing food aid in the form of soup kitchens had also experienced growth in demand and a change in their users who were no longer mostly single men but a much wider cross-section of the community, including families with children (*Dominion*, 6 December 1989).

In the absence of any national organization or systematic monitoring exact quantification of the growth in food banks is difficult, however it is thought that the numbers of food banks doubled in both 1990 and 1991 and although the rate of growth has lessened there is still about a 20 per cent per annum increase (Old, 1991, p. 19; SPA, 1994, pp. 2–4). The pattern of growth has also varied in different parts of the country. The total number of food banks is now estimated to be 365, with over a third of these being in the Auckland area although there are likely to be small food aid programmes operating which have not been included in this overall figure. Demands on food banks tend to be at their highest during the winter months when people face high heating costs, and at Christmas time, although there is local variation, for example, in areas in which seasonal work such as fruitpicking is an important but variable source of income.

Just as the number of food banks has increased dramatically so has the scale of help which they provide. There are no national statistics on the volume of food parcels distributed, but the SPA in a recent review of food banks quotes the figures for the Salvation Army's programmes; these are set out in Table 4.1.

Table 4.1 Number of People Receiving Food Parcels, 1990–4

Year	Food Parcels
1990	1 226
1991	2 124
1992	10 261
1993	14 347
1994	14 906

Source: SPA (1994, p. 3).

It is estimated that during 1994 around 43 000 food parcels will have been distributed with a monetary value of $25 million. Whilst the momentum for the growth in food bank numbers was established by 1990 the dramatic increase in the scale of assistance is generally agreed to be a result of major changes in policy concerning benefit levels which were introduced in April 1991.

It is the voluntary welfare sector which has found itself at the forefront in providing food banks and within the voluntary sector most although not all food banks have close affiliations to the churches. A survey of a selection of food banks in 1991 found that very few had any paid workers, being almost entirely reliant on volunteers who usually worked for less than 10 hours each week. The volunteers are mostly women and usually aged 60 years and over (Old, 1991, pp. 11–23). Whilst there may be some limited resources from charitable trusts or governmental sources, food banks have been funded predominantly by the churches and through individual donations. Similarly, the food for distribution has come from the churches and their congregations, with perhaps limited support from donations through local food supermarkets. The volume of food for distribution has been affected by the increase in the number of food banks and the demands placed on them. In addition, donations of food and money to food banks have become an established and ongoing demand upon charitable giving rather than a temporary emergency. Food banks have become anxious about 'donor fatigue' and their ability to ensure continuity of food supplies. An agency such as the Salvation Army has reported having to purchase around 80 per cent of the food being provided (*Dominion*, 3 June 1992). Most food parcels provide only basic commodities such as bread, cereal, margarine, tea, sugar and milk. Food banks provide parcels which are designed for a particular household size and composition. The two most common approaches are parcels for 2–4 days or for 5–7 days, although some food banks give parcels merely to cover the immediate situation over a night or the next day (Old, 1991, pp. 14–15; SPA, 1994, pp. 6–8). The SPA report also identifies concerns about the quality of food provided and in particular the presence of damaged goods in food parcels and that the amount and composition of food parcels may be inadequate (1994, p. 7).

Food banks have developed additional services such as help with furniture, clothing and advice on budgeting and some offer counselling assistance too. These services aim to respond to a range of perceived needs amongst those coming to food banks but are also seen as a way in which food banks have sought to control, monitor and moderate demands for food by users, for example by making use of budgeting services as a requirement for receiving food aid or by limiting the frequency at which food aid can be given (*Listener*, 19 December 1992; SPA, 1994, pp. 7–8). The pressures placed on food banks have also been felt by other agencies in the non-profit sector, especially those who provide broad-ranging advice services, such as the CAB, which had increasing numbers of people seeking help about food access and budgeting (CAB, 1992; NZCSS, 1992). A widely shared concern is that food banks have had to find ways of deciding whom to help and how they will help with limited resources, including limited knowledge and expertise amongst food bank workers about what resources and services might be available to particular users. In these circumstances those seeking help have few if any rights and are almost entirely dependent on the goodwill of the food bank workers (McGurk and Clark, 1993, pp. 8–20).

These problems have been compounded by the actions and public perceptions of the Income Support Service (ISS) which is part of DSW, the government agency responsible for income maintenance services. There is ample evidence that ISS has had substantial problems in administering discretionary assistance measures which are meant to help people in circumstances such as inadequate food security. The ISS has also allowed a situation to develop in which agency staff regularly send those receiving social security benefits to food banks for additional assistance almost as a standard procedure (SPA, 1994, pp. 14–15). Community agencies report growing resistance from people to return to ISS because of the perception that their staff lack adequate knowledge of the assistance programmes which they are administering, the physical location of ISS offices and the personal treatment of applicants by staff (CAB, 1992; McGurk and Clark, 1993, pp. 18–19). Whilst it could be argued that these problems are the result of repeated policy and organizational change, the implications are that the legal rights of beneficiaries to special assistance are compromised. Food banks face a dilemma in the sense that most believe that government, through the ISS, should be the main source of assistance in achieving food security but in the face of inaction by government they cannot stand by and let people experience hunger. In this respect food banks in New Zealand face the same dilemma as that encountered by food banks in other countries (Riches, 1992–3).

It has already been noted that the growth of food banks reflects a move away from food assistance being confined to itinerant single men and towards a much more diverse range of people. There are, however, some common elements among those coming to food banks. The vast majority are in receipt of a social security benefit from government either in the form of an UB or a DPB which is paid predominantly to women caring for children on their own (Old, 1991, pp. 15–16; Jackman,

1993, pp. 14–20; SPA, 1994, pp. 8–9). The higher the number of children in the beneficiary family the more likely they are to need food aid. The identification of female-headed single-parent families and larger families confirms a wide range of research material which reports that these groups are at high risk of material hardship. Single-parent households with children have also been recognized as major users of food aid in other countries (Riches, 1992–3). Maori and Pacific Island migrants are substantially over-represented in both these groups, which means that there is an overlay of ethnicity in food bank use. It is thought that about 10 per cent of food bank users are young people aged under 20 years. This group has been particularly affected by the incidence of unemployment and specific reductions in both the level of unemployment benefit and conditions under which benefit can be claimed (*Signpost*, 1994).

Even as early as 1990 the Wellington Inner City Mission was reporting that while most people seeking food aid had a detailed family budget against which they were trying to live, they found themselves unable to achieve that budget because of unexpected bills (Inner City Ministry, 1990). These problems have worsened in the face of high levels of unemployment including long-term unemployment, changes in health, housing, taxation and other social polices and in particular cuts in social security benefit levels in 1991. Added to these problems are those related to the operation of the social security system which include delays in processing benefit applications, delayed or inaccurate payments and unexpected withdrawal of benefit (Old, 1991, pp. 20–5; SPA, 1994, pp. 14–15).

The financial pressures on budgets obviously affect the kind of food which people can consume. The Public Health Commission on the basis of the National Household Expenditure Survey data for 1992 concluded that low-income households have high consumption of cheaper foods such as bread, cereals, sugar, milk and low consumption of higher cost foods such as fruit, vegetables, fish and meat (PHC, 1993, p. 81). There seems to be agreement that food is in some ways seen as a discretionary area of expenditure in the sense that faced with demands related to housing, health, education, energy costs or meeting debts incurred by borrowing, altering food consumption is one of the few ways in which expenditure can be modified to meet an immediate budgetary problem (*Dominion*, 9 June 1992; People's Select Committee, 1992, pp. 6–10; SPA, 1994, pp. 11–14). It now seems that food parcels have become incorporated into the regular budget expectations of an increasing number of families. Regular food aid is obtained either from a single food bank or by going to several food banks over time, perhaps in a regular rotation (Jackman, 1993, p. 14; SPA, 1994, p. 5). Again, this picture of continual reliance on food parcels for groups within the population has been reported from other countries (Riches, 1993).

There is particular anxiety about the impact of hunger amongst children. The Plunket Society, which monitors the care of very young children, has expressed apprehension about the impact on babies of hunger during pregnancy, upon breast-feeding and families being unable to afford feeding formulas and either using cow's milk or diluting formula feeds (Jesson, 1991). The People's Select Committee found that schools were worried about children coming to school inadequately fed (1992, p. 7) and these fears have been especially evident in the Auckland region (Fowler and Schmidt, 1994). This issue has been subjected to a national survey of schools commissioned by the PHC. On the basis of that survey it is estimated that schools believe that about 3.4 per cent or 22 600 children regularly come to school hungry. Hunger is more likely amongst secondary school children and for Maori and Pacific Island children. Some schools are running food programmes of their own with these mostly being focused on a small group of children within the school who are regarded as being at high risk of hunger. The report to the Commission points out that there is not only the worry about the impact of hunger on school children in the here and now, but also about the long-term impact on their future well-being (Food and Nutrition Consultancy Service, 1995, pp. 1–3).

WHY FOOD BANKS? SETTING INSTITUTIONAL CHANGE IN A BROADER CONTEXT

Whilst the dramatic growth of food bank provision in New Zealand has been concentrated in the post-1990 period, it would be wrong to ignore earlier changes in New Zealand society which were effectively creating greater levels of risk to the achievement of food security. Throughout the 1970s and early 1980s New Zealanders were partly insulated from the effects of a deteriorating economic and fiscal position by successive governments who sought to control prices and wages, to maintain a closed and highly protected domestic economy and a highly subsidized export sector and who retained a commitment to full employment. A significant growth in social expenditure which occurred in other OECD countries in the late 1960s and early 1970s did not fully impact on New Zealand until the late 1970s and early 1980s.

This substantial increase in social spending partly reflected policies introduced between 1973 and 1976 which included a statutory social security benefit for sole parents, a universal accident compensation scheme which included cover for non-earners and a generous universal superannuation benefit payable to everyone aged 60 and over.

The Labour government which came to power in the election of 1984 was faced with an immediate financial crisis, including a currency crisis. Over the subsequent six years two successive Labour governments radically reformed the economy and public sector in accordance with economic liberal thinking in a more extensive manner than the Thatcher or Reagan governments. What had historically been a highly protected economy was rapidly opened up and tariffs, import quotas and subsidies were substantially lowered or removed. Government and government activities were scrutinized with a view to reducing the size of the state and returning trading activities wherever possible to the private sector. By 1989 the dominance of monetary policy was enshrined in the requirement that New Zealand's central bank pursue a 0–2 per cent inflation target as its overriding objective.

The extensive and radical nature of these reforms has had an impact on everyone. However, two areas of policy change had particular importance for those in low-income households. The taxation system was substantially reformed. What had been a highly progressive personal income tax system with a high top rate of tax was compressed to just two tax rates. These changes substantially assisted those on higher incomes, especially as they took place in a high inflation environment. The tax base was also reformed in 1985 with the introduction of a goods and services tax (GST). Such taxes are generally viewed as regressive, but the New Zealand scheme was distinctive for its comprehensiveness, with the inclusion of almost all goods and services. Despite opposition, food and clothing were made subject to the levy of GST. A compensatory payment in the form of an income-tested payment to families caring for children was introduced but inflation seriously eroded its real value even prior to its being enacted and a subsequent lack of regular indexation of the payment has further reduced its value.

Continual restructuring of both private and public sector activity, euphemistically referred to as 'downsizing', has resulted in the continued shedding of labour and large increases in unemployment. Until 1977 New Zealand's unemployment rate was less than 1 per cent and well below the OECD average. It rose to around 5 per cent by the mid-1980s, still well below the average, before increasing rapidly from 1987 to 1992 when the rate was above 10 per cent and well in excess of the OECD level (Prime Ministerial Task Force on Employment, 1994, pp. 21–2). There has been concern about the increasing presence of significant long-term unemployment and a fear that even with a return to higher levels of employment it might not be possible to reintegrate those people into the workforce. Table 4.2 describes changes in unemployment levels. A relatively high rate of economic growth in recent years has reduced unemployment rates and had some impact on long-term unemployment. Increases in part-time and casual work within that employment growth pattern and the necessity for multiple jobs still remain as sources of concern to some, as does a return to higher unemployment rates as the economy is being constrained to forestall inflationary pressures.

The Labour Party lost the 1990 election and the National (Conservative) Party was returned to power. The National government was committed to the continuation of economic and public sector reforms but was also committed to two further areas of change, namely labour market and social policy reform. It is not possible to discuss labour reforms in any detail here other than that they were driven by market liberal notions of individual freedom and involved the removal of perceived 'rigidities' in the labour market, a reduction in the influence of trade unions and the replacement of collective wage agreements by individual contracts.

Whilst changes in access to employment and work conditions are important, food banks themselves have focused on social policy changes as being a more direct contributing factor to their growth and some of the more significant changes are briefly described below.

Education

There has been ongoing change in the structure and organization of education services since 1988. The aim has been to increase parental influence, control and responsibility for what goes on in schools. Whilst public education is still nominally free, funding changes related to reform have seen 'donations' become an important component of school budgets. These payments, and those linked to a wide variety of school activities, can pose an impossible dilemma for families on low incomes with several school-aged children. The concerns of school staff about children coming to school hungry have already been described. The Special Education Services in a recent submission to a parliamentary committee estimated that one in five children are at risk of educational failure in New Zealand schools. They argued that poverty increased the likelihood of absence from school as children tried to deal with the effects of crises within their family and noted that when at school the combination of the physical and emotional consequences of poverty meant that these children were unable to make use of educational opportunity in the classroom (*Auckland Herald*, 29 December 1994).

Housing

New Zealand has a history of publicly provided rental housing through central government. There have been various changes in recent policy including making state rental units available for sale and the introduction of income-related rental levels. The system of housing support payments for those on low incomes or receiving benefits was modified in 1993 in a way which made a payment available to those in private sector rental units but decreased the level of assistance to some in public rental units. Food banks have continually expressed concern about the impact of housing costs on food security. A survey of northern New Zealand conducted by NZCOSS and the Salvation Army in 1992 found that about a third of all food bank users were in state rental houses. They were concerned about the likely effect of the new housing support payment and surveyed food bank workers in south Auckland shortly after the policy change. Most users were estimated to be spending over 30 per cent of their net income on housing costs and about 50 per cent in state rentals and 60 per cent in private rentals were spending over half their income. Around 90 per cent of users had faced an increase in rents during the policy changes and around a third had seen their rents doubled. Sole parent-headed households were thought to have been particularly harshly affected (NZCCSS/Salvation Army, 1994). These findings actually confirm the forecasts of the government agency responsible for implementing the policy, which expected a substantial increase in the numbers of households paying over 50 per cent of their income on housing (Jackman, 1993, p. 16). There seems general agreement that housing policy changes have placed household budgets under considerable additional strain.

Health

Whilst the New Zealand welfare state has featured free hospital care and medicines, access to primary health care has been based on a fee for service by the patient, supplemented by a universal subsidy from government. The balance of cost between government and patient has generally moved in such a way as to leave the patient facing an increasing proportion of that cost. The policy since 1990, and indeed in the 1984–90 period, has been to introduce more part-charges, including experimenting with charges for hospital care and increasingly stringent charging regimes for medicines in the face of a continuing escalation in costs. Government has argued that its targeting system should ensure that those on low incomes will have access to the full range of health services at minimal direct cost. There have been longstanding concerns about the reality of access for low-income people and much anecdotal evidence of people trying to access the lowest cost part of the system and deferring use of services either for themselves or for other family members. Whilst governments have maintained that there is no hard evidence to substantiate such concerns, it could be argued that having claimed that access for low-income people would be enhanced through targeting the onus of proof rested on the government. Successive governments have conspicuously failed to set up research to monitor and evaluate health policy performance in this way.

Evidence about health status does little to allay concerns, especially where the health of children is concerned. New Zealand has one of the highest infant mortality rates in the OECD, the highest post-neonatal mortality rate and in the case of Maori children the lowest birth weights (Department of Health, 1989, p. 216). New Zealand also finds itself continually at the 'top of a league table' for suicide rates among 15–19 year olds (*ibid.*, p. 210; UNICEF, 1994).

Data from a longitudinal study of children born in Christchurch in 1977 have confirmed that there are long-term effects of stress and poor physical environment. Studies in South Auckland have shown that where there is poor nutritional status amongst children there will be an increase in skin infections, head lice, gastroenteritis, respiratory infections and anaemia. Children who experience these home circumstances frequently fail to achieve the developmental milestones at the same rate as other children (Jackman, 1993, pp. 21–2). In addition to concerns about child health the enthusiastic adoption of deinstitutionalization policies for those with a mental disability has placed large numbers of adults into the community. Inadequate housing, lack of employment and inadequate levels of income support have meant that this group has been identified as being at risk of material hardship as well as repeated periods of brief hospitalization (Mason Report, 1988). Those placed in community care have also been identified as a distinct group of users of food banks (*Listener*, 1 April 1991).

Income Maintenance Policy

Table 4.2 describes changes in the pattern of number of benefits being paid for unemployment benefit and domestic purposes benefit since 1981.

Table 4.2 Unemployment and Domestic Purposes Benefits, 1975–94

Year	Unemployment Benefit	Domestic Purposes Benefit*
1975	2 891	17 231
1980	20 850	37 040
1985	38 419	56 548
1986	12 405	62 570
1987	63 922	69 146
1988	86 782	74 862
1989	123 565	85 615
1990	139 625	94 823
1991	153 259	97 000
1992	170 367	96 722
1993	170 339	96 335
1994	157 182	100 256

* Payment predominantly to sole parents caring for children introduced as a statutory benefit in 1973.
Source: Department of Social Welfare, *Statistical Information Report* (Wellington: DSW, 1994).

New Zealanders have faced a sustained period of reductions in their living standards. It is estimated that between 1981 and 1991 the average loss of purchasing power for wage and salary earners was in the order of 3.6 per cent (Jackman, 1993, p. 14). The fall in living standards, however, was not evenly distributed between all households in the community with the bottom 10 per cent of income households experiencing a fall in the order of 20 per cent in their purchasing power. Single parents with children figure prominently in that bottom 10 per cent of households and it is estimated that this group faced an especially sharp drop in living standards from March 1990 to March 1991 (Mowbray, 1993, p. 20). Even a study sponsored by the New Zealand Treasury which analysed 1988/9 household expenditure survey data and using a stringent poverty line based on the proportion of income spent on food identified sole parent-headed family households as being at high risk of poverty (Brashares, 1993, pp. 193–204).

When the National Party government was elected in the latter part of 1990 there was substantial evidence of increasing hardship amongst low-income households. This situation was emphasized in briefing papers prepared by DSW for the incoming government. These papers reiterated the problems for sole parents and concluded from the available evidence that: 'A dollar taken from Domestic Purposes Benefit would create more hardship than a dollar taken from other benefits' (DSW, 1990, p. 30).

In an economic and social statement issued in December 1990 the new government announced a range of benefit cuts to take effect on 1 April 1991. All beneficiaries were affected by the cuts, although the most severe reductions were imposed on sole parent-headed households and on young unemployed people whose access to benefit was restricted as well as having the level of their benefit reduced. The serious implications of these cuts for women and children, and especially for Maori and Pacific Island women and children because of the high incidence of sole parenthood amongst these groups, has been noted by many analysts (Frater *et al.*, 1991, pp. 57–65; Easton, 1993). Dann and Du Plessis (1992), in an in-depth study of 23 sole parents in Christchurch, describe the gradual and sustained deterioration in the financial position of these families and their attempts to cut costs across all areas of expenditure including food. These families talked about their feelings of being ground down by the cumulative impact of policy changes. It is the cuts in social security benefit levels in April 1991 which has been seen as the major catalyst for the surge in growth in food bank numbers.

There is provision within the social security system to make additional payments to reflect hardship either because of special circumstances in which beneficiary households find themselves (Special Benefit [SB]) or where they face an emergency situation (Special Needs Grants [SNG]). These measures were included in the legislation in order to provide discretionary power to respond to specific individual circumstances. During the final stages of the 1987–90 Labour government SB and SNG payments had increased rapidly. The government's response at that time was to reduce the level of payments and to cap total expenditure on these grants for the June 1990–June 1991 year at a level about 30 per cent below that paid in the previous year. Capping of these payments was widely regarded by food banks as the cause of the initial increase in the number of food banks during 1990 (*Listener*, 1 April 1991). The National government has placed considerable emphasis on targeting resources on those in greatest need and therefore access to SB and SNG payments is a crucial part of achieving that objective.

However, those working in food banks have increasingly come to see these special payment provisions and how they are administered as part of the problem their clients face rather than, as they should be, a crucial element in a system to relieve hardship and ensure food security access.

Since the National government came to power, community agencies have been critical of the way in which the Income Support Service (ISS) sends beneficiaries to food banks almost as a matter of course. They have questioned whether the discretionary options provided by SB and SNG payments under the social security legislation have in fact been properly used. A litany of problems has been highlighted in the way these payments have been administered, information about payments is not given to beneficiaries, the rules are so complicated that both beneficiaries and staff do not understand them, staff fail to make use of flexibility in the system and try subsequently to recover payments that have been made even when this is not required, and people who have their eligibility established are not given payments for the period in which they were eligible prior to their application. In general ISS staff seem to have developed a wide range of unofficial practices which effectively exclude applicants either permanently or temporarily from accessing these payments (McGurk and Clark, 1993). Despite highlighting these problems publicly in 1993, further research work has confirmed that there has been little or no improvement in the way in which ISS administers these payments (Barwick and McGurk, 1994). Government did respond to growing public concern about poverty, food security and access to special discretionary payments by relaxing the eligibility requirements for the payments just before Christmas 1994. The criticisms of the ISS unit of the DSW have however recently been upheld by the High Court, which has found that the Department failed to take into account the financial circumstances of applicants for special benefit since April 1992. In the absence of records from that date the Court ordered DSW to complete a review of all applications since February 1994. This judgment of course excludes those people who were discouraged or prevented from applying for an SB payment because of the way in which ISS staff were operating the system.

DIFFERING PUBLIC EXPLANATIONS FOR FOOD SECURITY PROBLEMS AND FOOD BANKS

Whilst there are many alternative explanations for the rapid growth of food banks the government and non-governmental agencies, especially the churches, find themselves at opposing ends of a continuum. Governments in New Zealand have not found themselves in the position of having to defend their actions concerning the incidence of poverty and deprivation in the community since the 1930s. Unlike other countries studied in this text New Zealand had no 'rediscovery' of poverty in the 1960s. The stance of the government is mainly based on two aspects of its overall approach to policy which are first, the need to pursue a more deregulated labour market policy and second, their explicit commitment to reform the welfare state and to diminish long-term dependency on welfare.

The labour market policy has been aimed at removing what are perceived as restrictions or rigidities in the operation of the market which are believed to keep the price of labour high and consequently affect the supply of jobs. The social security system itself is seen as having become a barrier to a competitive labour market. The Royal Commission on Social Security in its 1972 report expressed a commitment to ensuring that all social security beneficiaries have access to sufficient income so that they feel that they can participate and belong to the wider New Zealand society. In order to further that objective the Commission supported the continuation of a policy in which the rate of benefit was set at a rate higher than that of the base of the wage structure. The Commission's report also led to the introduction of indexation of benefit levels. Whilst the system of indexation has varied over time the usual method has been to relate benefit levels to changes in price movements rather than changes in wage movements. For much of the 1980s price movements exceeded wage movements and one effect of this was to alter the relativity between wage-earners and beneficiaries. In 1972 the married couple benefit rate was just over 68 per cent of the average, ordinary time weekly wage, by 1981 the figure was 66.5 per cent.

As can be seen from Table 4.3 the position of beneficiaries relative to wage-earners improved significantly from 1981 to 1986 reflecting both the price indexation of benefit rates and the inability of workers to get pay increases which matched inflation.

The Labour government sought to modify those relativities and in the 1989 budget signalled that the core benefit rate would be fixed within a band of 65–72.5 per cent of the net average wage. This was in line with the historical relativity between wages and benefits (Caygill, 1989, p. 82). The National Party government of 1990 onwards has had a clear commitment to see that those in full-time work will always be better off than those on benefit. The extent to which the cuts in benefit rates which they introduced in April 1991 has eroded the position of

Table 4.3 Wage–Benefit Relativities, 1981–95

Year	(1) Married Couple $	(2) Married +2 child $	(3) AOTTW $	(1)/(3) %	(2)/(3) %
1981	110.00	139.92	165.40	86.5	84.6
1982	127.28	159.96	188.16	67.6	85.0
1983	146.76	173.40	202.57	72.50	85.6
1984	152.04	180.46	205.42	74.0	87.8
1985	166.36	214.48	214.39	77.6	100.0
1986	191.76	228.18	247.47	77.5	92.2
1987*	214.80	278.80	326.83	65.7	85.3
1988	232.88	296.88	359.30	64.8	82.6
1989	243.84	307.84	369.71	66.0	83.3
1990	255.08	319.08	391.19	65.2	81.6
1991	229.88	293.88	406.85	56.5	72.2
1992	232.18	296.18	416.84	55.7	71.1
1993	235.24	299.24	419.63	56.1	71.3
1994	238.52	304.52	429.41	55.6	70.9
1995	245.20	314.20	438.00	56.0	71.7

(1) Basic benefit payment for a married couple with children.
(2) Benefit payment incorporating child related payments for couple with two children.
(3) Average ordinary time take home wage rate after tax.
* The 'jump' in the AOTTW series is attributable to changes in personal income taxation which accompanied the introduction of a Goods and Services Tax on all expenditures.
Sources: Department of Labour Quarterly Employment Series, 1981–8.
        Department of Statistics Quarterly Employment Series, 1989–95.
        Department of Social Welfare Annual Reports.

beneficiaries is clearly apparent in Table 4.3. The growth of food bank provision has closely paralleled this policy change.

The National Party government expressed a clear view on the future direction of the welfare state 1991 in a document from then Minister of Social Welfare, Jenny Shipley, released as part of the 1991 budget. She described the welfare state as being an institution which had been a product of affluence and minimal levels of social need and that it was not sustainable in its present form in the face of economic problems and increasing levels of social need. She was asserting that the level of social need in the community and the level of government income are always inversely related, so that a generous public welfare response to social need fashioned in a time of prosperity cannot be maintained in terms of either coverage or level of provision during periods of economic adversity. The welfare state accordingly requires reform so that there is a safety net, but one below that achievable in paid work thereby motivating people to move away from long-term dependence on the state. Scarce resources must be focused on those in greatest need and this is to be done through extensive use of means testing, work tests and stand-down periods between loss of employment and claims for a social security benefit. A return, in other words, to systems more akin to the less eligibility ethos which applied before the contemporary welfare state came into being.

Given the increasing evidence of poverty and reduced food security as demonstrated by the growth of food bank numbers, the government has adopted several public strategies. One has been to say that it is not possible to establish a causal link between government policy and food security problems. Given the government's expectations about the desired impact of their policies on work-seeking behaviour amongst beneficiaries one might reasonably ask, however, why the government has not put in place a system of monitoring the impact its policies have had on beneficiary behaviour. A second response has focused on the public concern about hunger amongst children and especially school children. The Prime Minister and Ministers of Education and Social Welfare have all attributed this to poor parenting rather than access to inadequate resources within families (Fowler and Schmidt, 1994). A third strategy has been to use the opportunity to press the argument for welfare pluralism. The Prime Minister has publicly accepted that government bears an important responsibility to tackle the problem represented by increasing food bank usage, but has argued at the same time that government shares this responsibility with the churches, communities and individuals (*Dominion*, 20 October 1993).

Since 1984 non-government agencies (NGOs) have faced considerable difficulty in deciding how to respond to changes in social policy in general, and more recently, the issue of decreased food security in particular. The government's commitment to welfare pluralism and with it an increasing role for NGOs alongside private and public sector provision has meant that the voluntary sector has been confronted by large increases in demand across a whole range of social services whilst at the same time government services have been either eliminated or reduced. At the same time these agencies have experienced growing uncertainty about their funding both from government and from traditional sources of donations. Competition between agencies for the 'donor dollar' has intensified, as has the range of community agencies.

This uncertainty has been further heightened by the introduction of service contracting, which, as in other countries, tends to reduce flexibility and place NGOs under restrictive monitoring arrangements in the name of public financial accountability. Research in other countries suggests that these changes may stifle innovation and restrict NGO advocacy activities (Lewis, 1993; Kramer, 1994). Some NGOs with varied interests in community issues have tried to mobilize collectively to respond to the growing issue of poverty and hunger. For example, in Wellington a poverty action group was formed in 1990 made up of representatives from the Citizen's Advice Bureaux, Mental Consumer Union, Domestic Purposes Benefit Action, Wellington Unemployed Workers Union and the Community Law Centre (*Dominion*, 17 June 1991). Similar groups were formed in other parts of the country. As has been the case in mobilizing action to respond to reforms since 1984, it has proved difficult to mount sustained, coherent and successful opposition. The reasons for this are complex and relate to much wider social changes such as the move away from social class as the organizing factor and the rise of multiple interests linked to gender, ethnicity and service user identity.

The churches have been placed in a particularly difficult position. They have been at the forefront of both the provision of food banks and of advocacy on behalf of the poor. Their dilemma has been well expressed by the New Zealand Council of Christian Social Services (NZCCSS) when they write: that 'Christian agencies face a moral dilemma in times of social crisis. It can be argued that we are letting the government off the hook by stepping in to fill the charity gap. We feel obliged to respond to immediate needs of the community. We must speak out for those people whose humanity is being violated' (1992, p. 4).

The churches have been one of the most prominent voices questioning government policies over the last decade. They have argued against placing priority on economic policy goals as opposed to social goals and the need to hold fast to the values of community and collective responsibility alongside individual freedom, choice and responsibility (Randerson, 1992). The severity and level of need in the community has placed the churches and church agencies under immense strain in order to keep the flow of food aid available. Jenny Shipley, the Minister of Social Welfare from 1990 to 1993, used the churches' actions as an example to the public of how government and voluntary agencies can forge a partnership in providing solutions to social problems! (*New Zealandia*, 1992/3).

A polarization of public opinion around the stance being taken by the churches was well illustrated during 1993 and early 1994. A Methodist minister made a public statement in line with the sentiments expressed by Boerma quoted at the beginning of this chapter, namely that we have a right to life and if that right is threatened, and there are no other alternatives, then it would be justifiable to steal food in order to ensure survival. This view was publicly supported by New Zealand's Catholic Cardinal. This argument was further pressed by another member of the clergy contrasting food bank queues alongside the dumping and destruction of food in New Zealand where 'overproduction' had occurred (Consedine, 19 January 1994). These ideas caused howls of protest in the press from the business community and retail sellers who saw such sentiments as representing a denial of Christian strictures against theft. Such protests about the churches' pursuit of a social mission in the public arena are not confined to the business community and the churches' adoption of a very public advocacy position highlights divisions within church congregations.

As in other western countries the established churches face falling attendances, ageing congregations and the development of small subgroupings with very definite values and beliefs. At one end of the spectrum are views such as those of the Auckland Methodist Mission who argue that the churches must express compassion and care and that 'In its prophetic role, the Church stands in judgement on government beliefs, policies and directions' (Auckland Methodist Mission, Social Policy Unit, 1991, p. 37). At the other end of the spectrum are those within the churches who believe that the churches should confine themselves to the spiritual care of their members. As Bryant (1986) says, advocacy on social issues has had the effect of dividing rather than unifying the churches and in particular has emphasized a gap between the clergy and many of the laity.

DISCUSSION AND CONCLUSIONS

Learning from the Past: Historical Experience of and Response to Food Insecurity

Despite possessing a large land area relative to population, and an abundance of natural food resources, the 1990s has not been the first period in New Zealand's post-colonial history in which food security has been regarded as a problem. It would be wrong to ignore the significance of those past experiences of organizing food aid and the roles which government, churches and the community played to an understanding of contemporary events.

European colonial settlement of New Zealand is quite recent. In the 1840s private charity was the only form of help available and there is ample evidence for the existence of hardship, unemployment and very limited food supplies for settlers. Wife desertion was a common event because there was not enough food for everyone in the household and the 1846 Destitute Person Act was passed in an attempt to make extended families accept responsibility for family members unable to support themselves (Sutch, 1969, p. 51).

By the 1860s provincial institutions had been made responsible for providing a relief system for the poor. In 1866 a report on the increasing levels of pauperism in Auckland identified the major reasons as being a combination of a trade depression with a flow of new immigrants who had brought few if any material resources with them. Food relief was provided by the provinces through a system of service contracting with suppliers such as bakers, butchers and soup kitchen providers although the actions of contractors were carefully scrutinized by relief officers. In 1867 over 80 000 rations were issued through soup kitchens in the Auckland province (Sutch, 1969, pp. 49–50). Rations in the Auckland relief system at that time were one of three different types; a grocery ration consisting of 1/2 oz tea, 2 oz sugar and 1 lb bread per person per day, a meat and bread ration of 1/2 lb meat without bone and 1/2 lb bread daily, although this form of ration was seldom granted, and a soup kitchen ration for those who attended a soup kitchen of 1 pint of soup and 1 lb bread daily (Tennant, 1989, p. 17). By the 1870s economic recession had resulted in wage rates being driven down as people competed for work, and this fed through into public sector employment where wages were cut. Things were so bad that in 1880 some of the unemployed organized a petition to send to the President of the United States asking for them to be taken to be taken from New Zealand and resettled in America (Sutch, 1966, p. 61).

New Zealand historians have generally paid little explicit attention to poverty. A recent article by Husbands (1994), however, has examined poverty and relief systems in Freeman's Bay, a suburb of Auckland, from 1886 to 1913. He reports that limited relief was provided through the Auckland Hospital Board (Hospital Boards had been given responsibility for relief in legislation passed in 1875) with approximately 2–5 per cent of households in the area being granted assistance. The majority of those seeking help were women, and when applications were being made for a household nearly all of these contained children. Households economized by buying cheaper cuts of meat or no meat at all, and meals often consisted of continual rounds of bread and butter. The churches were active in providing help with clothing and furniture whilst shopkeepers and pawnbrokers helped by allowing households access to credit.

The early stages of economic depression in 1922 heralded cuts in wage rates for civil servants and in award wages determined by the Arbitration Court. The Arbitration Court adjudicated on what the basic wage levels should be for different types of occupation. Soup kitchens reappeared and the food aid rations system described by Tennant (1989) was still operational. It was based on a tendering system for food supplied by local merchants, and tenders were usually awarded to those submitting the lowest tender and as a result the food was often of poor quality and supplied in measures which were frequently underweight. Between 1928 and 1931 New Zealand faced a collapse in primary produce prices. Simpson (1974, p. 6) describes the response of the government of the day as being obsessed with dealing with debt and achieving a balanced budget which had serious implications for incomes and employment including the circumstances of farmers and shopkeepers. An Unemployment Board was set up to administer money collected by a poll tax, which was intended to provide relief of hardship associated with unemployment during the depression. This fund proved to be totally inadequate to deal with the scale of the problem during the 1930s. The government's response was to make cuts in both the level of relief payments and in the amount of food relief provided to those seeking help. Unable to cope with the large numbers of people seeking help from Board agencies and the severity of their circumstances, those responsible for administering the relief system put in place practices which effectively tightened the criteria for gaining assistance. Sutch described these events as a return to a kind of English Poor Law system of relief from which the original migrants to New Zealand had sought to escape (1966, p. 134). In 1932 over 10 000 people were seeking help each week and the Auckland City Mission provided over 102 000 meals during that year. The long-term impact of such a degree of hardship became evident as New Zealand moved out of the depression. Between 1934 to 1937 seven out of every ten school children with physical defects in Canterbury area were identified as suffering from malnutrition (Simpson, 1974, pp. 7–8).

The churches were the prime instigators in developing systems of assistance for people during the depression and they set up organizing committees in all main population centres. As government services were reduced or eliminated, church groups found themselves facing a growing demand for soup kitchens, homeless shelters and the general provision of food and clothing. Churches were placed in a similar position to that which they had found themselves in during the 1880s and were confronted with the need to adopt a public position which was in general opposition to government policies. In July 1935 a deputation of Anglican, Baptist, Church of Christ, Congregationalist, Methodist, Presbyterian and Roman Catholic clergy saw the then Minister of Labour. They argued for increases in relief rates and for the government to adopt a positive plan for tackling unemployment. The Reverend H. F. Wilkinson, a Presbyterian minister from Wellington, said the situation was 'really a disgrace to a civilization which regards itself as Christian' (Sutch, 1969, p. 223). In 1935 twelve Auckland clergy from many denominations pleaded that 'Widespread malnutrition in a primary-producing country is nothing short of a national scandal' (Simpson, 1974, p. 7).

While it would be silly to class the events of the 1860s/1870s, late 1920s/1930s and late 1980s and early 1990s as identical, there are quite striking parallels. The linkage between economic recession and reduced food security has produced government policies in which budgetary control, cuts in wages and relief payments, contracting out of services and less eligibility have figured prominently. Community agencies have found themselves in the position of trying to respond to both reductions in public assistance and increased levels of hardship. The churches in each case have found themselves as key agencies in trying to mount opposition to the public policies being pursued whilst undertaking a substantial part of the burden of offering practical help to those in distress.

Learning from the Successes of Developing Countries

The problem of food adequacy and security is thought by many to have become a problem of distribution rather than a problem in the level of production and, therefore, as Dreze and Sen argue 'If politics is "the art of the possible" then conquering world hunger has become a political issue in a way it could not have been in the past' (Dreze and Sen, 1989, p. 4).

Countries which have been successful in combating famine and hunger amongst their populations such as China, Sri Lanka, Chile and Costa Rica have achieved this through government action, which both supports change and offers public provisions. Such actions may be expressed in a variety of different ways according to the type of regime, but they nevertheless do succeed in engendering an environment of support for change. Within this idea of change public support of education, health programmes and access to employment is as important as specific actions on food distribution systems. Dreze and Sen stress the importance of public participation in social change processes. Participation can take two separate forms and both are important. The first is collaborative support from the public for government-sponsored programmes and the second is adversarial participation in which public demands of various kinds are brought to bear on government.

If we were to accept these ideas about what constitutes a favourable strategy to defeat food security problems in developing countries, then the irony is that a so-called developed country like New Zealand appears to be intent on creating the conditions in which food insecurity may flourish. If access to employment and to publicly supported health and education programmes is important, then a variety of indicators suggests increasing problems for members of low-income households in New Zealand. If public participation in both supportive and adversarial roles is a key factor, then there is evidence of a loss of public engagement within the policy environment during the process of economic and social reform since 1984. Dreze and Sen see hunger as a reflection of inequality in developed economies and that market liberal reforms will increase the level of vulnerability for some within those developed economies. This vulnerability has been offset in the past by social security and social insurance provisions which have been in existence since the creation of the modern welfare state. Income support programmes not only offer protection but also promote certain living standards and basic capabilities within the whole population (Dreze and Sen, 1989, pp. 16–17). The level of protection for the most vulnerable has clearly been deliberately reduced by government action since 1984 and especially since 1990 with cuts in benefit levels and by implication corresponding increases in the level of food security risk.

Rights

In the process of economic reform, have successive New Zealand governments abandoned their responsibilities to ensure basic social and economic rights, including a right to food? Has the safety net within the welfare system been lowered to such a point that it can no longer guarantee even food security for all? One could argue that New

Zealand governments have merely repeated responses which their predecessors have adopted since the late nineteenth century. Faced with severe economic difficulties those governments froze or cut wage rates and reduced the level of payments in relief and benefit systems. Since 1984 governments have emphasized that the level of government and national debt had reached a point where further borrowing to fund current spending could not be sustained. The 1987 Labour government and National Party governments since 1990 have also maintained that social spending had to be constrained in order to achieve the goal of reduced government spending. Constraint has also been deemed necessary to prepare for the future impact on social spending of marked numerical and structural ageing of the population from the year 2011 onwards.

There are, however, important differences between the environments in which past and contemporary governments have decided upon their actions. New Zealand is a signatory to two important UN declarations, *The International Covenant on Economic, Social and Cultural Rights* (1966) which was ratified in December 1978 and the United Nations *Convention on the Rights of the Child* (1989) which was signed in March 1993. Have governments since 1984 met their obligations under those agreements? On the basis of Table 4.1 it would be hard to argue that beneficiaries were seriously disadvantaged relative to wage-earners in the 1984–90 period. The policy to peg benefit rates to a 65–72.5 per cent band relative to the net average wage announced in 1989 was in line with historical relativities and was a response to a substantial shift in favour of beneficiaries in the mid-1980s. The cuts in benefit rates which were introduced in April 1991, however, seriously eroded the relative position of all beneficiaries and particularly sole parents and young unemployed people. There seems little doubt that these cuts have been closely related to the growth of food banks and greater levels of risk in terms of food security.

One should also look beyond wage–benefit relativities at increasing levels of inequality in New Zealand society. Real wages for most people have fallen for well over a decade. 1986 saw the introduction of a comprehensive expenditure tax of a type that is generally viewed as regressive despite the introduction of some compensatory payments. At the same time the progressive personal income tax system was largely dismantled with consequent substantial tax cuts for those on higher incomes. In addition the abandonment of a national wage adjustment system, collective awards covering all in certain occupations, the move to individual contracts of employment and the reduction of union influence have all had serious implications for the New Zealand welfare state. New Zealand and Australia are unusual in being tax based and not insurance-based welfare systems. They have been described by Castles (1985) as wage-earners' welfare states in which wage-setting procedures and access to employment have been central features rather than government-provided or regulated social services. Significantly, New Zealand reserved the right not to apply Article 8 of The *Covenant on Social, Economic and Cultural Rights* and Article 32 of the *Convention on the Rights of the Child*, both of which concern employment and trade unions (Ministry of Foreign Affairs and Trade, 1994, p. 49; Henaghan, 1995, p. 33). The foundations of the New Zealand welfare system have therefore been seriously eroded by changes in the workplace. Despite union complaints to the International Labour Organization that New Zealand has breached the 1948 ILO convention the government maintains the validity of its position. Whilst New Zealand has had historically high levels of working-class mobilization around a welfare state it was a welfare state based in the workplace with a safety net system for those not in work. Reduction in union power and the lack of a focus in the past upon underlying welfare provisions has contributed to an inability of unions to protect low-income earners and beneficiaries against cuts in their living standards since 1984. The move to targeting and discretionary provisions has not just led to what many regard as inadequate payment levels, but has also created an environment typical of less eligibility systems – low levels of takeup of benefits and abuse of discretionary power as evidenced by the recent High Court decision on Special Benefit payments.

Responsibilities

Alongside rights it is always necessary to examine the question of responsibilities, and this is an important facet to providing an explanation for erosion in food security for citizens in New Zealand. As with any government of a market liberal persuasion emphasis is placed upon the importance of self-help, personal responsibility and effort and by implication those who require assistance, especially for any period of time, are regarded as deficient. How is the responsibility of government viewed? The general trend might be accurately described as one of claiming diminished responsibility. Since 1984 successive governments have pointed to the globalization of world economic markets combined with the dictates of international financial institutions that own New Zealand's debt to argue that they have little choice in many aspects of policy – 'don't blame us we have no choice'.

Historically, New Zealanders, since European colonization, have placed central government in a dominant position in the organization of institutional life including the welfare state. Services have been provided through government departments with decision-making of all types being highly centralized. There has been neither a federal system as in Australia, Canada and the US nor a strong local government role as in Britain. Institutional reform of the public sector has featured privatization, splitting responsibility for funding and providing services, dividing policy advice from operations and a more generalized commitment to welfare pluralism in terms of social services. The net effect is to fracture responsibility both within government and between government and an increasing variety of semi-public, private and non-profit agencies. One result, and a frustrating result for those seeking to identify and challenge government social policy decisions, is what might be best described as a 'pass the parcel' syndrome. Seeking to deflect responsibility is rampant, whether between ministers, between Departments, within Departments, and rippling outwards in a similar manner towards the periphery of the 'mixed welfare economy'. This problem is further compounded by a claim of 'commercial sensitivity' preventing the release of information, especially in relation to health care, and a lack of any monitoring of major policy decisions such as the impact of benefit cuts on work-seeking behaviour. Dispersion and distortion of the lines of responsibility have played an important role in diverting challenges to social policy changes which have been introduced.

CHALLENGING CHANGE

How has it been possible for radical changes in social, economic and political life to be introduced in New Zealand to the extent that the possibility of deprivation of basic food security rights can be seriously debated? That question is beyond the scope of this chapter, however the dismantling of trade union power, the role of the Labour Party as the representative of working people in instigating these reforms and a dispersion of responsibility by political and governmental institutions would be crucial elements in any answer. To these factors one would add the emasculating of professional power through the impact of sustained criticism of the role of professional workers in the welfare state aligned with New Right arguments of vested interest and the restructuring of the setting for professional work. The churches have been left as almost the sole champions of those dispossessed by change along with groups formed from within the increasing underclass itself, such as unemployed workers groups. The challenge presented by the churches has had some impact but that impact is largely confined to mitigating the sharp edges of policy rather than its underlying direction. Opposition is being channelled into the traditional welfare rights movement technique of scrutiny of policy and procedure against practice. Only one political party, the Alliance, which as the name implies is a coalition of quite disparate groups, offers any substantive alternative to an economic growth, market driven political perspective.

The lack of sustained opposition to measures which have substantially increased inequality and fundamentally changed institutional life is not confined to New Zealand. Postmodernist analysis would locate the lack of opposition in terms of a disintegration and fracturing of collective action which leads to the loss of mass support for universal services such as those provided under the welfare state umbrella (Taylor-Gooby, 1994, pp. 74–6).

The way in which a rise of new social movements can contribute to such a disintegration of support for existing welfare institutions is well illustrated in New Zealand in terms of the impact of both the women's movement and a renaissance of Maori political influence. The women's movement has been strong and well organized in both New Zealand and Australia. Feminist analysis in both countries has been rightly critical of past social policies and their gender implications. A group of Australian writers have recently characterized such welfare systems as 'the Men's Welfare State' (Bryson, Bittman and Donath, 1994, pp. 118–21). Since the mid-1970s the position of Maori as the indigenous people of New Zealand has been given much greater prominence. Part of the ongoing debate has focused on the incidence of unemployment, low income, poor housing, poor education performance, high mortality rates and generally poor health status for Maori. The welfare state has been implicated as a partial agent of such a picture of deprivation rather than a proven means of rectifying and promoting the welfare of Maori.

It is not surprising, then, that in New Zealand two potentially important social movements which may seek to challenge the direction and impact of economic liberal reform exhibit what Habermas refers to as 'ambivalent attitudes toward the welfare state' (1989, p. 62). Habermas has characterized the welfare state as historically part of the broader utopian vision of a society based on social labour and the emancipation of the working class. He describes that utopian vision as having been exhausted, assailed by critics from many sides including the newer social movements whose focus has been on the failings of welfare states rather than their achievements. The problem for those who wish to oppose the market liberal stance is that at present there is no new utopian vision to replace that of social labour. In a country like New Zealand where the protection of working men and women lay at the heart of the welfare state that void is both more obvious and more difficult to bridge.

FUTURE IMPLICATIONS

The picture of large numbers of people queuing for food parcels on the streets of the richest countries in the world at a time of great material wealth for many individuals and corporations is one in which New Zealand can now feature. The agricultural industries of the developed world have regularly generated large surpluses which, despite GATT, are built upon extensive systems of subsidies which transfer resources to producers and indirectly to the large food manufacturing and distribution companies. Large multinational companies are key agencies in all aspects of policy related to food (Joffe, 1990/1). As Bennett and George (1987, p. 185) observe, the very same countries are at the same time operating, supporting or encouraging food assistance programmes for their own citizens. Rather than a necessity of life the amount and quality of food consumed by a family becomes one of the few ways in which the budget can be adjusted to meet the kind of financial pressures which they experience.

These problems are not new in New Zealand nor are they new in other countries within this study. This is well illustrated by the way in which both during wartime and conscription the impact of a lack of food security is clearly demonstrated when recruits are found to be in poor health and often unsuitable for military service (for example, British volunteers for the Boer War and American conscripts for the Vietnam War). What becomes evident at that time are the long-term implications for those who suffer from inadequate access to food. Just as improvements in nutrition have been a key factor in past improvements in many health indicators such as infant mortality, so undernutrition has been closely related to health problems such as infectious diseases and deficient physical and mental development (Joffe, 1990/1; Warnock, 1987). We have evidence of poor nutrition in low-income households in which more fat, more sugar and fewer fruit and vegetables are consumed. Issues of access are further compounded by a tendency for women in low-income households to deprive themselves of food and the possible impact of this behaviour on both them and, if pregnant, on their unborn children at birth and beyond is serious. Given the incidence of sole female-headed households amongst those receiving food aid this is a major concern. There is evidence that children in low-income households are at risk of undernutrition, and this is likely to impact on their growth, educational performance and future prospects. Bennett and George quote the 1984 report of the American Physicians Task Force which stated that 'We will end up with a generation – or maybe two or three generations, depending on how long this lasts, of individuals who have not grown intellectually or physically to their full potential. It will weaken this country' (Bennett and George, 1987, p. 187).

If food security is a question of inequality, as Dreze and Sen argue, then a further dimension to the problem is not just its material impact, but also the effect of an increasing social distance between the recipients of food aid and an increasingly small well paid elite within society which includes political decision makers. As Scrimshaw observes, 'the frequent famines in various regional populations of Europe in the past centuries were more the result of poverty and social inequity than an actual lack of available food' (cited in Rotberg and Rabb, 1983, p. 335).

Famines and hunger are not 'acts of God', but rather are caused by social and political acts. The long-term effects of the decisions which have been made in the name of economic and social reform in New Zealand may offer increased material well being for some, yet they also involve a very substantial cost for others.

NOTE

1. The Department of Social Welfare was created in 1971 when the Department of Social Security and the Child Welfare Division of the Department of Education were combined into a single entity. This Department has been subject to repeated reorganization since 1984. Its present structure was put in place in 1992 and consists of three 'business units', the Income Support Services which is responsible for social security, the Children and Young Persons Service which is responsible for child welfare, and the Social Policy Agency whose function is to provide policy advice and research to the Minister and on contract to the other units in DSW and outside the Department.

5 Let Them Eat Cake! Poverty, Hunger and the UK State

Gary Craig and Elizabeth Dowler

INTRODUCTION

In this chapter, we review the issue of hunger and poverty in the UK. Our particular concern is to explore the extent to which anyone may be said to be in absolute poverty, in terms of not having the resources to eat adequately. The chapter is in four sections. The first reviews the extent and characteristics of poverty in the UK, situating our analysis in a European context where possible. In the second section we examine the role of the British state in deepening and widening poverty in the UK, particularly since the 1979 Thatcher government, and the state's response to these trends. Third, we look at hunger in the British context, summarizing research on diet, nutrition, health and income. Finally, we review activities of national and local organizations which respond politically and practically to the growing problem of hunger in the UK and conclude by briefly drawing out some implications for future policy.

POVERTY IN THE UNITED KINGDOM: RECENT TRENDS[1]

There is a considerable recent literature on the definition and measurement of poverty in the UK (Roll, 1992). The historical pedigree of absolute and relative approaches to poverty within the UK is reviewed by, respectively, Rowntree (1941) and Townsend (1979). Although Victorian social reformers and investigators such as Booth, Mayhew and Mearns had 'rediscovered' poverty in the late nineteenth century, it was the pseudo-scientific work of Rowntree which first began seriously to address the issue of the adequacy of benefits. Rowntree differentiated between 'primary poverty' (where earnings were insufficient to obtain the minimum necessaries for the 'maintenance of mere physical efficiency') and 'secondary poverty', which was the result of gambling, drinking and betting, 'ignorant and careless housekeeping and other improvident expenditures' (Rowntree, 1913, pp. 116–17, 176). However, maintaining the highly judgemental approach to the poor of earlier investigators, Rowntree's poverty line 'was drawn at a level of income which... meant the barest of subsistence' (Andrews and Jacobs, 1990, p. 178) – never travelling by bus, buying newspapers, giving to church collections, smoking, drinking or buying sweets for children. Beveridge drew in 1942 on Rowntree's work to propose the first scales for a national assistance benefit which 'would need to provide food, clothing, fuel, light and "household sundries" and he costed these... by reference to data on the spending patterns of average households, suitable reduced to... subsistence levels.... [T]hese... became the rates of benefit levels in 1948... and that was the last any British government has attempted to devise social security rates which have an empirical basis' (*ibid*). Beveridge's adaptation of Rowntree's punitive subsistence income was also statistically flawed (or, at least, politically manipulated) since the final 1948 benefit levels only allowed for about 40 per cent of the inflation which had occurred since Rowntree's second survey in 1938. Nor, of course, did Beveridge view it as necessary to disaggregate household expenditure, which would have exposed the relatively greater poverty of women and even within poor households.

Here we review definitions of poverty which encompass absolute and relative dimensions: that is, in terms of *whether or not people have the resources to provide for basic necessities within the UK context* (food, clothing, shelter and fuel) and in terms of *the difference between the standard of living of poor people and that of other defined groups*, for example, those in the top decile of income distribution. Growing consensus among academic commentators over the broad parameters of poverty notwithstanding, successive UK governments have consistently denied the basis of this consensus by technical argument.

Unlike a number of other countries the UK does not have an official 'poverty line'. Debates about poverty are thus controversial (for example, Piachaud, 1987, pp. 147–64; Donnison, 1988, pp. 367–74; Ringen, 1988; Oppenheim, 1993). The definitions above each implies that in order to characterize an individual or household as poor, income has to be interpreted in terms either of the cost of basic necessities, or of comparative living standards. Such comparisons are explicitly resisted in relation to means-tested benefits by the Department of Social Security (DSS: the Department responsible for income maintenance), and other branches of the executive (the Department of Health [DH] or Ministry of Agriculture, Fisheries and Food [MAFF], for example).[2] In the

absence of a formal definition of poverty, most commentators and researchers choose one of two options. One is to use state-published statistics, either for households/individuals whose income is at or below a
rough-and-ready 'poverty line', the level of minimal state means-tested
support (currently Income Support – IS; and in practice, the numbers
in receipt of IS are often used) or on distribution of income. The numbers on IS itself understate those who may be defined as poor since
many people are on wages below IS level and many others do not claim
IS for some reason. Additionally, any definition of the numbers of
poor people based on IS levels would tend to underestimate the real
level of poverty because, as we show below, IS is insufficient to purchase
basic needs.

The alternative approach is to use one of a number of deprivation indices derived from census or other quantitative datasets (Mack and
Lansley, 1985; Townsend *et al.*, 1987; McLoone and Boddy, 1994, pp.
1465–9; Phillimore *et al.*, 1994, pp. 125–8).

In relation to officially collected data, the decennial UK census
(1991 was the latest) does not include an income question. The major
sources of quantitative data on UK income distribution are govern-
ment-funded surveys, particularly the Family Expenditure Survey
(FES). This data source, being household-based, does not take account
of intra-household income distribution or gender differences in poverty
(Jenkins, 1991, pp. 457–83; Glendinning and Millar, 1992). By definition
those living in institutions (prison, hospital, residential homes) and the
homeless are excluded. Additionally, the 1991 census was the first to
ask an 'ethnic' question: data on race and poverty are thus very hard to
come by (Craig and Rai, 1996). A major research programme funded
by the Joseph Rowntree Foundation (JRF, 1995) drawing on both new
data and a reworking of existing sources, has allowed researchers to address issues such as the distribution of poverty between differing family
types and within different contexts such as rural areas, where the additional costs of access to goods and services require that we view fixed
'poverty lines' with some caution.

The annual Households Below Average Income (HBAI) data series,
itself based on FES data, provides data on those falling below certain
cut-offs, e.g. below 50 per cent, 40 per cent average income, etc. The
HBAI was introduced in 1988, shortly after a major restructuring of income-related means-tested benefits. It is widely believed that the introduction of a new means of recording income differentials was in part
an attempt by government to diffuse widespread concerns that the restructuring package would increase the extent of poverty. Prior to 1988,

the government published a regular dataset known as the Low Income Statistics, which compared family incomes with existing means-tested benefit (up till 1988, supplementary benefit – SB) levels. One consequence of this change in measurement has been to make direct year-on-year comparisons over the period 1979–93 (the last year for which data are currently available) difficult, although independent analysis by researchers at the Institute of Fiscal Studies (e.g. House of Commons, 1992) and pressure on government to issue 'backdated' HBAI figures from 1979 have mitigated the extent of these difficulties. The numbers in poverty derived from HBAI and LIS data series differ from each other, but both show significant increases in those numbers over time.

Together, these datasets show that about 4 million households (over 10 million people) are now dependent on IS. In the ten years since 1979, the number of those on or below SB/IS, increased by more than a half to over 11 million (one fifth of the UK population), or 29 per cent, taking Townsend's (1979) 'poverty threshold' of 140 per cent of SB/IS. Three times as many children were dependent on IS in 1993 as were on SB in 1979; and ten times as many as were on national assistance in 1948. The latter was the first national social assistance benefit, introduced to replace Poor Law arrangements in the wake of the 1942 Beveridge Report and which, it was claimed at the time, would 'abolish poverty' (Craig, 1992a, pp. 65–80).

In recent years, UK researchers have begun to make cross-national comparisons with other EU member states. The proportion of UK older residents, for example, dependent on means-tested benefits is actually higher than almost any other EU country. The British social assistance 'safety net' could thus be said to be working in the sense that these older people are apparently better protected than their counterparts in other European countries. However, this is 'only with respect to the severest definition of poverty' (Laczko, 1990, p. 269). In fact, there has long been more than adequate evidence that state social assistance benefits fail to meet the cost of even the most commonly accepted basic needs (including an appropriate diet) of adults or children (see, for example, Piachaud, 1979; Stitt and Grant, 1993; Kempson *et al.*, 1994).

Use of the HBAI figures as one definition of poverty is interesting in that the threshold of 50 per cent average income is used as a working definition of poverty by the European Union and this threshold may increasingly be used as such within the UK. In the ten years to 1989, those with an income below 50 per cent of the UK average increased from 4 million to over 10 million which, apart from Portugal, represents the highest proportion in any EU member state. The rate at which the number of poor people was growing in the UK was greater during the 1980s than in any other EU state.

If we look at real increases in the standard of living, that is, comparing changes in income against a constant standard of living, and compensating for price increases using the British Retail Price Index, we find an even more disturbing picture. The standard of living, measured in this way, rose for the UK population as a whole on average by a third between 1979 and 1991, a trend which allowed Prime Minister Thatcher to claim that 'everyone had benefited' economically from her government's policies. However, the bottom 10 per cent of the population saw their living standards drop by one-sixth (after housing costs) over this period (DSS, 1994). These losses to the poorest were obscured for a while by government statistical 'miscalculations' and only came to light in 1991 after a group of MPs commissioned independent researchers to re-evaluate the official data.

These trends throughout the 1980s have been captured in the phrase, 'the rich get richer and the poor get poorer'. As Alcock and Craig (1995) observe, 'these official statistics therefore suggest that in both absolute and relative terms, poverty has been deepening in Britain towards the end of the twentieth century.' Confirmation of this trend was provided in the government's annual social statistical review (HMSO, 1995, pp. 83–100), which commented that 'although real household disposable income per head is now 80 per cent higher than it was in 1971... [this] does not mean that everyone is equally better off... the gap has been widening. Moreover, there are proportionately more people who have less than half of average income. This has increased from 10 per cent in 1971 to 20 per cent in 1992.'

The trend of widening and deepening poverty has been confirmed by reports emerging from the Rowntree research programme (for example, Jenkins, 1994; Goodman and Webb, 1994). Complementary studies of incomes from employment suggest that these growing economic (and hence social) disparities are mirrored in wage structures. Gosling *et al.* (1994) have shown that wage levels polarized from 1979 onwards and the Low Pay Unit (1994) that wage differentials are now wider than they were in the late Victorian period. In the meantime, the new JobSeekers' Allowance, replacing national insurance-funded unemployment benefit, will only be available to those unemployed people who are prepared both to state the lowest wage for which they will work and be available for work at 24 hours' notice regardless of any care responsibilities they may have.

Research (e.g. Townsend *et al.*, 1987; McLoone and Boddy, 1994) uses deprivation indices, that is, 'things which society in general agree people should not be without' or factors from census data, as proxies for conditions about which there is agreement (e.g. lack of car as a proxy for income). This research suggests that the gap in health between rich and poor is also growing wider. Mortality rates have generally been falling throughout the UK but are doing so at a much slower rate in the most deprived areas and, in some of the latter, are increasing (Wilmott, 1992).

When we come to examine the composition of the lowest income decile in UK society, what emerges (as in the EU as a whole) is that a 'new poor' is in the process of creation (Cross, 1992), no longer focused on pensioners. This is due in part to improvements in the living standards of some pensioners, as a result of the growth of occupational pensions (Goodman and Webb, 1994). These improvements are, however, relative both to a low threshold and to those of past cohorts of pensioners (who formed the major group within the poorest) and of other groups in society (Hancock and Weir, 1994). Nevertheless, many pensioners *are* still poor: a 1994 survey conducted for Age Concern showed that 37 per cent were cutting back on basics such as food and clothing in order to meet their heating bills.

This changing profile of the poorest results also from the quadrupling of unemployment levels to over 4 million during the early 1980s. Although families with children receive both the targeted child benefit and, for those on IS, other 'passported' benefits such as free prescriptions, etc., child benefit has not kept pace with inflation. In addition, many parents with children have suffered the consequences of unemployment which, as well as substantially lowering family income, has also resulted in increased levels of stress. This has been one contributing factor to the growth of lone parenthood which is even more strongly associated with poverty. The bottom decile by income of UK households thus now includes fewer pensioners, more unemployed families, more couples with children and more single people without children than, say, ten years ago. The last group experienced the largest fall of income between 1979 and 1991, 18 per cent after housing costs, of any family group. As we shall see below, direct government policy, particularly social security policy, has contributed significantly to these trends. Population groups generally at greater risk of poverty include women (Glendinning and Millar, 1992), ethnic minorities (Amin and Oppenheim, 1992; Craig and Rai, 1995; Rai, 1995) and disabled people (Martin and White, 1988; Barnes, 1991). The likelihood of ethnic minority groups experiencing poverty is increased by their experience of direct and indirect discrimination within the social security system, which frequently acts as a disincentive to claim benefits to which they are entitled (NACAB, 1991).

Perhaps most worrying, socially and politically, is the extent of poverty among young people just leaving school. Such data as we have probably understate the problem since, as the Institute of British Geographers were told in late 1994 (*Guardian*, 6 January 1995), over 1 million people 'disappeared' during the 1991 census. This includes up to 30 per cent of young men between the ages of 20 to 30 in some inner city areas, a response to pressure created by a combination of government policies including the poll tax and the removal of automatic eligibility to benefit for unemployed 16–17 year olds.

Recent qualitative studies of poverty are an important complement to the quantitative data summarized above as they provide insights into the experience of poverty: what it feels like to be poor, what choices poor people have to make and how financial poverty impacts on other areas of their lives. For example, a study of poverty amongst young people living away from home (Kirk *et al.*, 1991) indicated that 'young people have been particularly affected by wider, long-term changes... in the family, housing and the labour market' (p. 63). The report rehearses a number of familiar issues particularly the extent of poverty amongst young people, poor levels of nutrition, growing homelessness and the failure of the government's youth training scheme (YTS) to provide proper, well-supported and adequately financed employment and training opportunities.

Research with family groups on IS, including Mirpuri Muslims (Cohen *et al.*, 1992), noted the psychological pressures and stresses of poverty, and the difficulties these could produce in relationships with friends and within the family. They explained how 'a shortage of cash could curtail their participation in social and community activities' (*ibid.*, p. 106) and constrain access to proper diet and nutrition. Researchers found many respondents who either went without food altogether (notably women 'donating' their share of household income to their children) or else ate an inadequate diet, or both. Lone parents were particularly disadvantaged by benefit arrangements which asserted the role of families in providing support for children whilst providing inadequate resources to enable them to undertake that task (Clarke *et al.*, 1994). It is perhaps appropriate to conclude this section, given the UK government's much-vaunted recent interest in a return to 'Victorian values', by reference to a study by the National Children's

Home (1994), which indicated that 'over one and a half million families in Britain could not afford to feed their children an 1876 workhouse diet at present Income Support levels'.

THE RESPONSE OF THE STATE

Depressingly, the most common government responses to deepening poverty in the UK have been denial and ridicule. When Oxfam, a UK international aid agency, announced it was exploring the need for an anti-poverty programme within the UK, press and government reaction accused Oxfam of being 'patronizing' and 'insulting'. Similarly, official response to the *UN Monitoring Committee on the Convention on the Rights of the Child* (UN, 1989) on human rights, which highlighted the growing number of British children living in poverty and 'that the phenomenon of children begging and sleeping on the streets has become more visible' in Britain, was that the UN should confine its attention to countries like Brazil where there were 'real' problems of poverty. Such a response misses the point of Oxfam's and the UN's interventions into national debates, namely the deteriorating situation within the UK. It also highlights the dangers inherent in conducting debates solely on the basis of internationally relative definitions of poverty.

As noted above, the development of a 'new poor' within the UK, and the European Union more generally, has been associated in particular with the rapid growth of unemployment in western economies, particularly from the early 1980s. The 1979 government's approach (and, broadly, that of the succeeding three Conservative governments) to social and economic policy emphasized the importance of the individual and of private enterprise, and the role of the family, counterposed to the so-called 'nanny state'. The rhetoric of Tory policy was thus about 'rolling back the frontiers of the state'. In reality, the 1980s have seen, for individuals, families and local government, the growth of the most interventionist central state in living memory, but a state which has intervened to worsen the position of the poorest.

Golding (1983, pp. 7–12) provides a list of ingredients as to what the 'New Right' ideology approach meant for social policy, the key ones being domestication, selectivity, control and remaking the welfare map. Selectivity, for example, meant a growing emphasis on the use of means-tested benefits; remaking the welfare map consisted of a process of redefinition, through the manipulation of statistical and other material. 'One solution to the problem of poverty is to render it invisible' (*ibid.*, p. 10), a 'solution' increasingly reflected in government responses to both unofficial and official reports on the growth of poverty. The family was required to accept greater responsibility (both in terms of care and financial provision) for those for whom the state had hitherto provided services – the sick, disabled, young people and children. Increasingly, individual, private solutions were to be advanced for the problem of poverty rather than collective, public ones, whilst government rhetoric attempted to obscure the causes and consequences of poverty.

There is not space here to review the whole range of government policies which flowed from this particular ideological stance towards social policy. Here we note only the more significant ones which have contributed, directly and indirectly, to the deepening poverty (for some) and widening inequality described above. In the economic sphere, the first Conservative government's major concern was with reducing inflation. Its economic policies led to a rapid increase in unemployment, the numbers dependent on SB tripling to 1.5 million between 1979 and 1982. This produced a tension for the government between its social and economic policies in that, despite its declared intention to reduce public spending, especially so-called 'non-productive' social expenditure, social security spending rose rapidly during the 1980s. Much of this was in the area of means-tested social assistance benefits.

The government also introduced growing constraints on eligibility for, and the value of, insurance-related benefits. This process has now encompassed restructuring of disability and work-related benefits. At the same time, official data were manipulated in an attempt to downplay the extent of these growing social problems. For example, during the early 1980s, the government introduced 29 measures in which official counts of the unemployed were altered (usually downwards) (Atkinson and Micklewright, 1989, pp. 17–51), resulting in an official unemployment figure some 1 million below the count arrived at by independent observers.

The major social security legislation of this period was the 1986 Social Security Act, described at the time by the government as the most substantial examination of the social security system since the Beveridge Report. In reality, it was the first concerted attempt significantly to rein in social security expenditure.

As a result of the Act, Income Support was introduced to replace supplementary benefit in 1988. Income Support payments are supposed to cover basic needs, including food, clothing, and so on. Premiums are paid for special needs and housing costs are met separately. The Act aimed to simplify the system of means-tested benefits which meant, in practice, a major restructuring of weekly benefit rates and significant losses in income, as Evans *et al.* (1994) later showed, to so-called 'targeted' groups. Perhaps most remarkable, benefit rates for under 25 year olds were set about 30 per cent below those for over 25 year olds, on the assumption that they lived at home and could therefore exist more cheaply.

The subsequent ten years have seen a series of further measures driven primarily by a desire to cut spending. Hiding behind the smokescreen of 'simplification' and targeting resources on those most in need, the 1986 Act redistributed expenditure from certain groups to others. The government's own contemporary projections suggested that the disabled, lone parents and couples with children would be amongst the main 'gainers'. Indeed, not only was the extent of gains in these groups considerably less than forecast but the aim of 'targeting' help to the most vulnerable failed (*ibid*). It should also be noted that Income Support benefits do not include a specific entitlement to food as such but are intended to cover a broad range of needs.

The government's reforms demonstrate that it is unprepared to address the issue of the inadequacy of benefit levels. Indeed, the consequence of the 1986 Act and subsequent legislation was to push more people either onto or below that inadequate safety net level. Meanwhile, in the consultation preceding the Act, the government argued against an agreed poverty line (HMSO, 1985). Sir Keith Joseph, one of Margaret Thatcher's key ideological advisers, argued that absolute poverty did not exist in the UK (Joseph and Sumption, 1979) and a later Secretary of State for Social Security that poverty had been 'abolished' (Craig, 1992b, pp. 129–43). Despite government resistance to extensive research evidence, academics and activists have continued to map the extent of poverty (see Mack and Lansley, 1985; Bradshaw, 1993; and Stitt and Grant, 1993 for three complementary approaches to this issue).

The government's ideological approach to poverty was most clearly revealed in the 1986 Act in the introduction of the so-called 'social' fund, a cash-limited, loan-based, discretionary system of payments to replace the previous regulated scheme of single payment grants (Craig, 1990, pp. 97–117). This was the most extreme example of the government's determination to 'privatize poverty'. Single payments had been available to those on SB as an entitlement to those with a need for large sums of money for big household goods such as cookers or beds: a safety net *beyond* the safety net. The social fund's structure ensured that few of those benefit claimants with similar needs to single payment claimants would in fact get help from it. The emphasis on loans was part of the government's drive to push responsibility (in this case for budgeting on inadequate benefit levels) back to the family; cash limits reflected its concern with constraining public expenditure and it supported these by arguing that growth in single payment expenditure had been driven significantly by fraudulent or inappropriate claiming.

The social fund not only represented a major reduction in overall spending (Craig, 1992c), even 'successful' applicants found their weekly income pushed below the social assistance level by 15 per cent or more of weekly income. Cash limits meant that, by 1993/4, more than 7 million applicants had been refused help, refusal rates for grants reaching 75 per cent (Craig, 1993, pp. 109–30) and more than 300 000 claimants were refused help as 'too poor' even to repay an interest-free loan from weekly benefit, being already in serious debt with bills for water, fuel, etc. (Ford, 1991). The fund itself was widely criticized as being ill-targeted and inconsistent (Huby and Dix, 1992): the government's response was that the 'fund was working well'.

As a result of deductions from benefit, some claimants received barely 50 per cent of their weekly benefit (Mannion *et al.*, 1994). Meanwhile, the privatization of utilities such as water and electricity pushed prices up towards more 'market' levels. One consequence of water privatization was that household water bills increased by 67 per cent in three years, with customers contributing £2 billion more than if charges had kept pace with general price inflation (NCC, 1994). A major current concern is that the impact of both privatization and the monitoring of water supply will force families with children and older people to cut back on necessary water consumption (with consequences for health) or go further into debt.

Recent changes in social security entitlement have also threatened the welfare of young people. In 1988, the government removed the automatic right to social security benefit for 16–17 year olds. With the exception of a few 'special cases', those under 18 years were able to claim state benefit only if they registered for a government youth training scheme. Although the government claimed that YTS places and allowances would be guaranteed to all 16 and 17 year olds not in full-time education, this guarantee was not met (MacLagan, 1992). The 1988 restrictions on entitlement also set the under-25 IS rate significantly lower than for older claimants, the government arguing that benefit levels should be related to wage levels, thereby effectively underpinning the growing low-wage economy. The policy was also justified in terms of the government's emphasis on family responsibilities, as it argued that most under 25 year olds lived at home, a 'fact' which was demonstrably false (Craig, 1991). Recent studies have identified, as a result of cash limits, increasing instances of young people who claimed to be starving or eating inadequate diets but who had failed to convince social security officials that they were facing a crisis (NACAB, 1989; NCH, 1993). The official view, as reported in the *Social Fund Manual*, the handbook for social fund officials, is that 'fit young people are... better able to cope with a crisis' and therefore of low priority for so-called 'crisis loans'.

Despite the manifest growth in both relative and absolute poverty since the early 1980s, Conservative governments continued both to deny its existence and to pursue policies exacerbating its dimensions, claiming that the benefits of government economic policy have 'trickled down' to the poorest. Mrs Thatcher was forced to qualify this claim when the Institute of Fiscal Studies revealed that income inequality had grown and that the position of the poorest had worsened both absolutely and relatively during the 1980s. John Major, however, has attacked the government's own HBAI figures, arguing that they 'did not prove that people had become worse off during the decade' (*Guardian*, 25 May 1994, p. 6) because the HBAI methodology did not track particular individuals and that, therefore, the specific composition of the poorest 10 per cent might have changed over time.

Ideological language has been an important part of this process. From the late 1970s onwards, Conservative spokespeople have, for example, placed a strong emphasis on the need for fraud detection in the drive to cut benefit expenditure. This emphasis not only discouraged many claimants from taking up benefits to which they were entitled; it also obscured major structural problems in social security such as the inadequacy of benefit levels and a deteriorating quality of service, as well as distracting attention from politically more embarrassing issues such as the extent of tax evasion. In the early 1980s, this was running at about ten times the alleged extent of social security fraud (Cook, 1989). Improving take-up of benefits (which never generally exceeded 75 per cent for means-tested benefits and was often considerably lower: DSS, 1995) would of course have exacerbated the government's spending difficulties. The UK government's obsession with minimizing public debate on poverty also extended to European collaboration. At its insistence, the word 'poverty' was removed from the Third European Anti-Poverty programme which became the programme for 'the integration of the excluded' (CEC, 1989).

Other ideological attacks by the current Secretary of State for Social Security have identified various groups of (in his view) fraudulent or undeserving claimants, including lone parents, the unemployed and 'benefit tourists' from other EU countries or further afield. At the same time, the government has increasingly subscribed to the theory of the 'underclass', propounded by US commentator Murray (1994), who argues that the UK government, as with its US counterpart, has contributed to the development of an underclass largely comprising lone parents (usually unmarried), unemployed and blacks, disconnected from the mainstream of social, political and economic institutions, whilst depending on the state for financial support. This stance is one of the most vivid examples of the government's tendency, both in policy and rhetoric, to 'blame the victims' of its own policies (Walker, 1990, pp. 49–58).

Government ministers increasingly feel free to wear their ideology on their sleeves, Prime Minister Major commenting that beggars are 'very offensive'. The Minister of Housing, responsible for policies to deal with the needs of the estimated 8000 sleeping rough in Britain and the 60 000 staying in emergency hostels nightly, characterized the homeless as 'the sort of people you step over when you come out of the opera.' These comments appear to disregard increasing evidence as to, for example, the growing problem of begging in most UK cities (Banister, 1993), or at best to explain it as a question of individual pathology. This is the context within which a major review aimed at further reducing the level of basic benefits is proceeding (DSS, 1993). Despite a few well-publicized cases of fraud, these attacks bear little relationship to accumulating research evidence about the deteriorating position of those, particularly the increasing numbers of long-term unemployed, on social assistance benefits or of those made ineligible for social assistance benefits at all. In the following section, we examine the real impact, in terms of forms of deprivation such as hunger and undernourishment, that results from attempting to live on (and increasingly, without) government social assistance benefits or poverty wages.

HUNGER AND POOR NUTRITION

The main thing [when I'm buying food] is price because sometimes you get it 2p cheaper. If you calculate 1p is nothing, 5p is nothing, but at the end of the day it might come to 50p and that stands for 2 bottles of milk.

(lone mother, early fifties, claiming IS, with two dependent and two non-dependent, unemployed children living at home, quoted in Dowler and Calvert, 1995, p. 39)

Poverty may mean not having enough for basic survival – which obviously includes food; it may also mean having to live in a way that excludes the experiences others take for granted, such as eating the same type of food as the rest of your peer group. 'Hunger' or 'poor nutrition' are difficult to define consistently even in extreme conditions, not least because the human body is highly adapted to survive. It is hard to demonstrate with absolute certainty that there are people in the UK whose immediate survival is in jeopardy because they are unwillingly starving. Even those who beg on the streets have day centres and soup runs that provide minimal nourishment (Rushton and Wheeler, 1993). None the less, for people managing on low incomes, food is usually the flexible item in the household budget; it is difficult to choose healthy diets or maintain mainstream food patterns on a tight budget (Milburn *et al.*, 1987; Graham, 1993; Dobson *et al.*, 1994).

We use two indicators here: inadequate intake of nutrients and limited food variety. In dietary surveys, the food people eat over a specific period is weighed and recorded, and converted to nutrient intakes using food composition tables. The results are compared to reference figures to assess the adequacy of nutrient intake. The UK Department of Health (DH) publishes reference figures,[3] known as Dietary Reference Values, derived by a committee of experts (DH, 1991, p. 9). People vary in how much of a nutrient they need to avoid deficiency and ill-health; the DH 'reference nutrient intakes' (RNI) are sufficient to meet the needs of most people. They are a yardstick for assessing the adequacy of dietary intakes by population groups. They show the likelihood that people are eating enough of a nutrient to avoid deficiency. For groups of people, if their average intake of a nutrient is equal to or exceeds the RNI, the risk that members of the group are not eating enough is very small (*ibid.*, p. 9). This gets us some way to an understanding acceptable in government circles of 'nutritional deprivation': the lower a group's measured nutrient intake is as a percentage of the reference intake, the less likely all members of the group are to be eating enough of that nutrient to avoid ill-health. The probability of deficiency increases as the percentage of reference value (DRV) achieved decreases (Dowler and Rushton, 1994). Surveys which use this indicator based on adequacy of nutrient intakes are summarized below.

Nutritional deprivation could also mean little food variety: it is very difficult to meet vitamin and mineral needs when diets are monotonous and based on few foods. A diverse food base is associated with healthier living and reduced risk of developing cancer or coronary heart disease, and therefore a longer life (DH, 1994a, pp. 14–22; Buttriss with Gray, 1995). No prescription of actual foodstuffs exists for a 'healthy' dietary pattern, but there are guidelines from government departments (Health Education Authority (HEA), 1993; DH, 1994b). Everyone has times when they have to make do with what is in the cupboard: being poor is having to 'make do' from a few basic foods week after week, because there is no money left for variety. Households which cannot afford to purchase a varied diet featuring recommended 'healthy' foods, or whose local shops/restaurants/canteens do not stock them, could also be described as nutritionally deprived, in terms of their ability to obtain a varied 'healthy' diet. Studies where variety and dietary patterns have been assessed in relation to deprivation or social class are also summarized below.

There is much current concern in medical and some government circles that members of poorer UK households are more likely to be ill, or to die in infancy, or at an early age when adult, than those in richer households. These differentials are particularly common for the diseases mentioned above – coronary heart disease and cancers – and they have widened over the last decade (Phillimore *et al.*, 1994; Sloggett and Joshi, 1994). Explanations for these differences have tended to be behavioural: that people eat the wrong things, smoke too much and exercise too little. Wilkinson (1992) asserts that inequality of income, rather than absolute levels of poverty, are associated with higher mortality rates and that rising income inequality in the UK during the last 15 years accounts for the rise in morbidity and mortality among those at the lower end of the scale. The mechanisms of this association have yet to be elucidated, though Davey-Smith (1994, p. 140) argues that the cumulative impact of materialist rather than behavioural factors are more able to account for these differences: the stress induced by inadequate housing, low income, poor education and job insecurity with contingent restricted food choice and poor diets. However, they also argue that 'research in this area has not advanced greatly since the appearance of the Black Report[4]...a major reason for the relative paucity of evidence concerning the link between material conditions and health is the lack of enthusiasm for investigating this area' (*ibid.*).

Given the government's hostility to acknowledging the growth and extent of poverty, it is unsurprising that there is debate over how much money is needed to buy and prepare a 'healthy' diet, and in turn, whether or not state benefits are sufficient to enable recipients to afford such a diet. The poorest households are regularly shown to buy foods which are the best value for money for nutrients, and to buy more of basic food items such as bread, fats, potatoes and sugar (MAFF, 1994a). But a varied diet which conforms to current healthy eating advice is more expensive than a monotonous 'unhealthy' diet, if real, typical diets are costed using the shops poor people have access to. Until recently there was little systematic research on nutritional deprivation among UK low-income groups or the contribution diets make to poor health and early death. The few dietary studies that have been done suggest diets in poor households are seldom deficient in macro-nutrients – energy, protein, fat – but are consistently lower in vitamins and minerals, and are monotonous, with low levels of fruits and vegetables (Dowler and Rushton, 1994), characteristics precisely those that healthy eating guidelines caution against.

Poorer People's Nutrient Intakes

National surveys of nutrient intakes commissioned and/or funded by the UK government are done annually at the household level (National Food Survey: for example, MAFF, 1994a) and less regularly on individuals of different age groups (school-aged children: DH, 1989; adults: Gregory *et al.*, 1990, MAFF, 1994b; toddlers: Gregory *et al.*, 1995: over-65s: current). In addition, national sample surveys (Bolton-Smith *et al.*, 1991) and many smaller studies provide one-off nutrient intake data about different age groups.

The National Food Survey (NFS) is a continuous survey of household food purchases by a representative sample of 7000–8000 British households a year, in which details of food for human consumption brought into the home during one week are recorded. The nutrient and energy content of foods is estimated from food composition tables. In the NFS for 1993 (MAFF, 1994a) those in Group A represent households with at least one earner and gross weekly incomes of £520 and above; those in Group D households with at least one earner and gross weekly incomes below £140 per week. These cut-offs represent respectively the top and bottom percent of target income distribution in the MAFF sample (MAFF, 1994a, p. 71). Characteristically, they are not comparable with the income distribution data by decile issued by the IFS, nor with the Social Security Statistics and HBAI data from the DSS.

There is a consistent trend that nutrient intakes per head were less likely to be adequate in Group D compared with Group A, although the difference is only marked for vitamin C. Those in Group E2 represent households without an earner where gross weekly income is less than £140, the majority of them mainly dependent on means-tested benefits. Their intake adequacy per head is consistently lower for all nutrients than other groups including even those in the category Old Age Pensioner (although this category is descriptive of status rather than a reflection of income). These patterns of nutrient adequacy distribution have remained much the same for some years. Differences in nutrient intake adequacy were more marked between households of different composition. Intakes per head of vitamin C, folate, iron, zinc and magnesium were much less likely to be adequate in households with more than three children, and in lone-parent households. Households in group D got much less energy from drinks, alcohol or sweets than those in group A.

No national data are available on income and nutrient intakes which have been measured on individuals. In the school children survey, the Adult Nutrition Survey (ANS) and Pre-School Nutrition Survey (PSNS), nutrient intakes were calculated from weighed dietary intakes recorded by each individual and are presented by various measures of socio-economic status: for individuals from households whose main source of income was means-tested benefits; by household composition (which identifies lone parents); by employment status of the informant or head of household (ANS and PSNS); and by mother's education level (PSNS). In these national surveys, and some smaller surveys, occupational social class is also used as a proxy for economic well-being of households and individuals (albeit with problems of heterogeneity of categories, gender and age biases). In the surveys on children's intakes, only absolute intake data, or nutrient intakes adjusted for differences in energy intake, are given by social class. Data on adequacy of nutrient intakes (proportion of children meeting UK reference values, where these exist for children) are only presented for the whole sample, and not by any socio-economic indicator.

In the ANS, unemployed men and women had significantly lower intakes of many vitamins and minerals, as did those who lived in households receiving benefits. Men and women in manual social classes had lower intakes of most vitamins and minerals than those in the higher social classes; these trends were most marked for calcium, iron, carotene and vitamin C (MAFF, 1994b). In the PSNS, young children from manual social classes had lower absolute intakes for most vitamins and minerals than those in non-manual households. When intakes were adjusted for differences in energy intake, children from manual homes had proportionately lower amounts of carotene (a form of vitamin A found mainly in vegetables), niacin, vitamin B_{12}, vitamin C and vitamin E. Blood levels of most vitamins were also lower in children from manual homes, or from less advantaged homes (where the head of household was unemployed, or where parents claimed means-tested benefits, or where the mother had a low education level). Children from lone-parent families had lower levels of carotene and vitamin C, particularly if there was more than one child in the family. Similarly, children in manual households, or those receiving benefits had lower intakes of iron, calcium, phosphorus and potassium. There were no significant differences in energy intake by any socio-economic characteristic (Gregory *et al.*, 1995). In the study on school children's diets, those who received free school meals (and were therefore from households in receipt of benefits) had lower vitamin and mineral intakes than those not from benefit households (DH, 1989). These data show that the poorest and most disadvantaged were not hungry in that they ate insufficient energy, but consistently had worse diets in terms of nutrients consonant with good health than those from better-off households.

Other national surveys – for example, the Scottish Health Study (Bolton-Smith *et al.*, 1991) and the 36-year follow-up to the national birth cohort study (Braddon *et al.*, 1988) – show similar results. Mineral and vitamin intakes were much lower among the manual social classes, or among the unemployed, even when the data were controlled for smoking. These findings from large surveys are comparable to those from smaller surveys looking at nutrient intakes in different age groups, and in households of different socio-economic circumstances (Schofield *et al.*, 1989; Gibney and Lee, 1993; Moynihan *et al.*, 1993; Doyle *et al.*, 1994), and among the homeless in bed and breakfast accommodation or sleeping rough (Sevak, 1987; Williams, 1989; Rushton and Wheeler, 1993).[5]

A recent survey by Dowler and Calvert (1995) of nutrient intakes in lone-parent households used adequacy of nutrient intakes and a number of indicators of household socio-economic status: income, occupational social class, attained educational level and a material deprivation score. Patterns of nutrient intake in parents were similar to previous surveys for all the economic indicators – the poorest achieved the lowest adequacy – but the differentiation was most marked when households were divided by the deprivation score. Those in the worst deprivation category – who had lived for more than a year in rented housing, who were unemployed, had no holiday and had fixed, regular deductions from a low budget – had much lower nutrient intakes than parents who were not poor. This finding was largely true whether or not parents smoked. Intakes of iron, 'fibre', vitamins A, C and folate, were particularly low. In other words, the poorest parents whose income from benefits was being stretched to pay back debts (NACAB, 1993) had very poor diets.

Parents who claimed IS had worse vitamin and iron intakes than those who did not claim it, whether or not they smoked, and the further from benefit collection day, the lower their intakes of iron, fibre and folate. In dependent children only vitamins C and A were significantly different by the deprivation score. For those who smoked, being poor made a big difference to the adequacy of vitamin C intake, and some difference to iron, 'fibre' and folate intakes. For those who did not smoke, being poor made a large difference to iron and folate intakes. Smokers particularly need to increase their vitamin C intake (found in fruit and vegetables) – the nutrient in fact often found to be lower in smokers' diets (DH, 1994a). In the lone-parent study the poorest smokers had the lowest vitamin C intakes: 42 per cent of the reference intake, as opposed to 130 per cent in the poorest non-smokers. Smokers were more likely to be unemployed and living on IS, although fewer than half those receiving IS smoked.

We could regard individuals' nutrient intakes (such as how much vitamin C they eat), indices of food variety (how many different sorts of fruit people eat, and how often) and diet patterns (how much lean meat or fish they eat), as *outcome* indicators of a household's *access* to food or to food security. Access can include effective demand: the amount of money a household or individual allocates to spending on food, which in turn includes how much money they have and how they balance competing expenditure demands. Access also includes where and how people shop, the price of foods and the range of food commodities available to them. As Williams and Dowler (1994) have noted, 'to achieve food security in the UK foods for a healthy diet must be available in the shops (availability), and households must be able to use shops with these foods, and have the means (income, benefits, affordable prices) to buy them (access) on a sustainable basis'.

Differential food allocation within the household, choosing to eat more of one food and less of another, use of the store cupboard or borrowed food, and borrowing money or getting into debt, are amongst the 'coping strategies' that low-income households adopt to contain their poverty, either adapting their expenditure to match their income, or expanding their 'income' to meet their actual expenditure. 'Failure to cope' can result in debt crisis, and evidence supports nutritional deprivation rather than hunger and consequent stress. It can also lead to adjustment of food intake and choice to levels which result in nutritional deprivation. Government policies – particularly, for example, rising fuel prices, limits on benefit levels and eligibility, and the social fund – simply place even greater pressure on the poorest groups such as lone parent families and single young people.

Foods: Variety and Patterns of Eating

> I'll cut down myself on food. Sometimes if we're running out the back end of the second week and there's not a lot for us to eat, I'll sort of give the kids it first and then see what's left. He [partner] is very good that way.
>
> (mother on benefit, quoted in Graham, 1993)

No consistent measure of 'variety' or 'healthy' dietary patterns is used in British surveys. Many investigators simply report the frequency of eating foods listed in healthy eating guidelines as 'healthy' or 'unhealthy' on the assumption that those who report eating more of the former and less of the latter have a healthier diet, and vice versa. The literature suggests that poor people are no less informed about 'healthy' eating (such as eating more fruit and vegetables or trying to limit fat and sugar intake) than the general population; when asked, people on limited incomes say they do not eat as much fresh fruit or lean meat as they would like to largely because they cannot afford them.

Most national surveys and smaller-scale surveys report a wide disparity in the types of food people eat according to socio-economic status, which may partly be a reflection of historical and cultural class differences in behaviour. However, ethnic minorities are not evenly distributed between occupational classes: a larger proportion are found in manual or semi-skilled occupations than skilled or professional classes. Asian and Afro-Caribbean or black British food and meal patterns are very different from the traditional white working-class eating patterns; so if 'manual' class groups eat less fruit than 'non-manual' it is not just because the former are white and working-class. There must also be an income effect. Secondly, a number of surveys use employment status of household head, or receipt of means-tested benefits, or family size/number of dependent children, as socio-economic indicators; those in poorer categories have similar food patterns to those in manual social groups (MAFF, 1994a, 1994b). Few studies disentangle the social and cultural aspects from income *per se*, or from the demoralizing impact of poverty on self-esteem and personal care.

In the NFS, high-income households spend more on food. None the less, poor households spend the highest proportion of income on food (HEA, 1989; Hobbiss, 1993; MAFF, 1994a). Members of the poorest households are the most efficient purchasers of nutrients per unit cost, using economies of scale and purchase of the cheapest sources of nutrients. They spend £8–9 per head a week to feed their family, much less than either MAFF or a leading supermarket chain recognize: MAFF simulated a low-income 'healthy dietary pattern' for £10 per head per week (Leather, 1992), and a supermarket costed a week's food for a low-income family of four that met health guidelines at £11.66 a head (Erlichman, 1994).

We also know from the NFS that high-income households consume more fruit and less bread and potatoes than those in low-income households. In the ANS and PSNS, those in non-manual households were more likely to consume fruit juice, fruit, fresh salads and oily fish (recommended as 'healthy') than those in the manual. Smaller surveys have found similar results (Anderson and Hunt, 1992; Abel and McQueen, 1994). In the lone parent study (Dowler and Calvert, 1995) parents in the worst category of the deprivation index, that is, who were long-term unemployed tenants, with deductions for fuel or rent from benefits, had lower dietary variety (derived from a food frequency questionnaire) and less healthy dietary patterns than parents in less extreme circumstances. They were also much less likely to be eating five or more fruits and vegetables a day or to be drinking fresh fruit juice. Other indicators (IS receipt, educational qualifications, income), also differentiated dietary quality. Those who are poor in UK society face nutritional deprivation in terms of monotonous diets with little diversity.

Several studies have used qualitative approaches to investigate diet and low income. Many interviewed described food as a flexible budget item, where economies could readily be made in their own diets rather than in their children's (for example, Burghes, 1980; Cole-Hamilton and Lang, 1986; HEA, 1989; McKie and Wood, 1991; and see above). Other household expenditure is of necessity regarded as 'fixed costs', and low-income households try to avoid arrears. People economize on food by buying cheaper or different items ('filling' foods rather than fresh fruit) or by omitting meals altogether in order to meet pressing financial demands. When food economies are made, consumption of fruit, lean meat, cheese and fish decreases, and that of cheaper foods (eggs, beans, cheap meats and chips) increases (Milburn *et al.*, 1987; Dobson *et al.*, 1994; Dowler and Calvert, 1995).

People living in bed and breakfast accommodation are very unlikely to have enough money for even a minimally adequate diet if IS is their main income source (Sevak, 1987; Falconer, 1988; Williams, 1989). No special provision for their needs is available through IS. Pregnant young, single women on low wages need to spend 50 per cent of income on food to purchase diets recommended for pregnancy (Durward, 1988; Craig, 1991). 'Healthy' food usually costs more than 'unhealthy' food, if prices in shops where people live are used (Mooney, 1990; Morton, 1988; NCH, 1991; Sooman *et al.*, 1993). This evidence reveals overall that it is not that the poor ought to be able to eat properly and only fail to do so because they do not manage their budgets and shop wisely, as government and right-wing commentators aver. The poorest spent the least per head on food and are the most efficient purchasers of basic macro-nutrients; many budget well, and are skilled managers (Pember Reeves, 1913; Kempson *et al.*, 1994). However, food is the flexible item in very tight household budgets, and 'healthy' eating is invariably more expensive. The result is, frequently, a conscious decision to trade the immediate need to maintain family security against future health.

ACTION INITIATIVES AND POLICY IMPLICATIONS

Food and nutritional issues tend to fall into several sectors' responsibilities in the UK, as elsewhere, with varying success at co-ordination. Until recently, no sector took responsibility for poverty and low income in relation to diet and nutrition. In the 1980s, UK policy focused on the individual making an informed choice to eat a healthy diet, by labelling foods with nutrient content and by nutrition education, and not on whether money was a limiting factor. Few targeted benefits in the UK have a direct impact on food intake: receipt of IS carries entitlement to free school meals, and milk tokens and vitamin tablets for children under five years old and pregnant women. School meals are an important source of nutrients for children from low-income households, some of whom qualify for free school meals (Nelson and Paul, 1983; Sharp, 1992; Coles and Turner, 1994), but they are an easy target for cost-cutting with current major changes in the organization of education budgets (Williams, 1994). The statutory requirement for a free meal does not stipulate what the meal should contain: cheap snacks would be a poor substitute for a good mid-day meal.

As noted above, where problems of nutrition in low-income households were addressed in the past, they were seen as caused by nutritional ignorance, or poor budgeting and shopping practices, and therefore the responsibility of health education and home economics. Now, public and state interest in appropriate research and action is growing, if unevenly, given this lack of any co-ordinated policy response and the downright opposition of some government departments, particularly the DSS, to engage in serious discussion about the growth of poverty in the UK. Nevertheless, there are some instances of appropriate official research and action (MacIntyre *et al.*, 1989). The national Nutrition Task Force created to implement the dietary goals in the *Health of the Nation* White Paper (DH, 1992), recognized that 'people on limited incomes may experience particular difficulties in obtaining a healthy and varied diet', and set up a Low Income Project Team in June 1994 to begin to address these problems. This interest has resulted in some practical help for those working with low-income people.[6]

The Working Paper produced for the Low Income Project Team highlighted household and individual *access* and *choice* as essential issues in identifying problems and potential solutions for those trying to eat healthily on a low income (Williams and Dowler, 1994). 'Access' includes effective demand (how much money can be spent on food), where and how people shop, food prices and commodity range. To achieve household food security, suitable foods must be available in local shops, and people must have the means to buy them on a sustainable basis. The foods the household 'chooses' to buy depend on access plus individual tastes, preparation skills and intra-household food allocation. Low-income households arguably have fewer choices open to them than richer households, and skill in using the store cupboard or borrowed food, going without foods or getting into debt are widely adopted 'coping' strategies.

Local actions/initiatives to support such strategies have included food co-ops, crèches and shopping transport (to improve local availability); cookery courses and demonstrations (develop preparation skills and confidence); food price subsidies (used on a limited scale to promote 'healthier' foods); community cafés (local food provision, 'healthy' food consumption, strengthen local empowerment); mobile shops (improve local healthy' food availability – current interest from major supermarkets); fruit distribution, for example, through schools or churches (local food availability, widen tastes). Few of these initiatives have addressed effective demand – increasing wages or benefit income or reducing competing expenditure. In Scotland, these initiatives are funded by local authorities; in England and Wales they tend to be sponsored by community health departments or by the HEA. In all parts of the UK, however, there is rapidly growing interest in general anti-poverty strategies which may increasingly encompass these kinds of initiatives (Craig, 1994). Few initiatives have been written up, however, in a systematic and easily accessible format (Kennedy-Haynes and Hunt, 1994, is one exception) and many are small-scale or pilot projects (Dowler and Rushton, 1994). The creation of a centralized, systematic database and information source may result from the Low Income Project Team and some momentum has been given in this direction by the National Food Alliance Pack.

CONCLUSION

Do these low levels of nutrients and monotonous diets specifically, and food more generally, matter? If they contribute to ill-health, general misery and reduced life expectancy, then the answer has to be yes, they do matter. This chapter has been concerned with exploring the issue of hunger in the UK, a phenomenon more commonly associated with third world countries. Many of the latter are finding that the impact of the structural adjustment policies forced on them by market-driven first world-led economic organizations such as the International Monetary Fund, is to increase poverty and inequality (Craig and Mayo, 1995). It is, of course, important to understand how the same sorts of policies pursued by the UK government have led to a parallel growth of poverty and deprivation in the UK. Such understanding is a necessary precondition for constructing radically different national and international political responses to the growth of poverty and hunger on a worldwide basis. Currently, the UK government seems more concerned to deny the extent of poverty within its own boundaries and to deflect criticism of that situation away from itself than to collaborate with others in developing international programmes which address the structural causes of poverty across 'developed' and 'developing' countries. Nowhere was this stance more evident in recent years than at the World Summit on social development in Copenhagen, March 1995, where the sharpest analysis of growing poverty within the UK and other so-called 'developed' countries came from an international consortium of NGOs protesting at their exclusion from key policy forums at the event.

There has been a long tradition of poverty research in the UK and a consensus now exists outside government as to the broad dimensions of poverty. Government response, however, as we have seen, has been to deny the extent of poverty or its own responsibility for exacerbating it. In recent years, its strategies for dismissing the evidence of well-founded research has been to manipulate statistics and blame the victims of its own policies whilst introducing further regressive measures. The virulent contemporary campaign against lone parents has been but the latest instance of this general strategy (Clarke, Craig and Glendinning, 1994). The more generous treatment of lone parents in other EU countries reveals the purely ideological basis of this approach. Whilst central government has withdrawn from any responsibility for addressing poverty and its effects, increasing numbers of local authorities and voluntary and community groups have established programmes and projects to mitigate the effects of central government policies.

Research and action on diet and nutrition in low-income families is not yet at such an advanced stage. However, the dimensions of the policy and political problematic seem clear: local palliative responses, official (with some exceptions, such as nutrition groups within the DH) inaction. The UK is currently passing through a phase of heightened interest in communitarianism, citizenship and an increased emphasis on community and family values. This might cynically be viewed as yet another ideological precursor to further lessening of state support for the poorest. The contradiction facing those who argue strongly for the values of self-help is that, until the poorest have the resources to do more than struggle to survive, in financial, dietary, social and health terms, talk of a reversal of the current trend to political alienation is, literally and metaphorically, immaterial and puts the cart before the horse. Government, of whatever political persuasion, has first to address the issue of meeting the most basic needs of all its population: without this, talk of citizenship is derisory to those who are most disadvantaged by government itself. Whether we should define the condition we have described in this chapter as 'hunger' or starvation in a first world context may, in the end, matter less than our ability to create a government prepared to act on it.

NOTES

1. Part of this opening section draws on Alcock and Craig (1995).
2. For example, the DSS rejects the use of budget standards to assess the adequacy of benefit levels (Bradshaw, 1993, p. 238; NCC, 1992, Annex 1).

3. Reference values, in particular the Reference Nutrient Intake, used to be called 'RDAs' or Recommended Daily Amounts for each nutrient, although they were not in fact, amounts that individuals or groups were recommended to eat. They were the average amount of a nutrient which should be provided per head to meet the needs of most members of a population group. To avoid confusion over whom the 'recommendation' was aimed at – providers rather than consumers – the committee used the term 'Reference Values' instead (DH, 1991, p. 1).

4. The Black Report (named after its Chairman, Sir Douglas Black) was the result of a Working Group on Inequalities in Health, commissioned by the then DHSS in 1977. Publication of the Report was restricted to a few duplicated copies of the typescript during a bank holiday weekend. However, the resulting publicity led to extensive press coverage, public and professional attention and a House of Commons debte in 1981. A slightly edited version of the report with some statistical updating, was published in 1982 by Townsend *et al.*

5. Most of the studies mentioned are summarized and their methodologies and findings discussed in Dowler and Rushton (1994). Local authorities have a statutory duty to house homeless families with dependent children. Many use so-called bed and breakfast accommodation (often one room per family with limited cooking facilities in old hotels) to do so.

6. *Food and Low Income: A Practical Guide for Advisors and Supporters Working with Families and Young People on Low Incomes* was produced in November 1994 by the National Food Alliance (an information centre and voice for the public interest on food policy matters) with funding from the Department of Health. It is a pack of information specifically written for advice workers, community nutritionists and dieticians, and other professionals working with low-income families, to give such workers the advice, information and support necessary to help those on low incomes to obtain the food they want. The pack contains: an overview of many UK local food projects and initiatives, with lessons learned; practical and technical advice on setting up a food project, including a list of who to contact in existing projects; and summaries of national information about benefits and about healthy shopping. The pack is being made widely available by the National Food Alliance, 3rd Floor, Worship Street, London, EC2A, 2BH. Pack compiled by Suzi Leather and Tim Lobstein.

6 The USA: Hunger in the Land of Plenty

Janet Poppendieck

INTRODUCTION

Hunger in the United States has demonstrated remarkable longevity and resilience as a social issue. In this media-saturated culture, social problems tend to come and go like fads or celebrities. In contrast, hunger has been an issue for much of the past 60 years. It was a topic of considerable discussion in the great depression of the 1930s, dropped from sight in the period of relative affluence following World War II, was rediscovered in the late 1960s, and has been on the public agenda, in one form or another, for nearly the last three decades. Each succeeding spate of attention has left a new layer of public programmes and voluntary responses. As a result, the United States differs from most other western industrialized nations in the extent and variety of its public food assistance programmes. At the latest count, there are twelve separate federal programmes which provide food or food-specific purchasing power to people in the United States, and these are supplemented by state and local programmes and by an immense variety of voluntary sector activities.

In order to analyse the contemporary problem of hunger in the United States, it is necessary to understand the remarkable longevity of the hunger issue, the host of organizations and activities that has grown up around it, and the way in which it has evolved over time. The first section provides a brief history of hunger as a public issue. Subsequent sections lay out the size and scope of the current problem, explore the dominant explanations for hunger in this affluent society and review a variety of remedies for the problem in the context of the current US political situation.

A BRIEF HISTORY OF HUNGER IN THE USA

During the depression of the 1930s, hunger was perceived primarily in contrast to enormous agricultural surpluses that troubled the farm sector, a situation characterized as the 'paradox of want amid plenty'. Both the Hoover and Roosevelt administrations responded to this definition of the problem with programmes to transfer surplus farm products to people in need. The national school lunch programme was begun in this way; a network of state and local agencies distributed surplus commodities free to needy families, and an innovative food stamp programme allowed poor people to obtain surplus products without cost at local grocery stores. The programmes were drastically cut back when World War II replaced surpluses with shortages, but the practice of using food assistance to dispose of farm surpluses was firmly established and remained the dominant policy for 30 years, ensuring that food programmes would be administered with a priority on benefits to agricultural producers (Poppendieck, 1986).

In contrast, the anti-hunger activities of the late 1960s and 1970s were shaped by the consciousness of the civil rights era. When hunger was 'discovered' by a group of US senators touring the Mississippi Delta, a whole host of citizens commissions, foundation field researchers, government agencies and documentary film makers undertook investigations. They found that the existing federal food programmes, the legacy of depression era politics and wartime cutbacks, reached too few of those in need and provided those whom they reached with too little assistance to permit them to achieve a nutritionally sound diet. Further, they were governed by a wide variety of arbitrary local rules, and local practice was marked by unacceptable levels of stigma, abuse and inequity (Kotz, 1969). In keeping with the rights consciousness of the era, hunger was portrayed as a failure of the federal government to protect the rights of citizens to due process and equal access.

Anti-poverty activists made a strategic decision to pursue the reform and expansion of food programmes, rather than the more adequate cash assistance that might have made such programmes unnecessary. A backlash against welfare payments and War on Poverty programmes had already set in, and, as journalist Nick Kotz (1984, p. 22) has recalled, advocates for the poor identified hunger 'as the one problem to which the public might respond. They reasoned that "hunger" made a higher moral claim than any of the other problems of poverty. Federally supported housing and jobs programs could wait; but no one should go hungry in affluent America.' A bipartisan coalition of churches, labour, foundations and groups dedicated specifically to eliminating hunger laid out an ambitious agenda for food assistance reform. It was designed to expand eligibility for and access to federal food programmes, upgrade the benefits offered by these programmes so that they would approximate a nutritionally adequate diet, and secure legal protections and funding mechanisms that would establish entitlements conferring legally enforceable rights (Kotz, 1969; Poppendieck, 1985). The Senate Select Committee on Nutrition and Human Needs provided a bipartisan base within the Congress, and the anti-hunger network, sometimes called the 'hunger lobby', became a force to be reckoned with in Washington (Berry, 1982).

The remarkable success of anti-hunger advocacy over the ensuing decade convinced many that the food assistance strategy had been the optimal choice. School lunch and breakfast programmes were drastically expanded, and child care feeding and summer meals programmes were created. A Special Supplemental Nutrition Programme for Women, Infants and Children (WIC) was established to improve prenatal and infant health and nutrition, and programmes were created for both home delivered (Meals on Wheels) and congregate meals for the elderly. The most significant reforms, however, were those that transformed the Food Stamp Programme (FSP).

In 1967, food stamps were available only at the discretion of county governments and only to those who could scrape together the money to pay for them; they provided a standard of assistance based on ability to pay rather than nutritional deficit, and contained virtually no protections for the rights of applicants and recipients. By the end of the 1970s, food stamps had become a nationwide entitlement, governed by national standards of eligibility, offering a benefit based on a standard of nutritional adequacy, available to eligible households free of charge, with built-in protections for the rights of applicants and recipients. The FSP had become the closest thing available in the United States to an income guarantee, the only means-tested programme available without regard to family structure, labour force participation, age or health. The success of food assistance reform presented a marked contrast to the general decline in the purchasing power of benefits in the nation's main family welfare programme, Aid to Families with Dependent Children (AFDC), and the complete failure of the guaranteed annual income plan put forward by the Nixon administration. Federal spending for food assistance grew over 500 per cent between 1967 and 1980 (Chelf, 1992, pp. 42–4).

Economist Sar Levitan (1980, p. 77) explained the achievements of food assistance reform as follows:

This dramatic expansion of food programs was the result of a highly diverse political coalition with very different interests and concerns.

Some saw food programs as a way of getting more for the poor by raising the cry of 'hunger in America'. Others favored food distribution because they were concerned that the poor would use their cash grants unwisely. Still others sought to sustain the demand for certain agricultural products. Yet the result was a strong and repeated preference in American public policy for providing food directly to the poor instead of allocating a portion of their cash assistance to food, and a corresponding growth in the federal network of in-kind assistance programs.

Others (Berry, 1982; Poppendieck, 1985, 1995) have noted that the food programmes lent themselves to precisely the tactics in which advocates had developed skills in the long civil rights struggle: lobbying, litigation, legislative drafting, expert testimony, coalition building, programme performance monitoring, and outreach and organizing at the grassroots level. Although Bread for the World, a Christian organization concerned with global as well as domestic hunger, succeeded in getting both Houses of Congress to pass a 'Right to Food' resolution rooted in the UN Declaration of Human Rights and subsequent international conventions, there is little evidence that this campaign materially influenced crucial votes on domestic food assistance reform. For the most part, gains were achieved not through dramatic declarations of new rights but through incremental techniques: marginal adjustments in existing programmes and pilot or experimental programmes.

Just as hunger activists were beginning to claim victory in the war on hunger, however, the election of Ronald Reagan brought to power the right wing of the Republican Party and inaugurated a new round of hunger discourse in the US. Calling for reduced social spending, tax cuts and a reduction of welfare dependency, Reagan sought and obtained from Congress deep cuts in a whole host of federal social programmes. The combination of long-term changes in the economy, a sharp recession and cutbacks in federal assistance to poor people led the mayors of several large cities to declare a 'hunger emergency', pointing to long lines at soup kitchens and food pantries as evidence (Physicians Task Force, 1985, pp. 11–15).

The 'emergency' designation caught on. It was already part of the language of soup kitchens and food pantries, which provided food to individuals and households experiencing 'food emergencies' and were thus called 'emergency food providers'. It resonated with the sense of urgency felt by the long-term anti-hunger activists who saw the gains of the 1970s slipping away. And it was convenient for the new conservative administration because it permitted the establishment of temporary programmes that did not create entitlements (Lipsky and Smith, 1989) and elicited an outpouring of effort by the voluntary sector, reducing pressure on the public treasury (Poppendieck, 1995). New soup kitchens and food pantries opened at a rapid rate, and existing emergency food providers expanded their capacity and operations. In New York City, for example, there were 30 emergency food providers in 1980; 487 by 1987 and more than 700 by the early 1990s, dispensing an estimated 30 million meals per year (Food and Hunger Hotline, n.d., p. 5).

As pantries and kitchens expanded and proliferated, they coalesced into a network. Central warehouses called food banks were established in many communities to receive and distribute large donations from food manufacturers and wholesalers, and programmes to 'rescue' prepared and perishable foods from restaurants, caterers and institutional and corporate dining rooms were developed in many cities. The food banks affiliated nationally into an association called Second Harvest, which receives and redistributes donations from food corporations at the national level, and the Prepared and Perishable Food Rescue Programmes (PPFRPs) organized a national entity called Food Chain which negotiates national-level donation initiatives with restaurants and fast food chains. The federal government fostered the proliferation of emergency food providers by offering large donations of surplus agricultural commodities, first through the Special Dairy Distribution Program, better known as the cheese giveaway, then through the Temporary Emergency Food Assistance Program (TEFAP), and more recently through Operation Desert Share, through which leftover supplies from the Persian Gulf War (Desert Storm) were distributed to kitchens and pantries.

The growth of the emergency food phenomenon did not do away with the major public programmes that had developed in the earlier decades, but it transformed the dominant image of anti-hunger activity from lobbying and budget politics to charity and donation, from food as a right to food as a gift. In the process, hunger underwent a process of depoliticization. It became detached from issues of rights and entitlements and taxes and fairness, and became attached instead to canned goods drives, walk-a-thons, food festivals and corporate public relations.

Local soup kitchens and food pantries and the food banks and PPFRPs that supply them have been enormously creative in raising both food and funds for their activities. In so doing, they have provided opportunities for literally millions of Americans to become involved in

anti-hunger activities. Churches and synagogues conduct special offer-
ings, grocery stores enable customers to 'check out hunger' by making
donations to the food bank right at the checkout counter. Service clubs,
school groups and youth organizations of all sorts have become involved. So have sports figures and celebrities, radio stations and rock
bands, gardeners and summer camps. The highly successful Taste of
the Nation, coordinated by Share Our Strength, raises funds for both
charitable feeding programmes and advocacy by offering donors an opportunity to sample the wares of a city's major chefs, and the Taste of
the NFL (National Football League) allows patrons at the superbowl
to attend a feast prepared by chefs from the superbowl's host city. The
postal workers conduct a major food drive in cities across the nation
each spring, and the Boy Scouts pick up bags of canned goods in hundreds of communities every autumn. Given the extent and variety of
these activities, and the possibility of participating through very small
donations of food or time, it is credible, though still remarkable, that
nearly four-fifths of voters in a random telephone survey of 1000 households claimed that they, personally, had done something to help fight
hunger (Breglio, 1992, pp. 14–16). Fighting hunger has become a national pastime.

This does not mean that the public programmes have diminished in
size. Average monthly participation in the FSP reached a record high
of 27.6 million persons during the first three-quarters of fiscal year
1994 (USDA, 1994, p. 6). Washington-based advocacy groups worked
hard for a restoration of benefits cut by Reagan's early budget moves,
and in 1988, 1990 and 1993, with leadership from a House Select Committee on Hunger, Congress passed legislation to expand food stamp
eligibility and benefit levels and increase funding for the WIC programme. Public food assistance remains the core of the nation's response to hunger, but charitable feeding programmes have captured
much of the public imagination.

For the most part, those most deeply involved with the charitable
food programmes recognize the centrality of public food assistance
and assert publicly that the role of the voluntary sector is to supplement, not replace, public sector provisions. Nevertheless, the constant
fundraising, solicitation of donations of food and general publicity
needed to keep the emergency food network functioning make that system very visible. Whilst those directly involved may recognize its limitations, the citizen who donates a can of food now and then, or gives a
dollar when the local radio station broadcasts a fundraiser from the
shopping mall, may believe that charitable feeding programmes offer

an alternative to provisions like WIC and food stamps. Since private feeding programmes rely heavily upon volunteer labour and donated space, they appear very cost-effective at first glance, far cheaper than public provisions. In this context, when politicians launch attacks on fraud and abuse in the FSP or plate waste in school lunches, or complain about the rising cost of food assistance, the mere existence of the emergency food system may undermine public commitment to adequate public provision.

By the end of the 1980s, impelled by concern about such public misconceptions and by anxiety that fatigue amongst volunteers, underpaid staff and donors would render the emergency system incapable of meeting growing needs, people in and around the feeding movement began looking for a new definition of the situation that would lead to more permanent, less fragile solutions. The notion of 'community food security', borrowed from the field of international development, began to be widely discussed. Food security is defined as 'access by all people at all times to enough food for an active, healthy life. Food security includes at a minimum a) the ready availability of nutritionally adequate and safe foods, and b) an assured ability to acquire acceptable foods in socially acceptable ways' (Leidenfrost, 1994, p. 173). The food security approach embraces food security for the entire community, not just the poor, and gives attention to the preservation of local agriculture. There was debate among hunger activists over whether replacing the term 'hunger' with 'food insecurity' would rob it of its emotive power and political clout, but the idea of establishing community food security as a goal was gaining ground among emergency providers, food assistance advocates and supporters of food systems and localized agriculture when the mid term Congressional elections in November 1994 gave elements of the emerging food security coalition more immediate challenges to address.

These elections brought the right wing of the Republican Party into the majority in both Houses of Congress. The ensuing Contract With America has largely eclipsed the community food security initiative in the anti-hunger movement as advocates have mobilized to prevent the destruction of food stamps, WIC and school meals, while emergency providers have tried to convince the new majority that they are already stretched to breaking point and cannot take over any larger share of the care of the poor. The champions of community food security are continuing to promulgate their idea, but for the time being, at least, both traditional anti-hunger activists and emergency food providers are otherwise occupied.

The Contract With America represents the most profound assault on public assistance for poor people since the infrastructure of the American welfare state was created in the New Deal. Responding to dissatisfactions with welfare dependency and big government that have been brewing for years, the newly empowered conservatives believe they have a mandate to restore 'family values', reinforce rugged individualism and shift power from Washington to the states. The Contract calls for a balanced budget, lower taxes, deep cuts in social spending, a virtual end to public assistance for able-bodied people, rigid time limits for assistance to families and transfer of control of many social programmes to the states through a procedure called 'block granting', lump sums for general policy areas to be used as the state sees fit. Block granting would effectively end the entitlement character of such programmes as food stamps and school meals. In addition, advocates for the poor oppose it because they predict that states, subject to the same fiscal pressures and taxpayer resistance as the federal government, would enter an all out meanness competition to reduce benefits in hopes that poor people would go elsewhere. Furthermore, block granting would end the countercyclical nature of entitlements; instead of funding that automatically expands when recession or a natural disaster strikes, each state would have a fixed amount in any given fiscal year. As written, the Contract also calls for scheduled reductions in the overall block grant amounts, so that states that fail to supplement will see a steady decline in benefits. If it becomes law, it will drastically change the rules under which anti-hunger advocacy proceeds and inaugurate a new era in the life of hunger as a public issue.

THE HUNGER PROBLEM NOW: SIZE AND SCOPE

Estimates of the incidence and prevalence of hunger in the US have virtually always suffered from the twin confusions of definition and methodology. What do we mean by hunger? Not simply the sensation we feel as mealtime approaches, obviously, but not necessarily starvation, either. In general, the hunger that we regard as a social problem is roughly embraced by the concept of poverty-related malnutrition, with malnutrition defined as 'a condition in which the intake of nutrients is not conducive to good health' (Latham, 1968, p. 51). Malnutrition, however, does not necessarily involve the painful sensations associated with consumption of too few calories; people who fill up on starchy foods with low nutrient density may experience few or none of the discomforts of hunger, but nevertheless, their diets may be inadequate to maintain health. On the other hand, short-term episodes of hunger in adults, even if acute, may not damage health. That is, you can have hunger without malnutrition as well as malnutrition without hunger. Finally, advocates of the emerging food security approach would include the notion of being able to 'acquire acceptable foods in socially acceptable ways' (Leidenfrost, 1994, p. 173) in their definition of food security. They specifically exclude soup kitchens and food pantries from the socially acceptable repertoire, along with begging, theft and scavenging. In fact, Cohen and Burt (1989, p. 4) define hunger as 'the state of being unable to obtain a nutritionally adequate diet from non-emergency food channels'.

Needless to say, these definitional issues render precise measurement difficult, but the controversies surrounding the measurement of hunger are political as well as technical. Ever since Herbert Hoover alienated sections of the electorate by his famous assertion that 'No one has starved', the ability to perceive hunger in America has been a dividing line. In her fascinating dissertation on the definition and measurement of hunger, Kathy Radimer (1990, p. 20) designated two sides in the hunger debate, the Believers and the Disbelievers. Among the Believers, she listed as prominent voices the Physician Task Force on Hunger in America and the Citizens Commission on Hunger in New England, both headed by Dr Larry Brown of the Harvard University School of Public Health, two Washington-based public policy advocacy organizations, the Food Research and Action Center, and the Center for Budget and Policy Priorities. An update would add the Tufts University Center on Hunger, Poverty, and Nutrition Policy, founded and directed by Larry Brown, both Second Harvest and Food Chain from the emergency food system, The United States Conference of Mayors, the American Dietetic Association, The Society for Nutrition Education, Public Voice for Food and Health Policy, The Children's Defense Fund, and a group of organizations originally and primarily concerned with global hunger which have begun to focus a greater share of their attention on hunger in the US: Bread for the World, World Hunger Year and Food First. Among the Disbelievers, she listed Dr George Graham of Johns Hopkins University, the President's Task Force on Food Assistance, on which Graham served, President Ronald Reagan, his adviser Edwin Meese and the US Department of Agriculture (USDA). An update of this list would move USDA under Bill Clinton to the Believers column and add very nearly the entire Republican leadership of the US House of Representatives to the Disbelievers tally.

Liberals tend to be Believers and conservatives Disbelievers, with exceptions on both sides, but these generalizations mask a more complicated underlying politics. The Believers, for example, include many whose primary concern is nutrition or getting food into the hands of hungry people, and others for whom hunger is only a symptom of poverty and for whom the politics of hunger are simply the most productive avenue to obtain public benefits for the poor. The Disbelievers seem to embrace both those who simply cannot believe the evidence that the economy is so profoundly failing a large number of Americans and those whose definition of hunger verges on starvation, for whom people receiving food from soup kitchens, for example, are not hungry because they are being fed.

In the United States, there have generally been three broad approaches to the measurement of hunger: inference from statistical information on income, behavioural indicators and surveys and self-reports. A fourth approach, clinical studies of the incidence of malnutrition, are often cited in hunger reports, but the clinical approach is limited in its ability to detect most US dietary inadequacy because, as Wheler, Scott and Anderson (1992, p. 29S) have summarized, due to 'the relatively high standard of living in the US, and because food assistance programs are in place to help the needy, starvation rarely occurs and physiological measures are not sensitive enough to detect the subtle nature of chronic but sub-clinical hunger among the poor of the United States'. Over time, the *inferential* approach has probably been the most frequently used. We know the amount of money required to purchase a minimally adequate diet. We have figures on the numbers of people living on incomes below levels that would reasonably permit them to allocate that amount to food purchase. Thus we can infer the number of people who are hungry or 'at risk' of hunger. In the United States, this may be easier than it is in some other first world nations because the entire US system of poverty income thresholds, the so-called poverty line, is derived directly from the cost of a minimally adequate diet, the Economy Food Plan (EFP), a subsistence diet for emergency use developed by dieticians at the Agriculture Department. The logic by which this system was constructed sheds further light upon the challenges of measurement.

In short, household consumption surveys from the 1950s showed that, on average, US households spent about a third of their income on food. Casting about for an operational definition of poverty in the early 1960s, Molly Orshansky of the Social Security Administration reasoned that a family could thus be considered poor if a third of its income was not sufficient to purchase a subsistence diet for its household size. She established poverty income thresholds for households of various sizes by multiplying the cost of the EFP by three. They are updated annually for inflation, but they do not change to reflect the declining share of income that the society as a whole spends on food purchases. That is, the poverty line embodies an absolute rather than a relative definition of poverty. Over time, the officially poor have fallen steadily further from the median (Bell, 1987, pp. 97–115).

The federal poverty line remains a topic of controversy among academics and advocates concerned with poverty, but it makes estimates of inadequate food purchasing power relatively easy to compute. This was the approach used by the US Senate, Select Committee on Nutrition and Human Needs (1969, pp. 20, 21) in the aftermath of the 1960s discovery of hunger. The Committee, in a study that became a prototype for subsequent inferential assessments, reported that approximately 5.1 million people lived on total incomes less than the cost of the economy food plan, and another 9.3 million had incomes less than twice the cost of the plan for their household size. These 14.4 million people, the Committee concluded, had incomes so low that they would almost certainly suffer hunger and malnutrition unless they received food assistance; another 10.4 million officially poor people were at risk, and yet another 13 million 'near poor' had incomes low enough to make hunger a real possibility. The Committee went on to point out that the patently inadequate family food assistance programmes were serving only a combined total of 6.4 million persons and that their aggregate expenditure fell far short of meeting the gap between poor people's incomes and the cost of the economy food plan.[1] More recently, the inferential approach was used by the Tufts University Center on Hunger, Poverty and Nutrition Policy to come up with an estimate of 28 million hungry Americans in 1991 (Center on Hunger, 1993).

A second approach to measurement might be labelled behavioural. We conclude that people are hungry if we observe them engaging in activities to obtain food that we believe most people would find distasteful: foraging in dustbins and skips, waiting in long lines under unpleasant conditions for a meal at a soup kitchen, taking food from plates left on tables at restaurants. In essence, we believe that most people would not do these things unless they were hungry, so we use them as behavioural indicators of hunger. In the early 1980s, in the aftermath of the Reagan administration budget cuts, the US Conference of mayors began conducting surveys of growing numbers at soup kitchens and food pantries. In subsequent years, the mayors issued annual updates on hunger and homelessness in American cities, reporting each year an overall growth in the numbers of people seeking emergency food. In 1994 the behavioural approach culminated in the release of a report by Second Harvest, the National Food Bank Network. A consulting firm that conducted a massive study of 34 member banks and then projected the results to the organization's total membership of 185 banks, reported that 26 million people had received food from soup kitchens and food pantries supplied by Second Harvest member food banks. Assuming that some of them had used more than one such programme, Second Harvest projected the 'unduplicated count' of emergency food clients to be in the vicinity of 21.8 million individual persons (VanAmburg, 1994, p. 24). Since Second Harvest does not collect statistics on agencies supplied by food banks that are not Second Harvest members, and since no one familiar with the haphazard nature of the emergency food network would claim that it reaches all who are hungry, the Second Harvest report of nearly 22 million people makes the Tufts estimate of 28 million appear quite credible, if one assumes that going to a soup kitchen or food pantry is an indicator of hunger. This last contingency, however, is a bone of contention which leads back directly to the difficulty of agreeing upon a definition of hunger.

For the advocates of the food security approach, resort to an emergency food provider, as noted above, is *prima facie* evidence of hunger. On the other hand, many observers question whether all clients at soup kitchens and food pantries would actually go hungry without this emergency food assistance; some would simply have less money to spend on other portions of the household budget. Ed Meese, an adviser to President Ronald Reagan, made his scepticism briefly famous when he told reporters questioning him about growing lines at Washington area soup kitchens that the Reagan administration had received 'considerable information that people go to soup kitchens because the food is free and that's easier than paying for it' (Newton, 1986, p. 12). The Reagan administration's contention that there were no reliable measures of hunger and that reports of hunger were based upon 'anecdotal stuff' led hunger activists to collaborate with social scientists and public health professionals to construct more reliable and convincing measures.

The largest of these efforts has been the Community Childhood Hunger Identification Project or CCHIP. CCHIP relies upon a point-prevalence survey in which members of households with at least one child and incomes below 185 per cent of the federal poverty line are

First World Hunger

asked a series of questions about household food supply and strategies for coping with household food shortages, that is, 'Thinking about the past 30 days, how many days was your household out of money to buy food to make a meal?' (Wheler, Scott and Anderson, 1992, p. 31S). Households are designated as 'hungry' if their answers on five of eight key dimensions indicate inadequate food resources.

The CCHIP approach was carefully designed and meticulously tested before local studies were conducted in seven sites across the nation, and, although it has its critics, its findings have received wide acceptance in both government circles and the medical and public health community. Based on its findings from 2335 interviews in seven low-income communities, CCHIP estimated in 1991 that there were approximately 5.5 million hungry children under the age of 12 and that another 6 million children were at risk of hunger because they lived in households experiencing food insufficiency due to inadequate resources. The results of a second round of CCHIP studies were released in autumn 1995. A far simpler survey approach was taken by Dr Vincent Breglio whose conservative credentials as a 'Republican Pollster' with clients including the *Wall Street Journal* gave special credibility to his efforts in some circles. Breglio, repeating a technique used a decade earlier by Louis Harris, simply asked the 1000 respondents in his random phone survey if they knew anyone who was hungry. He produced an estimate of 30 million hungry people. (Center on Hunger, 1993).

On a smaller scale, another very interesting effort to develop a means for measuring not only hunger but the broader notion of 'food insecurity', including distress experienced by mothers when they do not know how they will feed their children, has been developed at Cornell University (Radimer, 1990; and Radimer *et al.*, 1992).

Meanwhile, drawing on the CCHIP and prompted by the recommendations of the President's Task Force on Food Assistance, the Third National Health and Nutrition Examination Survey (NHANES III), conducted by the National Center for Health Statistics, began developing questionnaires to measure individual and family food insufficiency in ways that could be integrated with data on health and nutritional status. Finally, this flurry of measurement activity culminated in an effort by USDA, which, under Secretary Mike Espy had made a major commitment to dealing with problem of hunger, to devise hunger measurement questions for inclusion in the Census Bureau's annual update, a panel study of 60 000 households, known as the Current Population Survey (CPS). The Census Bureau has administered the first round of hunger questions (in April 1995), but the results will not be available to the public until approximately a year after the survey was completed. Regardless of the outcome of the inclusion of hunger questions in the CPS, however, the sheer volume of effort that has gone into trying to document the existence of hunger and measure its extent points to the underlying tension around this social problem. Hunger is so contrary to the nation's self-image that conservatives, who want to promulgate the idea that capitalism is basically working well and would work better with less government interference, are at great pains to deny or minimize its existence, creating a necessity for liberals and anti-poverty activists, 'Believers', in Radimer's terms, to expend significant energy and resources to 'prove' what they already 'know'. The measurement of hunger has become a minor industry in and of itself.

One of the advantages of including hunger questions in the CPS is that it will permit reliable measurement of the distribution of hunger among various demographic subgroups. Many local studies have included such data, but the diversity of American communities makes projection to the national level unreliable. National figures exist for the population in poverty, of course, but the whole point of including hunger questions in the CPS, which already measures poverty, is the assumption that not all poor households experience hunger and that some non-poor households do. Until the CPS data become available, the Second Harvest study described above is probably the closest thing to national data about the composition of the hungry that we have, again assuming that one is willing to define people as hungry if they seek emergency food.

The Second Harvest study looked at the housing situation of respondents as well as such standard demographic variables as age, sex, family structure and race and ethnicity. Second Harvest found that 18.1 per cent of clients served by its network were homeless and another 5.4 per cent live in marginal housing situations. Children age 17 or younger account for more than two-fifths (42.9 per cent) of all emergency food clients but make up 25.9 per cent of the total US population; whilst 8.1 per cent of all Second Harvest clients are elderly, a figure that rises to 22 per cent of soup kitchen clients, as compared with 12.5 per cent of the general US population. Women comprise more than two-thirds of adult pantry clients; whilst men comprise 62 per cent of soup kitchen clients. Single-parent households comprise 26.8 per cent of all households served by the Second Harvest Network and 55.5 per cent of those households with children. A majority of food recipients is white (50.9 per cent of clients as compared with 75.6 per cent of the US population), but minority groups are over-represented. African Americans constitute nearly a third (32.9 per cent) of food recipients as compared to 11.7 per cent of the US population. Native Americans are substantially over-represented and Latinos are slightly over-represented, while Asian Americans are under-represented, in comparison with their numbers in the total population. The study also collected data on employment and income and found that 17.2 per cent of all clients are disabled; nearly a third (31.6 per cent) of all client households have someone employed. Finally, nearly three-quarters of all client households have incomes under $10 000 annually and 87.9 per cent have annual household incomes below $14 000 (VanAmburg, 1994, pp. EX6–9).

EXPLANATIONS FOR HUNGER

Poverty has virtually always been the prime suspect in explaining hunger in the US. When reports of hunger began to appear with increasing frequency in the early 1980s, therefore, the search for explanations focused upon two related questions. Why were more people poor? And why were the food assistance programmes that advocates had worked so hard to expand and reform during the 1970s not preventing hunger among those who fell into poverty? On a day-to-day basis, these questions surfaced primarily in attempts to explain the rising demand for emergency food at soup kitchens and food pantries. As providers and advocates surveyed applicants in an effort to understand the rapid expansion of demand, there emerged a portrait of people caught between declining income and rising costs. Four factors were generally identified as contributors to the growing need for emergency assistance in the 1980s, and to varying degrees they all continue to explain the persistence of need in the 1990s: (1) cutbacks in food assistance programmes, (2) deterioration of the ability of the economy to generate jobs and incomes, (3) erosion of the value of public assistance benefits, and (4) sharp increases in shelter and other costs.

Cutbacks in food assistance are listed first, not because they are the primary explanation but because they were the trigger that put hunger on the public agenda. Ronald Reagan was elected in 1980 claiming a mandate to cut domestic social spending. By including food assistance programmes among those targeted for cuts, the administration almost guaranteed that the issue would be framed in terms of hunger, since food assistance had so active a network of dedicated advocates. The Congressional Budget Office has estimated that over the period encompassed by fiscal years 1982–5, $12.2 billion less was available for food aid than would have been true had the laws remained unchanged. Added to the effects of other cuts in social spending, and implemented in the midst of a particularly deep recession, the nutrition cuts hurt poor people and enraged advocates. Frustrated in their attempts to expand programmes or even resist cuts, anti-hunger activists threw themselves into the task of documenting the growth of hunger and specifying the social circumstances that led so many people to the soup kitchen and food pantry door.

The reality they found, however, was not simply the fallout from budget cuts. Writing in the early 1980s, Michael Harrington, whose book *The Other America* had aroused the nation to the plight of the poor in the 1960s, summarized the matter this way: the *New American Poverty* (1985, pp. 7, 8), he argued,

> is not... the creation of Ronald Reagan. He made the worst of a bad thing, to be sure, scapegoating the poor for imaginary wrongs. But the structures of misery today are not simply the work of the ideological rigidity of a President.... They are the results of massive economic and social transformations...

In short, as the economies of Europe and the Pacific developed and markets internationalized, US industries found themselves in competition with the products of a powerful combination of advanced technology and low-wage workers. Multinational corporations with little or no loyalty to particular societies moved capital around the globe to find its most profitable application, leaving behind empty smokestacks and ruined communities in the industrial heartland of the US. Even those firms that remained in the US adapted to the new reality in ways that hurt workers: they automated, streamlined, downsized and engaged in a frenzy of leveraged buyouts and hostile takeovers.

Recessions in both the early 1980s and the early 1990s intensified the pace of these trends and made them more visible. Average unemployment rates have been rising for the last quarter-century in virtually all western industrialized nations (McFate, 1995, p. 3). In the US, unemployment averaged 4.6 per cent in the 1968–73 period and 7.2 per cent in the 1980–9 period, reaching well over 9 per cent in the recession of the early 1980s and climbing to 7.7 per cent in the milder recession of the early 1990s. Coupled with a reduction in the proportion of the unemployed who received unemployment compensation and a drop in the fraction who ever got their old jobs back, these rates spelled disaster for many once independent families (Burt, 1993, pp. 99, 100; Center on Hunger, 1995, p. 17).

The recession of the early 1980s hit particularly hard at workers who had held manufacturing jobs that paid relatively high wages and provided health insurance. These were the among the people who acquired the label 'new poor'; the General Accounting Office described them in a 1983 survey of clients at emergency food centres as 'the breed of "new poor", members of families, young and able-bodied with homes in the suburbs. They now find themselves without work, with unemployment and savings accounts exhausted, and with diminishing hopes of being able to continue to meet their mortgages, automobile and other payments.'

When the new poor of the early 1980s did find new jobs, they encountered other aspects of the global restructuring of the economy, aspects that continue in full force today. The new jobs were less likely to be in manufacturing, less likely to provide comprehensive fringe benefits and very likely to pay lower wages. The proportion of the labour force employed in the manufacturing sector fell by nearly a quarter between 1975 and 1990. Real wages, adjusted for inflation, dropped in private non-agricultural industries between 1973 and 1993, and adjusted average weekly earnings during the same period declined by nearly a fifth (Center on Hunger, 1995, p. 15). The decline in purchasing power has been even more pronounced at the very bottom, for workers earning the minimum wage. Despite increases in the national minimum in 1990 and 1991, the minimum wage has fallen steadily in its ability to protect a family from poverty. Throughout most of the 1960s and 1970s, the income earned by a person working full time at a minimum wage job was sufficient to keep a family of three out of official poverty. By 1994, a minimum wage job, 40 hours a week, 52 weeks a year would not even keep a household of two above the poverty threshold; figured on the more typical 35-hour week, the minimum wage does not now pay enough to keep a single individual above the poverty line (Burt, 1993, pp. 73–5).

Wages are not the only source of income that has declined in value in recent decades. The erosion of the purchasing power of public assistance benefits is even more pronounced. By 1989, the average monthly AFDC benefit per family, adjusted for inflation, was worth only two-thirds of what it had been in 1970 (Burt, 1993, pp. 84–5). The decline in welfare benefits is not the result of a unified national policy; rather, it reflects the decisions of the 50 state legislatures. AFDC is a combined federal–state programme, with each state defining its own standard of need (the amount of money that the state believes that families need in order to subsist) and establishing its own benefit level, generally considerably below its declared standard of need. The erosion of public assistance benefits that has been in progress for several decades generally reflects the states' failure to adjust benefits to keep up with inflation. Even in the federal income transfer programme for elderly and disabled persons, Supplemental Security Income (SSI), which is indexed to inflation, state supplements are not tied to rising costs and most have failed to keep pace with prices. Single adults who do not qualify for either SSI or AFDC can turn to whatever state or local programmes exist under the rubric of General Assistance, called by a variety of different names in different localities, but these programmes are providing less support and are harder to obtain than in earlier years. The states of Michigan and Illinois recently ended general assistance altogether, and in the current assault on welfare, several other states are considering similar moves.

A peculiarity of American federalism, however, as well as a budget-driven parsimony toward poor people, has undoubtedly contributed to the states' reluctance to update their benefits. Food stamps, which contribute a significant portion of the income of AFDC households, are a federal programme funded with federal dollars. In purely financial terms, it is in a state's interest to have maximum food stamp participation by eligible people within the state, because the programme draws federal dollars into the state and cycles them through the food retailing sector, providing jobs. But the size of the food stamp benefit is based solely upon the gap between the applicant's food stamp relevant income and the cost of the Thrifty Food Plan (TFP) for her household size. Thus, the lower a state's actual public assistance benefit, the larger the number of federal food stamp dollars each recipient will draw into the state. For poor people and their advocates, this anomaly has posed a constant problem. A rise in the shelter allowance to cope with rising rents, for example, could actually make clients worse off. Their food stamps would decrease because they were receiving more 'income', but the income would often go directly to the landlord. The client would end up with less discretionary money, and the state would end up with fewer food stamp dollars. The gap between the steady growth of federal expenditures on food assistance and the steady decline in the purchasing power of state-determined welfare benefits may not be as contradictory as it appears.

Inflation is the other side of the squeeze that has sent so many Americans to emergency food providers in the last 15 years. As studies of the growing demand for emergency food piled up, one fact emerged with startling clarity: a sharp rise in shelter costs was forcing many impoverished Americans, both the working poor and those supported by public income transfers, into a dilemma often labelled heat or eat'. With shelter costs consuming an ever greater share of the household budget, more and more families were finding themselves without adequate resources for food. The rise in shelter costs, rooted in the fuel crisis of the early 1970s and driven by a frenzy of urban real estate speculation in the 1980s, has affected all segments of society, but it has been most onerous for the poor. In 1980, the federal government set a benchmark of 30 per cent of family income as the appropriate ceiling for rents; higher figures were defined as excessive (Chelf, 1992, p. 59). A 1985 Census Bureau survey found 22 million families paying rents in excess of this standard; 45 per cent of all households with incomes below the official poverty threshold spent 70 per cent or more of their income for rent and utilities. No wonder they could not afford to purchase adequate food!

For some the escalating burden of shelter became too much to bear, and homelessness joined hunger as both symbol and symptom of the escalation of poverty. Once a person becomes homeless, he or she almost automatically joins the ranks of the hungry, or at least the ranks of those dependent upon soup kitchens and other emergency providers for food. Without access to kitchen facilities, any hope of economical eating vanishes, and although food stamps can be used in restaurants under certain circumstances, they were never designed to cover the costs of eating out on a full-time basis. Since 'the homeless' constitute a fairly large segment of 'the hungry', nearly anything that causes homelessness contributes to the rise of hunger. The causes of homelessness have been the subject of numerous studies including several major books (Rossi, 1989; Burt, 1993; Snow and Anderson, 1993) and different scholars emphasize different explanations, but the list almost always includes deinstitutionalization of mental patients, epidemics of drug and alcohol abuse, rising housing costs, shrinking housing subsidies, the destruction of Single Room Occupancy (SRO) units, and of course, the same increases in unemployment and decreases in wages and public income supports already depicted above.

Taken together, these factors – the underlying deterioration of the economy, the impact of recession, the erosion of public assistance benefits and the rise in shelter costs – go a long way toward explaining why more Americans are poor, but they do not immediately explain why the public food assistance programmes that grew out of the New Deal of the 1930s and the War on Poverty of the 1960s have not been sufficient to prevent hunger among poor people. More specifically, they do not explain why the food stamp programme, the nation's first line of defence in any war against hunger, has permitted so many casualties.

Many of the nation's first emergency food pantries were established primarily to provide families experiencing a 'food emergency' with a three-day supply of food which would tide them over during the waiting period for expedited (emergency) food stamps. Once they were in business, however, many pantries began to see the same families returning month after month. Inquiring as to what had become of the food stamps, they received a simple answer: they ran out. Soon pantries were reporting a greatly increased volume of applicants during the last week of the month; many people's stamps were running out before the new ones were due. Other applicants whose need was convincing to pantry operators reported that they were unaware of the stamp programme, did not know how to apply for it, did not believe they were eligible, had applied and been turned down, or did not want to apply. Some were food stamp dropouts who had given up the attempt to secure the benefits, discouraged by the lengthy paperwork requirements and the demanding application and certification process, or unable for logistical reasons (hours of operation, location) to access a Food Stamp Office (Physicians Task Force, 1985; De Havenon, 1988; Clancy, Bowering and Poppendieck, 1991, pp. 153–74).[2]

Several factors combine to explain why food stamps run out before the month is over, why so many needy people are not eligible for the stamps and why others believe they are ineligible or do not want to apply. First, food stamps were never designed to provide a full month's supply of food, except for families with no cash income whatsoever. Benefit levels are calculated on the assumption that families can allocate 30 per cent of their income (after certain deductions) to food purchase. The stamp allotment is set at the cost of the TFP discounted by 30 per cent of household income. When the programme was first designed, the 30 per cent assumption, derived from the same information used to set the poverty line, may have made sense. Families could allocate 30 per cent of income for food when they could secure shelter for a quarter of their income, when fuel was cheap, when VCRs, fax and home computers had not yet been invented. Households now struggling to allocate 30 per cent of income to food are struggling against much greater odds. With rent consuming 60 per cent or more of income for well over half of poor renters, it is not surprising that they cannot find cash to supplement their food stamps up to the TFP level.

In fact, Congress has recognized the role of high shelter costs in creating a need for food assistance, and many years ago it created an 'excess shelter cost deduction' which is used in calculating both eligibility and benefits. That is, applicants can deduct from the income considered in calculating eligibility shelter costs in excess of 50 per cent of income. In order to slow the growth of programme costs, however, Congress established 'caps' or ceilings, both for the excess shelter cost deduction and for overall eligibility. At present, the cap on the shelter cost deduction is set at $231 per month. The overall cap is set at 130 per cent of the poverty line. No household can receive benefits if its income exceeds 130 per cent of poverty, regardless of the amount it must spend to secure shelter, the proportion of its income required for work expenses or taxes, child and dependant care costs, or any other allowable deduction. Given the very high shelter costs encountered in some areas of the nation, these two ceilings help to explain why people in sufficient need to turn to food pantries and soup kitchens are often ineligible for food stamps. Other needy households are barred by the 'assets screen'; that is, they are ineligible because they own liquid assets in excess of $2000 ($3000 for households containing at least one elderly person), or a vehicle worth more than $4600.

For those households that do overcome the eligibility barriers and obtain food stamps, the TFP presents another round of obstacles to the conquest of hunger. The TFP itself is technically a nutritionally adequate diet, but it provides a level of expenditure at which most participants cannot purchase nutritional sufficiency. In short, it presumes optimal circumstances for food purchase, transportation, storage and preparation. Recipients must have the knowledge, skills, time, equipment and utensils to prepare many dishes from 'scratch' (raw ingredients). And a whole series of factors relating to the location of supermarkets and the pricing policies of stores in poor neighbourhoods means that many food stamp customers cannot obtain foods at the competitive prices assumed in the calculation of the TFP or must pay for transportation out of their own neighbourhoods each time they use a supermarket. For many clients, the stamps would run out even if 30 per cent of household income were regularly allocated to food purchase simply because the prices they must pay are higher than those used to calculate the allotment. No wonder that so many emergency food providers have increased the frequency with which clients may receive food packages to once a month or more; reluctantly, they have accepted the role of regular supplement rather than emergency safety net.

What about those who simply don't apply? Studies of eligible nonparticipants have generally identified three factors: people were unaware of their eligibility, did not believe that they needed the stamps, or felt that the costs of participation in terms of stigma, travel to the programme office or the rigours of the certification process outweighed the benefits. In general, participation rates decline with the size of the expected benefits. Thus, while only 60 per cent of eligible households were participating in August 1984, nearly 80 per cent of the benefits payable if all eligible households had participated were disbursed (Allin *et al.*, 1990, pp. 23–35).

Food stamps are the only food assistance programme that might be expected to prevent hunger across the board. None of the other programmes is a general entitlement. Most are limited to specific groups – children or the elderly, for example. Several, like the WIC programme, are limited by available funding; they are not entitlements at all. Others are entitlements only if some local agency chooses to make the programme available. Free and reduced price school meals, for example, are an entitlement for income eligible children who attend schools that offer the programmes, but schools are not required to do so. And finally, none of these programmes is intended to provide access to a basic diet; all are supplemental in nature, providing a particular meal, or a meal and a snack. Packaged together, the school meal, child and adult care feeding, senior meals and WIC programmes can certainly help a poor household stretch its food dollars – and its food stamps – and it is probable that they provide a margin of safety that helps many families avoid hunger. Both the school meal programmes and WIC set eligibility ceilings at a more realistic 185 per cent of poverty, enabling them to assist families not eligible for food stamps. The following section identifies changes that would increase the hunger fighting capacity of these programmes as well as that of the FSP.

HUNGER IN THE US: WHAT CAN BE DONE?

At the start of this decade, a group of leaders in the US anti-hunger movement, following the example set by the Bellagio Declaration which called for an end to world hunger, convened in Medford, Massachusetts, to issue the *Medford Declaration to End Hunger in the US* (1991). The *Medford Declaration* conceptualized the ending of hunger in America as a two-step process – abolishing hunger itself and eliminating the causes of hunger:

In the short term we must use existing channels to see that food is available to the hungry on an adequate and consistent basis. If we fully utilize existing public programs – in conjunction with the heroic efforts of voluntary food providers in local communities – we can end hunger very soon. But we must move as a nation to end the causes of hunger as well. Many things can be done to increase the purchasing power of American households, and to fulfill the desire for independence and self-reliance which so characterizes our people.

Using the *Medford Declaration's* framework, let us look first at the major existing public food assistance programmes and how they might be improved, then at the activities of the voluntary sector, and finally at strategies for eliminating the causes of hunger. Food stamps are clearly the central strategy among public food programmes and will consume the bulk of the discussion, but let us look briefly at the major proposals that have been put forward over the years to improve nutrition among children, pregnant women and new mothers, and the elderly.

Child Nutrition

Child nutrition programmes include the School Lunch and Breakfast Programmes, the Summer Food Service Programme and the Child and Adult Care Food Programme. At present, all are entitlements; anyone who meets the eligibility requirements may receive benefits, yet most of these programmes, with the partial exception of school lunch, reach only a fraction of those whose health and well being could be improved by participation. The School Breakfast programme is a case in point; at present it is offered in only about 55 000 of the 93 000 schools that offer school lunches. The biggest obstacle has been the reluctance, or sometimes outright hostility, of local school principals who resist the added burdens of paperwork and the risk of sanctions for non-compliance with various regulations. Three major strategies are generally suggested for increasing participation in child nutrition programmes: vigorous outreach, nurturing of local sponsors and reduction of the stigma associated with participation.

Outreach has been hampered by lack of funding, but where local groups have undertaken aggressive campaigns, dramatic increases have frequently been achieved. Outreach projects involving sports figures and celebrities have also sought to reduce the stigma that inhibits some children from consuming free meals. Co-operation with local sponsors, including reduction of paperwork requirements, flexible and responsive administration, training in food preparation and presentation, and active recruitment of sponsors could make the benefits of these programmes more widely available, as would funds for equipment and other startup costs. Improvement of the nutritional quality and appeal of the meals served, a goal in its own right, would also undoubtedly increase participation.

School meals are by far the largest and most important of the child nutrition programmes. Over the years, the major proposal for improving the school meal programmes has been universal free school meals. Many industrialized nations offer lunch to all school children, *gratis*, as part of the school day. In the US, however, although all meals are partially subsidized, only poor children can get them free. In fact, there are three levels of cost, with children whose families have incomes under 130 per cent of the federal poverty threshold qualifying for free meals, those with incomes over 185 per cent of poverty paying 'full' (but still subsidized) price, and those in between eligible for reduced price meals. The system is a nightmare for school administrators who must keep track of the exact number of meals qualifying for each level of reimbursement. And, although the law provides that schools must protect the privacy of free and reduced price customers, this is very hard to accomplish in fact and children who use the programme are often stigmatized by their classmates.

Universal free school meals would eliminate the paperwork burdens that alienate school administrators, would be cheaper and more efficient on a per meal basis, would eliminate stigma and would permit the integration of school meals into the school day, providing opportunities for much needed nutrition education. Despite the power of these arguments, universalization has not received serious consideration in Congress since the mid-1970s, with cost and ideology the primary barriers. Advocates of universalization argue that the real cost per meal is in fact lower when the costs of record-keeping are figured in and the real issue is who pays and how. They assert that feeding children in school has social benefits that justify paying for the meals of middle and upper income children and then taxing middle and upper income households to pay for the meals. Certainly now, in the current anti-taxation, anti-spending atmosphere, such arguments stand little chance of success. Theoretically, the Nutrition Block Grants to the States proposed as part of the Republican Contract With America could permit states to experiment with universal free school meals, but since states are under similar anti-taxation pressures, such an outcome is unlikely.

Maternal and Infant Nutrition

The Special Supplemental Nutrition Programme for Women, Infants and Children, commonly known as the WIC programme, which provides highly nutritious foods and food supplements to pregnant and postpartum women and infants and preschool children is available to low-income families (185 per cent of poverty or below) found to be at nutritional risk; the programme provides nutrition education and improved access to medical care as well as foods rich in protein, iron, calcium, and vitamins A and C. WIC has demonstrated its effectiveness in improving health, and it has enjoyed broad bipartisan support in Congress, but it has never had sufficient funding to serve all who are eligible for its services. After steady growth from its inception as a small pilot programme in the early 1970s, WIC was reaching about half the eligible population by the late 1980s, when it became a priority for both anti-hunger and children's advocacy groups.

Efforts to convert WIC to entitlement status gave way, as the growing unpopularity of entitlements with both lawmakers and the public became obvious, to a call for 'full funding for WIC', that is, funding sufficient to permit the programme to serve all those eligible and in need, without the guarantee of access that makes a programme an entitlement. The Clinton administration proposed full funding for WIC by the end of 1996, and included sufficient funds in its 1995 budget request to move toward that goal. The Personal Responsibility Act, however, includes WIC in the proposed nutrition block grants, and since spending for these grants would no longer automatically increase if recessions bring increases in need, the likelihood that states would maintain the commitment to full funding is slim. Even if the Contract is never enacted into law, the spending caps imposed by the balanced budget legislation make additional increases in funding unlikely and reductions probable.

Elderly Nutrition Programmes

These programmes have also suffered from chronic underfunding. Local agencies have the responsibility for allocating funds provided under the Older Americans Act, and as the number of elderly persons being cared for at home has risen with the growth of home health care services and the trend away from institutional care, funds have increasingly been transferred from congregate meal programmes to home delivered meals (Cohen and Burt, 1989, p. 33). As a result, congregate meal programmes have become smaller, even while the demand for them has risen. The widespread perception that the combination of Social Security and Medicare has given elderly citizens an unfair share of the nation's social spending makes increased attention to the nutrition of even the poorest seniors unlikely.

Food Stamps

Part of the practical genius of food stamps lies in the programme's susceptibility to marginal improvements. Beginning in the mid-1980s, the hunger lobby, this time with co-operation from the bipartisan House Select Committee on Hunger, succeeded in recouping most of the cuts made in Reagan's early budgets and then resumed the politics of incrementalism that has characterized the FSP throughout its history. Automatic eligibility for anyone receiving AFDC or SSI, increases in the excess shelter cost deduction, a rise in the household assets limits and partial federal reimbursements for the costs of outreach all contributed to a rise in participation. A small add-on to the TFP slightly increased the value of the stamp allotment. Pilot programmes were established to experiment with the use of Electronic Benefits Transfer (EBT), a system of debit cards similar to credit cards that would reduce the stigma and increase the convenience of food stamps while helping to reduce fraud and abuse. In 1993, legislation honouring the late Mickey Leland (D. Texas), the founding chairman of the House Select Committee on Hunger who was killed in a plane crash while investigating hunger in Ethopian refugee camps, took the very significant step of phasing out the cap on shelter deductions, which will be removed entirely by 1997. According to one estimate, 1.5 million households will receive an average of $400 per year in additional food stamp benefits when the removal of the shelter deduction cap is fully implemented (Voichick and Drake, 1994, p. 22). In addition, the limits on the value of a vehicle that a family can own and still be eligible for food stamps will be raised in graduated stages and then indexed to inflation, and several changes in how various forms of income are treated in calculating eligibility will enable additional households to participate. In the current political and fiscal climate, however, the chances of preserving even these modest reforms seem limited.

Nevertheless, it may be useful at least to sketch out the parameters of a food stamp programme that could do the job of preventing hunger. As implied above, the ingredients of a programme that would really protect poor people against hunger would be a more adequate food plan, a more realistic household food expenditure assumption and a more generous eligibility standard. That is, revise the TFP, adjust the 30 per cent assumption and increase the eligibility ceiling.

The simplest approach to improving the hunger prevention capacity of the FSP would probably be to substitute the USDA's Low Cost Food plan for the TFP as the basis for stamp allotments. The Low Cost Food Plan is about 30 per cent more generous than the TFP and research shows that families spending at this level are far more likely to obtain a nutritious diet (Cohen and Burt, 1989, pp. 34–9). If the Low Cost Plan were substituted for the TFP, more people would probably participate, because those eligible households that have not found the benefit worth the trouble would be given a greater inducement. Larger benefits coupled with higher participation would impose substantial additional costs on the Treasury, an unlikely scenario in the current context.

Another approach would be to increase eligibility thresholds of the FSP. One possibility is to adjust the 'multiplier' used in Orshansky's original poverty thresholds to reflect contemporary realities. That is, in lieu of the 30 per cent assumption that underlies current poverty thresholds and eligibility criteria, substitute a multiplier that reflects the proportion of household expenditures currently allocated to food. Recent studies suggest that the average household no longer spends a third of its income on food, but rather a figure closer to one fifth (Ruggles, 1990, p. 182). If the cost of the TFP were multiplied by 5, rather than 3, much higher income thresholds would result, and millions of additional households would be eligible. A similar result could be obtained by simply raising the gross income eligibility level to something like the 185 per cent of poverty used for eligibility for reduced price school meals and the WIC programme.

In the immediate political and budgetary climate, such changes are clearly out of the question. Advocates are currently working to withstand an effort to block grant the FSP, a move that would, in effect, terminate its entitlement status. If stamp funds are turned over to the states without federal standards, we could see a return to the arbitrary and capricious regulations that ruled the Surplus Commodity Programme when hunger researchers began investigating its shortcomings in the late 1960s. Even if one assumes that states have made progress since the 1960s and would distribute available benefits in an even-handed manner, a block grant (or even a 'capped entitlement', a compromise now under discussion) would deprive the FSP of its countercyclical impact and its ability to respond to natural disasters or other disruptions of income. States would lose their incentive to perform out-reach, since new enrollees would no longer bring new federal dollars into the state, and the nation would retreat from its commitment to a floor under consumption.

The contrast between the advocates' dreams of increased eligibility and more generous benefits and the immediate political threat of shrinkage and disentitlement raises important questions. Has the food-specific strategy adopted by anti-poverty advocates in the late 1960s run its course? Is the *Medford Declaration* wrong in its implication that it is possible to end hunger before ending poverty? If the FSP cannot be updated to reflect current realities, is it still worth fighting for? Will we still, in Levitan's words quoted above, succeed in 'getting more for the poor by raising the cry of "hunger in America"'? Comparing the success of food assistance reform with the disastrous politics of welfare, most advocates would probably vote to stay the course, but the question is worth pondering nevertheless. Even without cutbacks, food stamps are increasingly falling short of the goal of insuring access to adequate nutrition, yet their high visibility makes voters assume that 'no one will starve'.

Voluntary Programmes

The concern that the visibility of food programmes may serve to divert public attention from the underlying problem of poverty is even more acute with regard to charitable feeding programmes. Their potential for undermining welfare state commitments was already an issue be-fore the Contract With America was articulated; as noted above, it was one of the concerns underlying the effort to shift the terms of the debate from 'hunger' to 'food security'. Once Newt Gingrich ascended to the position of Speaker of the House and began to share with the na-tion his vision of replacing government assistance with private charita-ble aid, the issue became both more concrete and more urgent. The *Medford Declaration*, as quoted above, calls for full utilization of exist-ing public programmes, 'in conjunction with the heroic efforts of vo-luntary food providers in local communities', but almost no one involved with the hunger issue at the national level, including the lea-dership of the major emergency food provider organizations, is urging an expansion of the role of these programmes. Catholic Charities, the Salvation Army, Second Harvest and Food Chain have been adamant in saying that they are already stretched to the limit and cannot absorb a new wave of need.

In fact, many emergency food providers criticize the 'band-aid' nature of their own work, and speak longingly of the day when they will no longer be needed, but they are caught in a bind that keeps them running in place to secure new donations to meet the growing demand. And with their energies absorbed by the numerous and urgent day-to-day challenges of running a food programme – refrigeration, pest control, volunteer co-ordination and the like – they have little time to address the underlying causes or hunger or the attack on public sector programmes. As Harry Hopkins, Franklin Roosevelt's relief chief put it 60 years ago, 'People don't eat in the long run; they eat every day' (Ellis, 1971, p. 506).

Some thoughtful elements within the anti-hunger community have argued that with appropriate leadership, the 'feeding movement' underlying the emergency food system can be transformed into an 'anti-hunger movement', using the pantries and the kitchens, many of which are based in churches and other religious organizations in poor communities, to create a new national movement for economic justice comparable to the civil rights movement of the 1960s. 'Hunger can be the "door" through which people enter an introduction to larger problems of poverty, powerlessness, and distorted public values' (Bread for the World Institute, 1993, pp. 11–19). Bread for the World has undertaken a major project aimed at stimulating precisely such a movement. Meanwhile, however, most local direct food providers are reluctantly gearing up for the escalation of need they anticipate if the cutbacks in welfare and other social supports proposed in the Contract With America are implemented, or scrambling for funds to keep their doors open.

The preoccupation of kitchen and pantry providers with fundraising and day-to-day operations and the focus of advocates on resisting cuts in public food assistance do not mean, however, that hunger activists have no vision of what is needed to prevent hunger. The *Medford Declaration*, for example, was quite clear in its vision of the appropriate next steps:

Promoting adequate purchasing power is the way to achieve the goal of a hunger-free United States. This nation will have defeated chronic hunger when its people achieve 'food security' – regular access to an adequate diet through normal means.

A variety of steps can be taken this decade to accomplish this end: market based employment and training programs to build skills and expand jobs, making sure child care is available so parents can work; expanding concepts such as earned income tax credits and children's allowances so that the tax system strengthens families. The goal is to increase the purchasing power of employed heads of households so that work raises families out of poverty.

Other elements of the anti-hunger community stress the need for more adequate and dignified income supports for people when they cannot work, and for improved access to health care and housing: in short, an income guarantee that goes beyond food. The vision is receding, however, in the face of the conservative onslaught.

The recent history of welfare politics in the US gives the champions of more fundamental solutions little reason to be hopeful, even apart from the Contract With America. The globalization of the economy, major demographic changes including longevity and migration, and the massive entry of women into the labour force in the twentieth century have transformed both our families and our economies in ways we barely understand. People who find their economic aspirations unfulfilled and their sense of security eroding have been encouraged by politicians on both sides of the aisle to blame their troubles on government in general and on welfare recipients in particular. 'Welfare reform' in the United States for most of the past 15 years has been synonymous with efforts to force welfare recipients into a labour force that has few jobs to offer them. The pressure to reduce expenditure has all but ruled out the sort of massive public works projects that helped the nation recover from the Depression of the 1930s, and the resurgence of a conservatism focused on behaviour and lifestyle rather than economic opportunity has clouded and confused the terms of the debate. In this context, it is not surprising that the incremental approach to reducing destitution by expanding food assistance programmes has produced far more in the way of concrete benefits than the welfare rights movement or appeals to international law; nor is it surprising that anti-hunger activists continue to pursue the food specific strategy that has yielded this comparative success.

As happened after the election of Ronald Reagan in 1980, the advocates of progressive social policy in general and the anti-hunger network in particular are focusing their energies on resisting the most damaging of the immediate threats and finding little time or energy for consideration of the profound restructuring of the global economy that is probably necessary to eliminate hunger from the land of plenty or the wider world. In one sense the advocates of adequate food assistance are caught in the same bind that constrains thoughtful emergency providers. They know that food assistance alone is not the answer, but in the hostile atmosphere created by the Contract With America, they feel that they cannot let up the pressure to preserve the hard-won benefits on which million of Americans rely for tonight's supper or tomorrow's groceries. The same emotional salience and day-to-day urgency that have made hunger so comparatively successful as a means to increase spending for the poor make it nearly impossible for hunger activists to step back from their struggles to contemplate and design a broader and more fundamental politics of interdependence and social solidarity.

NOTES

1. Assuming that food assistance benefits reduced the incidence of actual hunger, the Committee calculated what it called a 'food income gap'; that is, it estimated that the total aggregate income of households below the poverty level fell 10 billion dollars short of what they would need to avoid poverty, and that a third of that gap should be allocated to food, and it subtracted total spending on food assistance benefits from this figure to come up with a total figure by which the income of poor households, including food assistance as in-kind income, fell short of the minimum they would need to purchase the economy food plan (United States Senate, Select Committee, *The Food Gap*, 1969, p. 22).

2. This overview, culled from local reports and extended interviews with emergency food providers, was recently confirmed by a large-scale study of emergency food clients conducted on behalf of Second Harvest, the food bank network (VanAmburg, 1994, pp. 150–6). The Second Harvest study found that just under half of the more than 6000 pantry clients interviewed for the study were currently receiving food stamps; of those, 65 per cent had been receiving them for a year or more. Interviewers asked clients who received food stamps how long their stamps usually lasted; more than four-fifths reported that they ran out by the end of the third week of the food stamp month. Among those not receiving stamps, close to half had ever applied for them. Of these, 43.2 per cent were awaiting approval, 37.6 per cent had been rejected and another 16.8 per cent had previously received them but were no longer doing so at the time of the interview. Among the slightly larger group who had never applied, 28.6 per cent believed that they did not qualify and another 28.6 per cent did not want to apply, while approximately 11 per cent did not know about the programme or did not know enough about it to apply and additional, smaller percentages were deterred by logistical reasons such as lack of transportation to a programme office.

7 Hunger, Welfare and Food Security: Emerging Strategies

Graham Riches

A number of common themes and some points of difference emerge from this study of hunger in the final decades of the twentieth century in Australia, Canada, New Zealand, the UK and the USA. Essentially it is a story of increasing hunger and unacceptable hardships, inadequate benefits and punitive welfare policies, government denial and uncoordinated public policy and valiant but inadequate charitable and community responses.

The case studies provide concrete evidence of the failure of the 'liberal' welfare state to protect the hungry and the poor. While each case study presents ideas and proposals about what to do, the fact is that the values of the private marketeers and the principles of New Right liberal economics have social policy tightly in their hold with the result that the rights and entitlements of millions of people living in some of the wealthiest countries in the world to adequate and nutritious food are being abandoned. Breaking the mould of the 'liberal' welfare state and its residual approaches to hunger and poverty thus seems highly problematic, at least in the short term. The purpose of this discussion is not to review the findings of the national case studies in order to suggest precise lessons that can be picked up and applied within another domestic situation, but to see what can be learned by teasing out certain ideas and approaches which may help inform progressive welfare reform strategies directed at the elimination of hunger and the establishment of the right to food security.

THE EXISTENCE OF FIRST WORLD HUNGER

As the contributions to this study make clear, despite the fact that hunger has not been a research topic of much interest to historians, hunger is not a new problem in any of the countries studied in the book. Indeed, as Wilson comments in Chapter 2, the practice of sheep stealing

to assuage hunger by Australia's early swagmen has been commemo-
rated in the country's informal national anthem *Waltzing Matilda*.
Only in the USA, as Poppendieck explains in Chapter 6, has hunger
been on the political agenda for the last 60 years and been the subject
of a variety of federal, state and local responses. Yet in each of the other
societies, hunger has only been rediscovered in recent years. Despite
this rediscovery the problem is growing.

Evidence about hunger derives from direct and indirect indicators
and anecdotal sources. Direct indicators refer primarily to hunger
surveys and prevalence studies and clinical studies of malnutrition; indirect evidence is based on the existence of emergency feeding programmes, including food banks and soup kitchens, school meal
programmes, inferential data from nutrition and dietary studies, welfare benefit statistics, poverty lines and unemployment data, the adequacy of welfare benefits and public opinion surveys. Anecdotal
descriptions of hunger and of the issues confronting those providing
and receiving emergency food assistance have also been included by a
number of the authors. Each study therefore provides a considerable
range of evidence that hunger and food insecurity have become major
health and welfare issues in their respective countries.

Whilst there are reasonable grounds for caution in terms of the relia-
bility and validity of much of the indirect data, particularly that of food
bank usage and the problems of double counting, the evidence for the
existence of hunger is compelling when understood within the context
of each country's high rates of poverty, unemployment and underemployment. More to the point, perhaps, if legitimate criticisms can be
made of the data on hunger it is also necessary to be aware of the ways
in which governments are prone to manipulate official data. For example in the UK, Craig and Dowler in Chapter 5 write that in the early
1980s 'the government introduced 29 measures in which official counts
of the unemployed were altered', thereby considerably reducing the official unemployment count.

The incidence of hunger revealed in the national case studies is considerable. Poppendieck, noting varying estimates of hunger in the
USA, reports a 1991 figure of 28 million hungry people derived from
poverty line data and reported by the Tufts University Center on Hunger, Poverty and Nutrition Policy as well as the finding of a major survey undertaken on behalf of Second Harvest, the National Food Bank
Network, which estimates 21.8 million people (based on an unduplicated count) receiving emergency food in 1994. She also notes that for
the first three months of 1994 average monthly participation in the

Food Stamp Programme reached a record high of 27.8 million persons. In Canada evidence of hunger began to appear in the early 1980s with the emergence of food banks and the estimate of 2.5 million people (8.6 per cent of the population) turning to these emergency food outlets in 1994 seems reasonable in light of a national poverty rate of 17 per cent in 1993. Food banks also helped highlight the issue in New Zealand though, as Uttley notes in Chapter 4, it was not until the 1990s that hunger and access to food became established on the political agenda. National food bank data are not available in New Zealand though the distribution of the Salvation Army's food parcels alone rose from 1226 in 1990 to 14 906 in 1994. Similarly, in Australia, Wilson observes that whilst benchmark studies do not exist, the experience of hunger is widespread and the demand for emergency relief increased in the early 1990s. Between 1990 and 1992 one in eight Australian households were estimated to be living below the poverty line. In the UK, Craig and Dowler suggest that the existence of hunger can be inferred from the statistical information on welfare benefits and they quote from the 1994 study by National Children's Home report that 'over one and a half million families in Britain could not afford to feed their children an 1876 workhouse diet at present Income Support levels'. Moreover the UK authors note that 'there is much concern in medical and some government circles that members of poor UK households are more likely to be ill, to die in infancy, or at an early age when adult, than those in richer households'.

In terms of the profile of hungry people it is clear that the image of the single able-bodied unemployed man tells only a small part of the story. Children comprise a significant proportion of those deemed to be hungry and women, as mothers and as single parents, too often go without food themselves in order that their children may eat. Too many children are having to go hungry to school. Significantly over-represented are Aboriginal peoples in Australia, Maori and Pacific Islanders in New Zealand, First Nations peoples in Canada and American Indians in the US. Infant mortality rates of indigenous peoples are consistently reported as being higher than those of the general population, a fact which may well be caused by the poor diets, malnutrition and poverty of their mothers and their families. Visible minorities and members of immigrant groups also suffer disproportionately from hunger as do young people, and there is evidence that the elderly are at risk. Hunger is both a family matter, likely to be more pressing in that period each month when the welfare cheque has run out, and a daily concern for the homeless and those living on the streets. The 'new poor', those who had good jobs and secure lives but were made redundant by public and private sector downsizing, have also found themselves joining the food bank lines and being forced to beg for their next meal. Whilst the existence of hunger is not new in economically advanced societies, what is problematic is that these are wealthy countries with adequate supplies of food. They are also countries with publicly financed safety nets established to guarantee income entitlements and ensure that basic needs, including that of hunger, are met.

THE CAUSES OF HUNGER

While there are undoubtedly unique and specific reasons for the growth of hunger in each of the five 'liberal' welfare states, there are certain explanations which are common to each study. Two categories of explanation suggest themselves: one has to do with changing economic conditions and the adequacy of welfare programmes in the face of the magnitude of the problems while the other reflects the responses of the state and civil society to the health and welfare needs, including that of hunger, of increasing numbers of people.

As each of the studies demonstrates, there can be little doubt that hunger is an outcome of prolonged high rates of unemployment and underemployment, growing inequality in terms of wealth distribution and the declining value of real wages and welfare benefits or the purchasing power of households. These factors are directly related to massive economic restructuring generated by the forces of market globalization and the pursuit by nation-states of economic growth and increased international competitiveness through committing themselves to anti-inflation and deficit reduction policies, free trade and labour market deregulation and social spending cutbacks. As the individual case studies show, this New Right economic agenda has been pursued with varying degrees of application in each country but always at the expense of secure and protected jobs and livelihoods and always on the backs of the most vulnerable. Massive unemployment since the beginning of the 1980s has placed tremendous pressures on unemployment insurance and public assistance programmes which, it must be recognized, were originally designed as short-term stopgaps.

The evidence is also unequivocal in its condemnation of inadequate welfare benefits being the immediate cause of hunger. The fact is that in none of the countries studied is it possible to provide for an adequate nutritious diet on the basis of social assistance incomes alone. Whilst there is evidence from the UK to suggest that those seeking to manage on welfare incomes are efficient managers of their food budgets, the unassailable fact is that when food expenditures have to be weighed against the increasing price of rent, utilities, clothing and other essentials it is the food bill which invariably suffers. Healthy eating, which means access to nutritious food and to a varied diet, as Craig and Dowler note, is expensive.

In addition, state-supported supplementary welfare programmes intended to provide emergency support and discretionary lump-sum payments for those with special needs are also failing. Government-provided emergency assistance in Australia often runs out before the year's end; eligibility criteria for the discretionary payments of the Social Fund in Britain, where emergency loans can be obtained, are difficult to meet; in New Zealand the policies for claiming special benefits are so complex that not even the social security staff understand them; in the US food stamp benefits are inadequate for providing adequate nourishment and food assistance programmes have been cut back; and in Canada, as in the other countries, public welfare officials frequently refer clients to charitable food banks, a clear sign that the right to a guaranteed social minimum is an illusion and that the public safety net is in tatters.

We might therefore want to ask whether it is the magnitude of the unemployment problem and rising welfare caseloads which has overwhelmed the capacity of public welfare systems effectively to respond or if there are there other agendas at work? In particular to what extent have the welfare reform policies of governments in the 1980s and 1990s taken the issue of hunger and food insecurity into account and how adequate has the response of the community sector been in responding to the growing crisis of hunger in their societies? What can be learned from these responses that might inform a new politics of welfare reform and the establishment of food security as a basic right?

RESPONDING TO THE HUNGER CRISIS

It must be emphasized that none of the countries studied suffers from an undersupply of food. It may be that, as the example of Australia shows, natural disasters such as bush fires, droughts and floods from time to time create emergency food crises, but the fact remains that each of these societies are food producing and exporting countries and import additional requirements. First world hunger it is not therefore caused by a country's failure to provide sufficient food, though there may well be problems with its system of production. Hunger is primarily an issue of distributional justice engaging broad questions of work and income distribution, food policy, agricultural practices, health and welfare reforms, nutrition education, charitable aid, community development and the role of the state and the community sector. Hunger is essentially a political question and one which demands a committed response both by the state and civil society. Yet as the evidence shows government has largely refused to respond to the issue and community action, despite a number of progressive NGO initiatives, has been divided and barely effective.

First, in terms of welfare policy the record is not good. Neo-liberal welfare reform strategies, informed by the structural adjustment policies of the New World Order, have been widely adopted in each country as a means to reduce both social spending and welfare dependency by encouraging and frequently coercing those in receipt of social assistance to re-enter the labour market. Workfare, less eligibility and the Active Society notion of reciprocal obligations whereby the continued receipt of welfare benefits is conditional upon participation in training and work schemes and upon the acceptance of any reasonable job offer have taken centre-stage in the reform of public welfare. The problem, of course, is that there are insufficient well-paying jobs to absorb the numbers of unemployed people particularly when governments are looking to private, not public, investment to create the necessary employment. The welfare recipe on offer is principally designed to manage large-scale unemployment by attaching stringent conditions to the receipt of welfare and by coercing people into low-wage work thereby disciplining labour and exerting downward pressure on wage demands. Welfare reform has resulted in increased targeting of services, cuts to benefits and the capping of social expenditures. It has also been a story of offloading welfare responsibilities from national and federal governments to lower levels of government, of developing partnerships with churches and voluntary sector and insisting that individuals and families which, of course, means women, once again, should pick up the burden.

Second, the state has responded to the problem of hunger by denying its existence, by neglecting its legislated and public responsibilities, by framing the issue of welfare costs in terms of fraud and abuse and by blaming the victim. In New Zealand the official response has been to deny a causal link between government policy and food security problems, to blame child hunger on poor parenting and to press the case that governments and the voluntary sector should work together on the issue; the UK government attempted to turn aside criticisms about the extent of child begging and sleeping on the streets made by the UN committee monitoring the *Convention on the Rights of the Child* by suggesting that the UN turn its attention to Brazil where 'real' poverty existed; in Canada, the Mulroney government similarly sought to dismiss criticisms of reduced welfare support for the poor made by the UN committee monitoring the *Covenant of Economic, Social and Cultural Rights* by claiming that its research was flimsy and inadequate; in Australia there is government denial of the need to address hunger and undernutrition as a genuine priority as the main issue is seen to be that of overconsumption; in the USA general welfare has been abolished in Illinois and Michigan and, as in Canada, the federal government is cutting welfare funding and shifting responsibility for public welfare programmes back to the states, thereby undermining national standards and rights to benefits. In terms of domestic welfare policy increasing hunger has been met by government denial, inaction, neglect and is best typified, as Uttley observes in the context of New Zealand, by the analogy of 'pass the parcel' or as Wilson notes in Australia of 'the raffle after raffle' welfare state. It is also appropriately summed up by Poppendieck's evaluation of welfare reform in the US as an 'all out meanness competition'.

Third, it should be noted, there is some evidence that the public health sector in the majority of the countries, at least since the *World Declaration on Nutrition* (Rome, 1992) has begun to take an interest in hunger and under nutrition. New Zealand's Public Health Commission (1993) has argued for the adoption of the United Nation's definition of food security, arguing that elimination depends on the purchasing power of households though in Australia, according to the Australian Institute of Health and Welfare (1994), undernutrition is believed to be uncommon. In the UK the national Nutrition Task Force established a Low Income Project Team in 1994 to address the dietary problems of low-income people. Community food security is emerging as an important policy goal in the USA. Community health initiatives are being developed at the local and municipal level. In Canada similar developments are occurring in the community health sector, and the country's food policy councils in Toronto, Edmonton and Kamloops, British Columbia have been promoting the idea of local food security. Federally, a national plan of action in relation to nutrition is being developed and Agriculture Canada has promoted a bold initiative by inviting the Canadian Hunger Foundation to consult both international and domestic food aid agencies and welfare organizations in an attempt to inform food security policy. In the buildup to the World Food Summit hosted by FAO in Rome in 1996, this is a bold initiative. Yet it must be recognized that in none of the countries studied is there evidence of political commitment to promoting co-ordinated national food policies which effectively link the knowledge and expertise of health, welfare, agriculture, and so on.

Fourth, despite such indications that the public health sector is more active in pursuing the issue of hunger than their welfare counterparts, it would appear that there is a cynical attempt by governments in the international arena to demonstrate a commitment to uphold basic human rights while at the same time undermining commitments to food security at home. With the exception of the US, all the countries studied in this book are signatories to the *International Covenant on Economic, Social and Cultural Rights* (1966) and the UN *Convention on the Rights of the Child* (1989), both of which commit ratifying governments to meet the basic needs of their citizens. Each society has also committed itself to achieving the goals of the *World Declaration on Nutrition* (1992) and of the *World Social Summit* (1995) and its commitment to eradicate poverty. Yet, for example, in Canada whilst the federal government proclaims the right of its poorest citizens to adequate food, clothing and shelter in international law, it has recently repealed the Canada Assistance Plan, thereby stripping social assistance claimants of these very rights.

It is not difficult, therefore, to believe that officially there is a cynical and deliberate attempt to jettison the idea of a guaranteed social minimum and right to food security and instead reassert the commodified notion that a person's welfare is entirely conditional on her or his ability to participate in the labour market. Given the incapacity of the economy to generate the necessary jobs and adequate incomes this approach to welfare reform, as the lessons of history show, can only result in increased hunger and deprivation. The sole response therefore for governments committed to neo-conservative welfare reform, and its rejection of the idea of social and economic rights, is publicly to deny the hunger its policies are creating and to do whatever they can to depoliticize it as an issue. Unfortunately, they are frequently aided in this process by the voluntary community.

Lastly, it should be stated that while community responses to hunger have been impressive they contain troubling dilemmas and contradictions. There can be little doubt that for many people the assistance provided by charitable food banks and emergency feeding programmes has kept hunger at bay and that their presence serves as a constant reminder that food insecurity is a critical public issue. In each country studied it can be seen that they are an important expression of community altruism yet despite the work of food banks and other feeding agencies the evidence of different countries confirms that they are not solving the problem of hunger. Far from being an emergency response they have become an institutionalized extension of a failing public welfare system. Governments refer their clients to them and food bank parcels are factored into the calculation of welfare benefits. Yet food banks cannot guarantee that hunger will be met: they are subject to donor fatigue and run out of food, they cannot necessarily provide nutritious or culturally appropriate food, they depend on volunteers who cannot always be counted upon and people's experience of having to ask for charity is often degrading and stigmatizing. More problematic is the effect which food banks have on community attitudes: they allow us to believe that the problem is being met and they deflect attention away from government and its legislated responsibilities. They serve to undermine social and economic rights. In this sense they play a key role in the depoliticization of hunger as a public issue, particularly when they enlist the services of the media to support them in the food drives. In this way the media come to portray hunger and the work of food banks as just another charitable cause. This is precisely what government wishes to hear and helps them promote their argument that it is only in partnership with the community that the hunger problem can be solved.

This is not to say that food banks either locally or through their national associations and in conjunction with national pressure groups do not also seek to educate the public and advocate on behalf of the hungry but in none of the countries studied have they been able to mount a successful challenge to punitive welfare reform policies. Whilst food bank organizations may well have progressive critiques of existing policies and support the right of people to support adequate welfare benefits, affordable social housing and full employment they, along with so many other organizations, have been unable to have their voice heard. They also have to contend with other food banks who regard charitable service as the real work of food banks. In the current climate food banks are necessary but in essence reactive organizations, which are more often than not overwhelmed by the magnitude of the task which faces them. In terms of naming the issue of hunger, promoting food conservation and advocating for the rights of public assistance claimants to adequate benefits they have important messages. Yet in the current political climate their progressive voice is unlikely to be heard, particularly if it is not part of a broader, sustained and well co-ordinated public critique.

THE RIGHT TO FOOD SECURITY: EMERGING STRATEGIES

The key goal in addressing hunger should be to establish the right of food security for all. In terms of an agenda for change there is no one approach to achieving this objective which will apply in five different societies whatever the nature of their common structural parameters and the similarities of their welfare systems. However, given the comparable experiences which each of these first world nations has had in recent years in responding, or failing to respond, to the growth of hunger, it is useful to sketch out some strategies for challenging and moving beyond the current impasse. Five broad approaches are suggested by the national case studies: understanding the nature of the hunger problem and the forces which oppose its resolution; creating long-term policy goals which focus on the structural preconditions of hunger; mobilizing for public action and devising both short- and long-term strategic objectives for working within and against the system.

If the problem of hunger in wealthy and technologically advanced countries is to be eliminated it must first be recognized that hunger is essentially a political question and a fundamental issue of human rights and distributive justice. In recent years hunger has been caused by massive economic restructuring, rising unemployment and poverty, growing inequality and the impact of New Right economic ideology on political decision-making. The state has pursued a range of labour market and welfare reform policies which have led to increased pauperization, and in so doing has turned its back on the poor and hungry. Whilst there have been some positive developments in the community health sector and by voluntary and charitable agencies in terms of providing emergency assistance, these efforts have not been sufficient to stem the growth of hunger. Moreover in a contradictory manner food bank activity has assisted the state in eroding people's rights and entitlements to basic welfare assistance and has aided the depoliticization of the hunger issue. Any strategy which seeks to eliminate hunger and establish a right to food security must therefore acknowledge the failure of current policies and practices. If food security is about the right of access to affordable and nutritious food and obtaining it in normal and socially acceptable ways (i.e. through supermarkets, corner stores, food co-operatives, and so on), it must be acknowledged that charity and food banks are not part of the long-term answer to hunger.

If the right to food security is to be achieved, comprehensive policies need to be developed not just by anti-poverty advocates health and welfare experts and proponents of sustainable agriculture but also by those who have to date been on the receiving end of charity. The debate about the right to food security will need to consider what it means for individual households, local communities, national society and within the global context. Rights to food security must be justiciable. In other words, there must be legal remedies at hand if people are deprived by the state of the right to adequate food allowances and to other necessities such as shelter and clothing.

Sustainable economic welfare which puts the needs and rights of vulnerable people (and environments) ahead of project maximization suggests a way ahead. Elements of a comprehensive strategy should include commitments by the state to adequate incomes and welfare benefits irrespective of one's formal employment status, full employment (redefined in terms of promoting socially useful work as well as the right freely to choose one's work), progressive taxation policies which effectively redress the balance between personal and corporate taxation, imposition of the Tobin tax on the financial transactions of international money markets, universal health and child care and effectively co-ordinated national and local approaches to progressive agricultural food and nutrition policies.

A more specific food and nutrition strategy could well look to the ideas of the Ontario Public Health Association and its policy objectives of equal access to food, a sustainable food supply, and the promotion of food for health which are discussed in greater detail in the Canadian case study (OPHA, 1995). Community control of the food supply and distribution system, greater access to farmers' markets, community kitchens and food co-operatives, more effective nutrition education, sustainable agricultural practices and the requirement of high nutritional standards in situations of mass catering are important aspects of this approach. Food self-reliance is a key objective of these proposals. If hunger and undernutrition are a function of people's lack of control over the food production and distribution system, then it is essential that empowerment strategies are developed in order to reassert ownership. Community development and locally based solutions are fundamental to the process of change.

In order to advance the debate about people's right to food security and the elimination of hunger the role of public action must be considered. As Uttley observes in the New Zealand case study, Dreze and Sen (1989) provide a useful framework for thinking about public action not just as government intervention and the public delivery of services (which is of course essential) but as public participation, both in terms of collaborative and adversarial processes. In other words, NGOs and civil society need to support governments in their initiatives to resolve the hunger problem, but at the same time must also challenge inappropriate policies and advocate progressive alternatives. This implies working within the system and outside it. Both approaches are necessary if the goal of food security is to be achieved and strategies need to be devised which recognize and meet the immediate needs of hungry people and work on the longer-term solutions. Given the New Right mindset of today's economic and social policy agenda this will not be an easy task.

In the short term, public action should focus on developing new forms of service with and for people who are hungry, seek to educate the public on why the problem of hunger exists and co-operate with governments at all levels in working to creating effective national plans for nutrition and food security and the promotion of progressive welfare policies. This may be easier said than done, but often the local or municipal level of government is responsive to ideas about community health promotion and this provides a useful way to enter the debate not just about policy but about practical responses to the hunger problem.

Adversarial action will also be necessary in terms of continuing to name the issue of hunger, in advocating with and on behalf of those who have had their benefits cut or who are homeless and hungry. Challenges will need to be mounted at the local level concerning the inappropriateness of welfare reform and work will need to be undertaken with like-minded welfare advocacy groups such as those representing women, labour, people with disabilities and immigrant and indigenous people's organizations. It will also be necessary to make effective links between the welfare, health, agriculture, environmental and development education sectors and ensure that those organizations that represent and speak on behalf of low-income people are centrally involved in the debate. International aid organizations and domestic food banks and food policy councils need to work together. Building effective anti-hunger coalitions is likely to prove difficult, particularly in terms of moving beyond the politics of difference which has so shaped the struggle for human rights in the post-modern era. Yet in both the short and long term, if universal basic needs such as hunger and poverty are to be recognized and addressed, coalition-building by progressive organizations will be a *sine qua non* of successful public action.

In the longer term collaborative strategies should continue to focus on working with governments on the development of a comprehensive policy framework. Useful starting points are the 1992 *World Declaration on Nutrition* and the *1995 Global Assembly on Food Security* as well as the commitments of governments to address the issues arising from the 1995 World Social Summit. The fact that the United Nations has declared 1996 to be the International Year for the Eradication of Poverty provides an important context for the development of progressive initiatives, as does the UN's World Food Summit being held in Rome in late 1996. Collaboration will also require educating not only the public but also the media as to the real causes of hunger and the consequences for society if the issue is left unaddressed.

In terms of challenging and contesting public policies which undermine the right to food security over the longer term the issues will undoubtedly prove difficult. One important mechanism for asserting the right to adequate food lies in international covenants which governments have ratified and public action should focus on making national, state and provincial governments accountable in terms of international law. Despite the fact that, as the Canadian and UK case studies show, governments will object to the international monitoring of their welfare policies, the opportunity exists for citizens' groups to raise the issue of social and economic rights with the UN monitoring committees. This could prove to be an important tool for maintaining public pressure and for requiring government accountability. In fact, it could prove to be a significant tool for organizing at the local level as it provides a politically useful way for educating people about human rights issues in both a local and global context. In the context of federal jurisdictions, state and provincial governments can also be held accountable for complying with international law.

Perhaps the essential question which must be addressed if hunger and absolute poverty are to be eliminated in the first world is whether the liberal welfare state regimes of Australia, Canada, New Zealand, the UK and the USA can recognize the social and economic rights of people to basic standards of living free from the requirement that benefits must always be attached to labour force participation. This is a particularly significant question given the inability of these societies to generate sufficient well-paying jobs. How possible is it to reject less eligibility and workfare and move beyond the commodification of social and economic rights? The signs are not hopeful in that the New Right economic agenda seems installed for a long time to come and given the forces of market globalization, it is difficult to see how the economic, social and environmental agenda can be reclaimed. Yet there is room for optimism. The social democratic Scandinavian welfare states have shown that hunger need not exist. Indeed, the growing awareness in the international and domestic NGO and community sector that hunger and poverty in 'advanced' and 'developing' countries are interrelated issues, and ones which require intersectoral analysis and collaboration if they are to be eliminated, is significant. It can only be hoped that the *UN International Year for the Elimination of Poverty* and the *World Food Summit* in 1996 create a positive context for progressive reform and advance.

References

Abel, T. and D. McQueen, 'Determinants of Selected Unhealthy Eating Behaviours among Male and Female Adults', *European Journal of Public Health* 4 (1994) pp. 27–32.

ACOSS, *Emergency Relief Handbook: A Guide for Emergency Relief Providers* (Sydney: Australian Council of Social Service, 1993).

Aitken, G. and A. Mitchell, 'The Relationship Between Poverty and Child Health: Long Range Implications', *Canadian Review of Social Policy* 35 (1995) pp. 19–36.

Alcock, P. and G. Craig, K. Dalgliesh and S. Pearson, *Combating Local Poverty* (Luton: Local Government Management Board, 1995).

Allin, S., H. Beebout, P. Doyle and C. Trippe, 'Current Perspectives on Food Stamp Program Participation', in C. Trippe, N. Heiser and H. Beebout (eds), *Food Stamp Policy Issues: Results from Recent Research* (Washington DC: United States Department of Agriculture, 1990).

Amin, K. and C. Oppenheim, *Poverty in Black and White* (London: Child Poverty Action Group/Runnymede Trust, 1992).

Anderson, A.S. and K. Hunt, 'Who are the "Healthy Eaters"? Eating patterns and health promotion in the west of Scotland', *Health Education Journal* 51:1 (1992) pp. 3–10.

Anderson, H., *Australia in the Depression* (Melbourne: Hill of Content, 1972).

Andrews, K. and J. Jacobs, *Punishing the Poor* (Basingstoke: Macmillan, 1990).

Atkinson, A. and J. Micklewright, 'Turning the Screw', in A. Dilnot and I. Walker (eds), *The Economics of Social Security* (Oxford: Oxford University Press, 1989) pp. 17–51.

Auckland Methodist Mission, *Social Policy Unit, Just Another Experiment? An Analysis of the 1991 Budget* (Auckland: Auckland Methodist Mission, 1991).

Avard, D. and L. Hanvey, *The Health of Canada's Children: A CICH Profile* (Ottawa: Canadian Institute of Child Health, 1989).

Backman, H., *No Loose Change: A Study of the Income and Expenses of Low-Income Families* (Melbourne: Action and Resource Centre Co-operative, 1988).

Banister, J., *Homeless Young People in Scotland* (Edinburgh: HMSO, 1993).

Barnes, C., *Disabled People in Britain and Discrimination* (London: Hurst and Co., 1991).

Barwick, H. and T. McGurk, *New Zealand Income Support Service Procedures for Assessing Application for Emergency Assistance* (Wellington: Downtown Ministry, 1994).

Battle, K. and S. Torjman, 'How Finance Re-formed Social Policy', Unpublished paper, Caledon Institute of Social Policy (Ottawa: March 1995).

Beaudry, M., 'A Nutrition Strategy for Canada Before 1995?', *Rapport* (National Institute of Nutrition) 8:3 (1993) pp. 1–5.

Bell, W., *Contemporary Social Welfare*, 2nd edn (New York: Macmillan, 1987).

Bennett, J. and S. George, *The Hunger Machine* (Cambridge: Polity Press, 1987).

Berry, J., 'Consumers and the Hunger Lobby', in D. Hadwiger and R.B. Talbot, (eds), *Food and Farm Programs. Proceedings of the Academy of Political Science* 34, 3 (New York: The Academy of Political Science, 1982).

Blainey, G., *The Tyranny of Distance* (Melbourne: Sun Books, 1966).

Boerma, A.H., *A Right to Food. A Selection of Speeches* (Geneva: Food and Agriculture Organization of the United Nations, 1976).

Bolton-Smith, C., W.C.S. Smith, M. Woodward, and H. Tunstall-Pedoe, 'Nutrient Intakes in Different Social Class Groups: Results from the Scottish Heart Health Study', *British Journal of Nutrition* 65 (1991) pp. 321–5.

Braddon, F.E.M., M.E.J. Wadsworth, J.M.C. Davies and H.A. Cripps, 'Social and Regional Differences in Food and Alcohol Consumption and their Measurement in a National Birth Cohort', *Journal of Epidemiology and Community Health* 42 (1988) pp. 341–9.

Bradfield, M., 'Macro Policy, Social Policy and the Debt – A Regional Perspective', Paper presented to the Second Annual Economic Policy Conference (Laurentian University, 25 February 1994).

Bradshaw, J., *Budget Standards for the United Kingdom* (Aldershot: Avebury, 1993).

Brashares, E., 'Assessing Income Adequacy in New Zealand', *New Zealand Economic Papers* 27:2 (1993) pp. 185–207.

Braudel, F., 'The "New History"', *World Press Review* 32:3 (March 1985) pp. 30–2.

Bread for the World Institute (BWI), *Hunger 1994: Transforming the Politics of Hunger*, Fourth Annual Report on the State of World Hunger (Silver Spring, MD: Bread for the World Institute, 1993).

Bread for the World Institute (BWI), *Hunger 1995: Causes of Hunger*, Fifth Annual Report on the State of World Hunger (Silver Springs, MD: Bread for the World Institute, 1995).

Breglio, V., *Hunger in America: The Voters' Perspective* (Lanham, MD: Research/ Strategy/Management Inc., 1992).

Brotherhood of St Laurence, *Easing the Pressure* (Fitzroy: Brotherhood of St Laurence, 1994a).

Brotherhood of St Laurence, *Poverty Facts* (Fitzroy: Brotherhood of St Laurence, 1994b).

Bryant, G., *The Church on Trial* (Whangerai: Whau Publications, 1986).

Bryson, L., M. Bittman and S. Donath, 'Men's Welfare State, Women's Welfare State: Tendencies to Convergence in Practice and Theory?', in D. Sainsbury, *Gendering Welfare States* (London: Sage, 1994) pp. 118–31.

Bull, N.L. and S.A. Barber, 'Food Habits of 15–25 Year Olds: II Living Accommodation and Social Class as Factors Affecting the Diet', *Health Visitor* 58 (1985) pp. 9–11.

Burghes, L., *Living From Hand to Mouth. A Study of 65 Families Living on Supplementary Benefit* (London: Family Service Units/Child Poverty Action Group, 1980).

Burt, M., *Over the Edge: The Growth of Homelessness in the 1980s* (New York: Russell Sage Foundation, 1993).

Buttriss, J. with J. Gray, *Nutrition and Cancer*, Factfile no. 12 (London: National Dairy Council, 1995).

Caledon Institute of Social Policy, *Colloquium on Child Poverty* (Ottawa, 1995).

Campbell, C.C., 'Food Security from the Consumer's Perspective: An Agenda for the 1990s', *Journal of the Canadian Dietetic Association* 52:2 (1991) pp. 83–8.

Canada, *Poverty in Canada*, Report of the Special Senate Committee on Poverty (Ottawa: Information Canada, 1971).

Canada, *The Charter of Rights and Freedoms* (Ottawa: Ministry of Supply and Services, 1982).

Canada, *Improving Social Security in Canada*, A Discussion Paper, Human Resources Development (Ottawa: Ministry of Supply and Services, 1994).

Canadian Association of Food Banks (CAFB), Submission to the Parliamentary Standing Committee on Human Resources Development, Canadian Association of Food Banks (29 November 1994) pp. 1–4.

Canadian Association of Food Banks (CAFB), Communities with a Food Bank (Toronto: Canadian Association of Food Banks, September 1994).

Canadian Centre for Policy Alternatives (CCPA), 'Federal Cash Transfers to Vanish by 2009/10', *Monitor*, Canadian Centre for Policy Alternatives 2:1 (May 1995).

Canadian Council on Social Development (CCSD), *Social Policy Beyond the Budget* (Ottawa, Canadian Council on Social Development April 1995) pp. 3–13.

Carter, S., 'Liberals Set to Dismantle the Standard They Established 30 Years Ago', Press Release (Ottawa: Canadian Council on Social Development, The National Anti-Poverty Organization and Lawyers for Just Reform, February 7, 1995).

Castles, F. (ed.), *The Comparative History of Public Policy* (Cambridge: Polity Press, 1989.

Castles, F.G., *The Working Class and Welfare: Reflections on the Political Development of the Welfare State in Australia and New Zealand, 1890–1980* (Sydney/Wellington: Allen and Unwin, 1985).

Caygill, D., *Securing Economic Recovery: Economic Strategy* (Wellington, Government Printer, 1989).

Center on Hunger, *Statement on Key Welfare Reform Issues: Empirical Evidence*, Center on Hunger, Poverty and Nutrition Policy (Medford: Tufts University, 1995).

Center on Hunger, 'Summary of U.S. Hunger Estimates; 1984 to the Present', Center on Hunger, Poverty and Nutrition Policy (Medford: Tufts University, March, 1993).

CCPI, Correspondence of B. Porter with Professor P. Alston, Chairperson, UN Committee on Economic, Social And Cultural Rights, Charter Committee on Poverty Issues (25 April 1995).

Chelf, C.P., *Controversial Issues in Social Welfare Policy: Government and the Pursuit of Happiness* (Newbury Park, CA: Sage Publications, 1992).

Choo, C., *Aboriginal Child Poverty* (Fitzroy: Brotherhood of St Laurence, 1990).

Citizen's Advice Bureaux, *Making Ends Meet. A Report from Citizen's Advice Bureaux* (Wellington: Citizen's Advice Bureaux, 1992).

Clancy, K., J. Bowering and J Poppendieck, 'Characteristics of a Random Sample of Emergency Food Program Users in New York: I. Food Pantries', *American Journal of Public Health* 81 (1991) pp. 911–14.

Clark, M., *A Short History of Australia* (New York: Mentor Books, 1963).

Clark, M., *In Search of Henry Lawson* (Melbourne: Macmillan, 1978).

Clark, M., *A History of Australia: Volume VI* (Melbourne: Hill of Content, 1987).

Clarke, K., C. Glendinning and G. Craig, *Losing Support* (London: Children's Society, 1994).

Cohen, B.E., 'Food Security and Hunger Policy in the 1990's', *Nutrition Today,* 25:4 (1990) pp. 23–7.

Cohen, C. and M. Burt, *Eliminating Hunger: Food Security Policy for the 1990's* (Washington, D.C.: The Urban Institute, 1989).

Cohen, R., J. Coxall, G. Craig and A. Sadiq-Sangster, *Hardship Britain* (London: Child Poverty Action Group, 1992).

Cole-Hamilton, I. and T. Lang, *Tightening Belts: A Report on the Impact of Poverty on Food* (London: London Food Commission, 1986).

Coles, A. and S. Turner, *Diet and Health in School Age Children: A Briefing Paper for Professionals* (London: Health Education Authority, 1994).

Commission of the European Communities (CEC), *Social Europe, the Fight Against Poverty* (Brussels: Commission of the European Communities, 1989), Supplement 2/89.

Commonwealth of Australia, *Australia's Health 1994*, 4th Biennial Health Report of the Australian Institute of Health and Welfare (Canberra: Australian Government Publication Service, 1994a).

Commonwealth of Australia, *Working Nation: Policies and Programs* (Canberra: Australian Government Publications Service, 1994b).

Community Childhood Hunger Identification Project (CCHIP), *A Survey of Hunger in the United States*, Food Research and Action Center (Washington, DC: Community Childhood Hunger Identification Project, 1991).

Consedine, J., 'Loving Means Feeding Your Neighbour', *The Dominion* (19 January 1994) 8.

Cook, D., *Rich Law, Poor Law* (Milton Keynes: Open University Press, 1989).

Council to Homeless Persons (CHP) (ed.), *Food For Thought: The Melbourne Food Bank* (Melbourne: Council to Homeless Persons, 1993).

Craig, G., 'Watching the Fund', in C. Ungerson and N. Manning (eds), *Social Policy Review, 1989–90* (Harlow: Longmans, 1990) pp. 97–117.

Craig, G., *Fit for Nothing?* (London: Coalition on Young People and Social Security, 1991).

Craig, G., 'Managing the Poorest', in T. Jeffs, P. Carter and M. Smith (eds), *Changing Social Work and Welfare* (Buckingham: Open University Press, 1992a) pp. 65–80.

Craig, G., 'Anti-Poverty Action and Research', *Social Policy and Administration* 26:2 (1992b) pp. 129–43.

Craig, G., *Replacing the Social Fund* (York: Joseph Rowntree Foundation, 1992c).

Craig, G., 'Classification and Control: The Role of Social Fund Loans', in G. Howell, *Aspects of Credit and Debt* (London: Sweet and Maxwell, 1993).

Craig, G., *Poverty and Anti-Poverty Work in Scotland* (Glasgow: Scottish Anti-Poverty Network, 1994).

Craig, G. and M. Mayo (eds.), *Community Empowerment* (London: Zed Books, 1995).

Craig, G. and D.K. Rai, 'Social Security, Community Care and "Race": The Invisible Dimension', in W. Ahmad and K. Atkin (eds), *'Race' and Community Care* (Buckingham: Open University Press, 1996, forthcoming).

Crean, P., *Survey of Low Income Families* (Christchurch: Low Income Working Party, 1982).

Cross, M., *The New Poverty and Strategies for Action* (Coventry: University of Warwick Local Government Centre, 1992).

Crotty, P., I. Ratishauser and M. Cahill, 'Food in Low Income Families', *American Journal of Public Health* 16 (1992) pp. 168–74.

Daily Bread Food Bank, 'Still Hungry' (29 May 1989); 'Ordinary People: The Real Facts about Toronto's Poor' (15 April 1990); 'Homegrown Hunger' (19 April 1995) (Toronto: DBFB).

Dann, C. and Du Plessis, R., *After the Cuts. Surviving the Domestic Purposes Benefit* (Christchurch: Department of Sociology, University of Canterbury, Working Paper No. 12, 1992).

Davey-Smith, G., D. Blane and M. Bartley, 'Explanations for Socio-economic Differentials in Mortality: Evidence from Britain and Elsewhere', *European Journal of Public Health* 4 (1994) pp. 131–44.

Davis, B., S. Katamay, E. Desjardins, E. Sterken and M. Pattillo, 'Nutrition and Food Security: A Role for the Canadian Dietetic Association', *Journal of the Canadian Dietetic Association* 52:3 (1991) pp. 141–5.

Davis, B. and V. Tarasuk, 'Hunger in Canada', *Agriculture and Human Values* 11:4 (1994) pp. 58–68.

De Havenon, A. L., *The Tyranny of Indifference and the Re-Institutionalization of Hunger, Homelessness and Poor Health* (New York: East Harlem Interfaith Welfare Committee, 1988).

Department of Health, *Contemporary Health Issues. Beyond the Facts* (Wellington: National Health Statistics Centre, 1989).

Department of Social Security, *Annual Report 1991–1992* (Canberra: Australian Government Publications Service, 1992).

Department of Social Security, *The Growth of Social Security* (London: HMSO, 1993).

Department of Social Security, *Households Below Average Income: A Statistical Analysis* (London: HMSO, 1994).

Department of Social Security, *Income-Related Benefits: Estimates of Take-up in 1992* (London: Department of Social Security, 1995).

Department of Social Welfare, *Key Issues for Social Welfare* (Wellington: Briefing Paper for the Minister of Social Welfare, 1990).

DH, *The Diets of British School Children*. Sub-Committee on Nutritional Surveillance, Committee on Medical Aspects of Food Policy, Department of Health. Report on Health and Social Subjects No. 36. (London: HMSO, 1989).

DH, *Dietary Reference Values for Food Energy and Nutrients for the United Kingdom*. Report of the Panel on Dietary Reference Values of the Committee on Medical Aspects of Food Policy, Department of Health, Report on Health and Social Subjects No. 41 (London: HMSO, 1991).

DH, *The Health of the Nation. A Consultative Document for Health in England* (London: HMSO, 1992).

DH, *Nutritional Aspects of Cardiovascular Disease*, Report of the Cardiovascular Review Group of the Committee on Medical Aspects of Food Policy, Department of Health, Report on Health and Social Subjects No. 46 (London: HMSO, 1994a).

DH, *Eat Well! Action Plan from the Nutrition Task Force to Achieve the Health of the Nation Targets on Diet and Nutrition*, Department of Health (Heywood, Lancashire: BAPS Health Publications Unit, 1994b).

Dilnot, A., 'From Most to Least: New Figures on Wealth Distribution', *Australian Society* (July 1991) pp. 14–17.

Dobson, B., A. Beardsworth, T. Keil and R. Walker, *Diet, Choice and Poverty: Social, Cultural and Nutritional Aspects of Food Consumption among Low Income Families* (London: Family Policy Studies Centre, with the Joseph Rowntree Foundation, 1994).

Dominion (Wellington) (20 October 1993) p. 9.

Donnison, D., 'Defining and Measuring Poverty. A Reply to Stein Ringen', *Journal of Social Policy* 17:3 (1988) pp. 367–74.

Dowler, E. and C. Calvert, *Nutrition and Diet in Lone-parent Families in London* (London: Family Policy Studies Centre/Joseph Rowntree Foundation, 1995).

Dowler, E. and C. Rushton, *Diet and Poverty in the UK: Contemporary Research Methods and Current Experience: a Review*, Department of Public Health and Policy, Publication No. 11 (London: London School of Hygiene and Tropical Medicine, University of London, 1994).

Doyle, W., S. Jenkins, M.A. Crawford and K. Puvadendran, 'Nutritional Status of School Children in an Inner City Area', *Archives of Disease in Childhood* 70 (1994) pp. 376–81.

Dreze, J. and A. Sen, *Hunger and Public Action* (Oxford: Clarendon Press, 1989).

Durward, L., *Poverty in Pregnancy: The Cost of an Adequate Diet for Expectant Mothers* (with 1988 update) (London: The Maternity Alliance, 1988).

Easton, B., *Poverty and Families: Priority or Piety?* (Wellington: Issues for Families Workshop, Barnardos/Birthright, 1993).

Echenberg, H. and B. Porter, 'Poverty Stops Equality: Equality Stops Poverty. The Case for Social and Economic Rights', in R.I. Cholewinski (ed.), *Human Rights in Canada: Into the 1990s and Beyond* (University of Ottawa: Human Rights and Education Research Centre, 1990) pp. 1–16.

Edmonton Food Bank, *Gleanings* (April 1995) pp. 1–2.

Ekos Research Associates Inc., *Rethinking Government* (Ottawa: 1995).

Ellis, E.R., *A Nation in Torment: The Great American Depression, 1929–39* (New York: Capricorn Books, 1971).

Emergency Relief News Victoria, 'Worrying Signs of Social Dislocation Reported by Agencies' (December 1992) p. 4.

Erlichman, J., 'Sainsbury's "Healthy" Diet Caters for the Poor', *The Guardian*, 7 September 1994.

Esping-Andersen, G., *The Three Worlds of Welfare Capitalism* (Cambridge: Polity Press, 1990).

Evans, M., D. Piachaud and H. Sutherland, *Designed for the Poor: Poor by Design?* (London: LSE/STICERD, 1994).

Falconer, S., *A Healthy Diet – A Basic Right Denied? A Survey of the Eating Patterns and Food Needs of the Homeless Living on Bed and Breakfast Accommodation* (London: Bloomsbury Health Authority, 1988).

Farquhar, L., *Food Banks: Who Are We Serving?*, Metro Food Bank Society (Halifax, 1993).

Food and Agriculture Organization (FAO), 'Food Security: Still Far From the Goal', Backgrounder, Global Assembly on Food Security, Quebec City (1995).

Food and Agriculture Organization (FAO), *World Declaration on Nutrition*, Food and Agriculture Organization International Conference on Nutrition (Rome: Food and Agriculture Organization, 1992).

Food and Hunger Hotline, *Thirty Million Meals a Year: Emergency Food Programs in New York City* (New York: Food and Hunger Hotline, n.d.).

Food and Nutrition Consultancy Service, *Final Report for the Public Health Commission on the Perceived Food Inadequacy Among Children in Schools* (Dunedin: University of Otago, 1995).

Ford, J., *Consuming Credit* (London: Child Poverty Action Group, 1991).

Fowler, J. and A. Schmidt, 'Hungry Mouths', *Metro Magazine* (Auckland) (June 1994) 72–82.

Frater, P., C. Waldegrave, S. Ward and R. Williams, *The National Government Budget of the First Year in Office: A Social Assessment* (Wellington: Hutt Family Centre/BERL, 1991).

Frederick, J., 'Running on Empty', unpublished dissertation (Melbourne: Monash University, 1994).

Gallup Canada Inc., 'Two-Thirds Believe Canada Has a Serious Hunger Problem', *Gallup Poll* (8 May 1989).

Gallup Canada Inc., *The Gallup Poll* 55:55 (1995).

Gibney, M.J. and P. Lee, 'Patterns of Food and Nutrient Intake in a Suburb of Dublin with Chronically High Unemployment', *Journal of Human Nutrition and Dietetics* 6 (1993) pp. 13–22.

Ginsburg, N., *Divisions of Welfare* (London: Sage Publications, 1993).

Glen Innes Citizen's Advice Bureau, *Survey of Family Income and Expenditure Patterns – Glen Innes 1975* (Auckland: Glen Innes CAB, 1975).

Glendinning, C. and J. Millar (eds), *Women and Poverty in Britain: the 1990s* (Hemel Hempstead: Harvester Wheatsheaf, 1992).

Globe and Mail, 'Food Bank for Veterans Called a First' (Toronto: 12 April 1995).

Globe and Mail, 'Welfare Benefits Cut 21.6 percent' (Toronto, 22 July 1995) A4.

Globe and Mail, 'UN Poverty Report Dismissed by Tories' (Toronto, 1 June 1993).

Golding, P., 'Rethinking Commonsense about Social Policy', in D. Bull and P. Wilding (eds), Thatcherism and the Poor (London: Child Poverty Action Group, 1983) pp. 7–12.

Gollan, R., *Radical and Working Class Politics* (London: Cambridge University Press, 1960).

Goodman, A. and S. Webb, *For Richer, For Poorer* (London: Institute of Fiscal Studies, 1994).

Gosling, A., S. Machin and C. Meghir, *The Changing Distribution of Wages in the UK, 1966 to 1992* (London: Institute of Fiscal Studies, 1994).

Graham, H., *Hardship and Health in Women's Lives* (Hemel Hempstead: Harvester Wheatsheaf, 1993).

Graham, J.R., 'Canadian Municipalities and Unemployment Relief During the 1930s Great Depression', *Canadian Review of Social Policy* 35 (1995) pp. 1–18.

Gregory, J., D.L. Collins, P.S.W. Davies, J.M. Hughes and P.C. Clarke, *National Diet and Nutrition Survey: Children Aged 1.5 to 4.5 years* (London: HMSO, 1995).

Gregory, J., K. Foster, H. Tyler and M. Wiseman, *The Dietary and Nutritional Survey of British Adults* (London: HMSO, 1990).

Guest, D., *The Emergence of Social Security in Canada* (Vancouver: University of British Columbia Press, 1985).

Habermas, J., *The New Conservatism* (Cambridge, Mass: MIT Press, 1989).

Hall, P., H. Land, R. Parker and A. Webb, *Change, Choice and Conflict in Social Policy* (London: Heinemann Educational Books, 1975).

Hancock, R. and P. Weir, *More Ways than Means* (London: Age Concern Institute of Gerontology, 1994).

Harding, A., 'The CEDA Vision and Enhancing Equity', Paper presented at *An Australia that Works: A Vision for the Future* Conference, Committee for the Economic Development of Australia (Regent Hotel, Sydney, August, 1993) pp. 3–4.

Harrington, M., *The New American Poverty* (New York: Penguin Books, 1985).

Harris, P., *Child Poverty, Inequality and Social Justice* (Fitzroy: Brotherhood of St Laurence, 1989).

Health Education Authority (HEA), *Diet, Nutrition and 'Healthy Eating' in Low Income Groups* (London: Health Education Authority, 1989).

Health Education Authority (HEA), *The Healthy Food Selection Guide* (London: Health Education Authority, 1993).

Henaghan, M., 'The 1989 United Nations Convention on the Rights of the Child', in *International Year of the Family Committee, Rights and Responsibilities* (Wellington: Bryce Frances, 1995) pp. 32–46.

Henderson, R., 'Banking on a Better Future', *Perception* 13:4 (1989) pp. 8–10.

HMSO, *Reform of Social Security, Programme for Change*. Vol. 1, *Summary* (London: HMSO, 1985).

HMSO, *Social Trends, 25* (London: HMSO, 1995) pp. 83–100.

Hobbiss, A., 'Managing Dietary Information whilst on Income Support: Implications for Government Policy', unpublished PhD thesis (University of Bradford, 1993).

Hobbs, K., W. MacEachern, A. McIvor and S. Turner, 'Waste of a Nation: Poor People Speak Out about Poverty', *Canadian Review of Social Policy* 31 (1993) pp. 94–104.

Horne, D., *The Lucky Country* (Melbourne: Penguin Books, 1964).

House of Commons (HC), *Low Income Statistics: Low Income Families 1979–1989* (London: Social Security Committee, 1992).

Huby, M. and G. Dix, *Evaluating the Social Fund* (London: HMSO, 1992).

Human Rights and Equal Opportunity Commission, *Our Homeless Children: Report of the National Inquiry Into Homeless Children* (Canberra: Australian Government Publication Service, 1989).

Husbands, P., 'Poverty in Freeman's Bay 1886–1913', *New Zealand Journal of History* 28, 1 (1994) pp. 3–21.

Industry Commission, *Charitable Organisations in Australia: An Inquiry into Community Social Welfare Organisations Draft Report* (Canberra: Australian Government Publication Service, 1994).

Inner City Ministry, *'Hand to Mouth', Life on a Benefit Long Term* (Wellington: Inner City Ministry, 1990).

Jack, C., 'Food Banks and the Politics of Hunger', *Canadian Forum* (December 1991) pp. 5–11.

Jackman, M., 'Poor Rights: Using the Charter to Support Social Welfare Claims', *Queens Law Journal* (1994) pp. 65–94.

Jackman, S., *Child Poverty in Aotearoa/New Zealand* (Wellington: New Zealand Council of Christian Social Services, 1993).

Jamrozik, A., *Class, Inequality and the State* (Melbourne: Macmillan, 1991).

Jenkins, S., 'Poverty Measurements and the Within-household Distribution: Agenda for Action', *Journal of Social Policy* 20:4 (1991) pp. 457–83.

Jenkins, S., *Winners and Losers* (Swansea: University College of Wales, 1994).

Jesson, B., 'The Poor Side of Town', *Metro* (August 1991) pp. 59–71.

Joffe, M., 'Food as a Social Policy Issue', *Social Policy Review* 1 (1990/1) pp. 43–59.

Johnson, F.A., S. McBride and P.J. Smith, *Continuities and Discontinuities* (Toronto: University of Toronto, 1994).

Johnston, G., *My Brother Jack* (Melbourne: Fontana, 1967).

Jones, C., *Patterns of Social Policy* (London: Tavistock, 1985).

Joseph, K. and J. Sumption, *Equality* (London: John Murray, 1979).

Joseph Rowntree Foundation, *Enquiry into Income and Wealth* (York: Joseph Rowntree Foundation, 1995).

Kalina, L., *Building Food Security in Canada* (Kamloops: Kamloops Food Share, 1993), p. 78.

Kaye, J,. *Food, Famine and Fact* (Melbourne: Council to Homeless Persons, 1991).

Kempson, E., A. Bryson and J. Rowlingson, *Hard Times?* (London: Policy Studies Institute, 1994).

Kennedy, G., *The Circumstance and Coping Strategies of People Needing Food Banks*, (Toronto: Daily Bread Food Bank, 1995).

Kennedy-Haynes, L. and C. Hunt, *Evaluation of 'Friends with Food' Programme*. An evaluation report on the development and field testing of a nutrition education package aimed at low income groups (Department of Food Nutrition and Hospitality Management, Huddersfield: University of Huddersfield, 1994.

King, A.J.C., A.S. Robertson and W.K. Warren, *Summary Report: Canada Health Attitudes and Behaviours Survey: 9, 12 and 15 year olds, Social Program Evaluation Group* (Kingston: Queens University, 1985).

Kirk, D., S. Nelson, A. Sinfield and D. Sinfield, *Excluding Youth* (Edinburgh: Bridges Project, 1991).

Kneen, B., *From Land to Mouth: Understanding the Food System* (Toronto: NC Press Ltd., 1993)

Kotz, N., *Let Them Eat Promises: The Politics of Hunger in America* (Englewood Cliffs, NJ: Prentice Hall, 1969).

Kotz, N., 'The Politics of Hunger', *New Republic* (April 30, 1984) pp. 19–23.

Kramer, R.M., 'Voluntary Agencies and the Contract Culture. "Dream or nightmare?"', *Social Service Review* (1994) pp. 33–60.

Laczko, F., 'New Poverty and the Old Poor', *Ageing and Society* 10 (1990) pp. 261–77.

Latham, M., 'Testimony before the Senate Select Committee on Nutrition and Human Needs', in US Senate, Select Committee on Nutrition and Human Needs, *Hearings... on Nutrition and Human Needs.* Part 1, *Problems and Prospects* (90th Congress, 2nd Session, December, 1968), p. 51.

Leather, S., 'Less Money, Less Choice: Poverty and Diet in the UK today', in *Your Food: Whose Choice* (London: National Consumer Council, 1992) pp. 72–94.

Lee, P., 'Nutrient Intakes in Socially Disadvantaged Groups in Ireland', *Proceedings of the Nutrition Society* 49:2 (1990) pp. 307–21.

Leidenfrost, N., 'Definitions Concerned with Food Security', in N. Leidenfrost and J. Wilson (eds), *Food Security in the United States: A Guidebook for Public Issues Education* (Washington, DC: The Cooperative Extension System, 1994) pp. 173–7.

Leonard, P., 'The Potential of Post Modernism for Rethinking Social Welfare', in L. Bella, P. Rowe and D. Costello (eds.), *Rethinking Social Welfare: People, Policy and Practice*, Proceedings of Sixth Biennial Social Welfare Policy Conference, St John's Newfoundland, 1993 (Memorial University, 1994), pp. 55–64.

Lester, I.H., *Australia's Food and Nutrition* (Australian Institute of Health Welfare, Canberra: Australian Government Publication Service, 1994).

Levens, B. and M. Clague, *Food Bank Users: A Profile of the Hungry in BC* (Vancouver: Social Planning and Research Council of BC, 1986) p. 49.

Levitan, S.A., *Programs in Aid of the Poor for the 1980s*, 4th edition, Policy Studies in Employment and Welfare No. 1 (Baltimore, MD: The Johns Hopkins University Press, 1980).

Lewis, J., 'Developing the Mixed Economy of Care: Emerging Issues for Voluntary Organizations', *Journal of Social Policy* 22:2 (1993) pp. 173–92.

Lifeline Brisbane, *Annual Report* (Brisbane, 1994).

Lightman, E., 'You Can Lead a Horse to Water, but...: The Case Against Workfare in Canada', in J. Richards (ed.), *Helping the Poor. A Qualified Case for 'Workfare'* (Toronto: CD Howe Institute, 1995).

Lipsky, M. and S. Smith, 'When Social Problems are Treated as Emergencies', *The Social Service Review* 63 (1989) pp. 5–25.

Longmore, J. and J. Quiggan, *Work for All: Full Employment in the Nineties* (Carlton: Melbourne University Press, 1994).

Low Pay Unit, *New Review* No. 25 (London: Low Pay Unit, 1994).

MacIntyre, S., E. Annandale, R. Ecob, G. Ford, K. Hunt, B. Jamaieson, S. MacIver, P. West and S. Wyke, 'The West of Scotland Twenty 07 Study, Health in the Community', in C. Martin and D. MacQueen (eds), *Readings for a New Public Health* (Edinburgh: Edinburgh University Press, 1989).

Mack, J. and S. Lansley, *Poor Britain* (London: George Allen and Unwin, 1985).

MacLagan, I. *A Broken Promise* (London: COYPSS, 1992).

MAFF, *National Food Survey 1993: Annual Report on Household Food Consumption and Expenditure* (London: HMSO, 1994a).

MAFF, *The Dietary and Nutritional Survey of British Adults – Further Analysis* (London: HMSO, 1994b).

Manning, L., 'Please, Mr. Minister, I Need Some More!' Poverty Action Group Brief, 5th revision (Regina: Regina Council on Social Development, 1995).

Mannion, R., S. Hutton and R. Sainsbury, *Direct Payments from Income Support* (London: HMSO, 1994).

Martin, J. and A. White, *The Financial Circumstances of Adults Living in Private Households* (London: HMSO OPCS, 1988).

Mason Report, *Psychiatric Care*, The Report of the Committee of Inquiry (Wellington: Government Printer, 1988).

McCaughey, J. *Where Now? Homeless Families in the 1990s* (Melbourne: Australian Institute of Family Studies, 1992).

McClelland, A., *Impact of Social and Economic Change on Women and Families: Dependency, Paid Work and Unpaid Work*, Social Policy Research Paper No. 9309 (Melbourne: Brotherhood of St Laurence, 1993).

McDonald, P. and H. Brownlee, 'Living Day to Day: Families in the Recession', *Family Matters*, Australian Institute of Family Studies, Melbourne, 31 (1992) pp. 8–13.

McFate, K., 'Introduction: Western States in the New World Order', in K. McFate, R. Lawson and W.J. Wilson (eds), *Poverty, Inequality, and the Future of Social Policy* (New York: Russell Sage Foundation, 1995).

McGurk, T. and L. Clark, *Missing Out: The Road from Social Welfare to Food Banks* (Wellington: Inner City Mission, 1993).

McKie, L.J. and R.C. Wood, 'Dietary Beliefs and Practices: A Study of Working-class Women in NE England', *British Food Journal* 93:4 (1991) 25–8.

McLoone, P. and F.A. Boddy, 'Deprivation and Mortality in Scotland, 1981 and 1991', *British Medical Journal* 309 (1994) pp. 1465–9.

McQueen, H., *A New Britannia* (Melbourne: Penguin Books, 1970).

Medford Declaration to End Hunger in the US. Available from the Tufts University Center on Hunger, Poverty and Nutrition (1991).

Metro Food Bank Society, *Food Banks. Who Are We Serving?* Summary Report (Halifax: MFBS, 1993).

Milburn, C., 'Record Numbers Clamor for Food, Shelter', *The Age* (1993) 21 May.

Milburn, J., A. Clarke with F. Smith, *Nae Bread: 440 Low Income Individuals in Relation to their Food Circumstances* (Argyll and Clyde: Health Education Department, Argyll and Clyde Health Board, 1987).

Mills, C.W., *The Sociological Imagination* (New York: Oxford University Press, 1959).

Ministry of Foreign Affairs and Trade, Human Rights in New Zealand, Report to the United Nations Committee on Economic, Social and Cultural Rights (Wellington, MERT, 1994).

Mooney, C., 'Cost and Availability of Healthy Food Choices in a London Health District', *Journal of Human Nutrition and Dietetics* 3 (1990) pp. 111–20.

Morton, S., *Local Food Shops Survey* (Manchester: Manchester City Council, 1988).

Mowbray, M., *Incomes Monitoring Report 1981–91* (Wellington: Social Policy Agency, 1993).

Moynihan, P.J., A.J. Admason, R. Skinner, A.J. Rugg-Green, D.R. Appleton and T.J. Butter, 'The Intake of Nutrients by Northumbrian Adolescents from One-parent Families and from Unemployed Families', *Journal of Human Nutrition and Dietetics* 6 (1993) pp. 433–41.

Mullaly, R., 'Why Workfare Doesn't Work', *Perception* 18:3&4 (1995) pp. 9, 13.

Murray, C., *Underclass: The Crisis Deepens* (London: Institute for Economic Affairs, 1994).

NACAB, *Income Support and 16–17 Year-Olds* (London: National Association of Citizen's Advice Bureaux, 1989).

NACAB, *Barriers to Benefit* (London: National Association of Citizen's Advice Bureaux, 1991).

NACAB, *Make or Break?* CAB Evidence on Deductions from Benefit, (London: National Association of Citizen's Advice Bureaux, 1993).

National Children's Home (NCH), *NCH Poverty and Nutrition Survey (1991)* (London: National Children's Home, 1991).

National Children's Home (NCH), *A Lost Generation?* (London: National Children's Home, 1993).

National Children's Home (NCH), *The Workhouse Diet* press release (London: National Children's Home, 1994).

National Consumer Council (NCC), *Your Food: Whose Choice?*, (London: HMSO, 1992).

National Consumer Council (NCC), *Water Price Controls Review* (London: National Consumer Council, 1995).

National Council Welfare (NCW), *Welfare in Canada: The Tangled Safety Net* (1987); *Welfare Reform* (1992); *Welfare Incomes 1993* (1994); *Poverty Profile 1993* (1995) (Ottawa: Minister of Supply and Services).

National Institute & Nutrition (NIE), *Nutrition for Health: 'An Action Plan for Canada'*, (Ottawa, 15 July 1995) pp. 2–18.

Nelson, M. and A.A. Paul, 'The Nutritive Contribution of School Dinners and Other Mid-day Meals to the Diets of School Children', *Human Nutrition: Applied Nutrition* 37A (1983) 128–35.

Nelson, M. and K. Peploe, 'Construction of a Modest-but-Adequate Food Budget for Household with Two Adults and One Pre-school Child: A Preliminary Investigation', *Journal of Human Nutrition and Dietetics* 3 (1990) pp. 121–40.

NZCCSS, *Windows on Poverty* (Wellington: New Zealand Council of Christian Social Services, 1992).

NZCCSS/Salvation Army, *Housing the Hungry: A Survey of Salvation Army Foodbank Recipients to Assess the Impact of the Government's Housing Reforms* (Wellington: New Zealand Council of Christian Social Services and Salvation Army, 1994).

NZCSS, *Families and Income* (Wellington: New Zealand Council of Social Services, 1976).

NZSDC, *Family Finances: Can the Community do Better?* (Wellington: New Zealand Social Development Council, 1977).

New Zealandia, 'Breaking the Banks. Lean Times for Foodbanks this Christmas' (December 1992/January 1993) 10–12.

Newton, E., 'All the Hungry People', *New York Daily News Magazine* (9 March 1986) p. 12.

Nutrition Taskforce, *Food for Health*, Report of the Nutrition Taskforce (Wellington: Department of Health/Shortcut Publishing, 1991).

Oderkirk, J., 'Food Banks', *Canadian Social Trends* (Ottawa: Statistics Canada, Spring 1992) pp. 6–14.

Old, B., *Food for Thought. A Report: Research on Food Banks Associated with Te Waahi Weteriana O Aotearoa* (Auckland: Methodist Mission, 1991).

Olson, K.W., *Food Security In Edmonton – Organizing For Action* (Edmonton: Edmonton Food Policy Council, 1992).

O'Neill, O., *Faces of Hunger* (London: Allen and Unwin, 1986).

Ontario Ministry of Health, *Ontario Health Survey Highlights* (Ontario, 1992).

Ontario Public Health Association, *Food for Now and the Future: A Food and Nutrition Strategy for Ontario*, Discussion Paper of the Food Security Work Group (Toronto: OPHA, 1995).

Oppenheim, C., *Poverty: The Facts* (London: CPAG Ltd, 1993).

Ormerod, P., *The Death of Economics* (London: Faber and Faber, 1994).
Pember Reeves, M., *Round About A Pound A Week* (London: G. Bell & Sons, 1913; reprinted London: Virago, 1979).
People's Food Commission, *The Land of Milk and Money*, The National Report of the People's Food Commission, (Toronto: Between the Lines, 1980).
People's Select Committee, *Neither Freedom Nor Choice* (Palmerston North: Massey University, 1992).
Phillimore, P., A. Beattie and P. Townsend, 'Widening Inequalities of Households in Northern England 1981–91', *British Medical Journal* 308 (1994) pp. 1125–8.
Physicians Task Force on Hunger in America, *Hunger in America: The Growing Epidemic* (Middletown, CT: Wesleyan University Press, 1985).
Piachaud, D., *The Cost of a Child* (London: Child Poverty Action Group, 1979).
Piachaud, D., 'Problems in Definition and Measurement of Poverty', *Journal of Social Policy* 16:2 (1987) pp. 147–64.
Poppendieck, J., 'Policy, Advocacy and Justice: The Case of Food Assistance Reform', in D. Gil and E. Gil (eds), *Toward Social and Economic Justice* (Cambridge, MA: Schenkman Publishing, 1985).
Poppendieck, J., *Breadlines Knee-Deep in Wheat: Food Assistance in the Great Depression* (New Brunswick, NJ: Rutgers University Press, 1986).
Poppendieck, J., 'Hunger in America: Typification and Response', in D. Maurer and J. Sobal (eds), *Eating Agendas: Food and Nutrition as Social Problems* (New York: Aldine de Gruyter, 1995).
Prime Ministerial Task Force on Employment, *Employment: The Issues* (Wellington: PMTFE, 1994).
Probert, B., 'The Overworked and the Out-of-work: Redistributing Paid Work, Unpaid Work and Free Time', *Future of Work* (Sydney: Australian Council of Social Services, 1993) pp. 40–9.
Public Health Commission (PHC), *Our Health Our Future. Hauora Pakari, Koiora Roa* (Wellington: Public Health Commission, 1993).
Queensland Council of Social Service Inc., *Building Queensland's Social Infrastructure* (Kelvin Grove: QCOSS, 1994).
Queensland Council of Social Service Inc. and Churches Community Services Forum, *Documents Accompanying Minutes of Brisbane Food Bank Establishment Meeting* (9 March 1994).
Queensland Poverty Research Project, Newsletter No. 2 (Brisbane, September 1994).
Radimer, K., *Understanding Hunger and Developing Indicators to Assess It*, Doctoral Dissertation (Ithaca, NY: Cornell University, 1990; University Microfilms, Ann Arbor, MI).
Radimer, K.L., C.M. Olson and C.C. Campbell, 'Development of Indicators to Assess Hunger', *Journal of Nutrition* 120 (1990) 1544–8.
Radimer, K.L., Olson, C.M., Greene, J.C., Campbell, C.C. and Habicht, J.P., 'Understanding Hunger and Developing Indicators to Assess it in Women and Children', *Journal of Nutrition Education* 24 (1992) 363–455.
Rai, D.K., *In the Margins* (Hull: University of Humberside, 1995).
Randerson, R., *Hearts and Minds. A Place for People in a Market Economy* (Wellington: Social Responsibility Commission, Anglican Church, 1992).
Raskall, P., 'The Widening Income Gap', *Modern Times* (March 1992).
Regina and District Food Bank Inc., *Annual Data 1986* (Regina, 1986).
Regina and District Food Bank Inc., *Annual Data 1994* (Regina, 1994).
Reynolds, H., *With the White People* (Melbourne: Penguin Books, 1990).

Riches, G., *Food Banks and the Welfare Crisis* (Ottawa: Canadian Council of Social Development, 1986).

Riches, G., 'Banking On Political Action', *Perception,* 13: 4 (1989) pp. 11–13.

Riches, G., 'First World Hunger: The Politics and Practice of Food Banks', *Welfare in Australia*, (1992–3) pp. 19–24.

Riches, G., 'Food Banks Fail to Provide the Right Answer', *The Age*, (Melbourne, 24 May 1993).

Riches, G., with M. Griffin, *On the Breadline: Hunger in Regina* (University of Regina: Social Administration Research Unit and Regina Food Bank, 1986).

Riches, G., with L. Manning, *Welfare Reform and the Canada Assistance Plan: The Breakdown Of Public Welfare In Saskatchewan 1981–9,* Working Paper Series No. 4 (University of Regina: Social Administration Research Unit, 1989).

Ringen, S., 'Direct and Indirect Measures of Poverty', *Journal of Social Policy* 17:3 (1988) pp. 351–65.

Rochford, M.W., *A Survey of the Living Standards of Beneficiaries* (Wellington: Research Section Department of Social Welfare, 1987).

Roll, J., *Understanding Poverty* (London: Family Policy Studies Centre, 1992).

Ross, D.P., E.R. Shillington and C. Lochhead, *The Canadian Fact Book on Poverty – 1994* (Ottawa: Canadian Council on Social Development, 1994).

Rossi, P., *Down and Out in America: The Origins of Homelessness* (Chicago: University of Chicago Press, 1989).

Rowntree, B.S., *Poverty and Progress* (London: Longmans, 1941).

Rowntree, B.S., *Poverty: A Study of Town Life* (London: Thomas Nelson and Sons, 1913; first published 1901).

Royal Commission on Social Security, *Report of the Royal Commission on Social Security* (Wellington: Government Printer, 1972).

Ruggles, P., *Drawing the Line: Alternative Policy Measures and Their Implications for Public Policy* (Washington, D.C.: The Urban Institute Press, 1990).

Rushton, C.M. and the late E. Wheeler, 'The Dietary Intake of Homeless Males Sleeping Rough in Central London', *Journal of Human Nutrition and Dietetics* 6 (1993) pp. 443–56.

Saunders, P., *Poverty, Inequality and Recession*, Study of Social and Economic Inequality Working Paper No. 5, Centre for Applied Economic Research (Kensington: University of New South Wales, October 1992a).

Saunders, P., *Longer-term Trends in the Distribution of Income in Australia: Study of Social and Economic Inequality,* Working Paper No. 3, Centre for Applied Economic Research (University of New South Wales, Kensington NSW, 1992b).

Saunders, P., *Welfare and Inequality, National and International Perspectives on the Australian Welfare State* (Melbourne: Cambridge University Press, 1994).

Saunders, P. and G. Matheson, *An Ever-rising Tide? Poverty in Australia in the Eighties*, Social Policy Research Centre Discussion Paper No. 30 (Kensington: University of New South Wales, 1991).

Saunders, P. and G. Matheson, *Perceptions of Poverty, Income Adequacy and Living Standards in Australia*, Social Policy Research Centre Reports and Proceedings No. 99 (Kensington: University of New South Wales, 1992).

Schofield, C., J. Stewart and E. Wheeler, 'The Diets of Pregnant and Post-pregnant Women in Different Social Groups in London and Edinburgh', *British Journal of Nutrition* 62 (1989) pp. 363–77.

Scott, E., *A Short History of Australia* (London: Oxford University Press, 1966).

Scrimshaw, N.S., 'The value of Contemporary Food and Nutrition Studies for Historians', in R.I. Rotberg and T.K. Rabb (eds), *Hunger and History. The Impact of Changing Food Production and Consumption Patterns on Society* (Cambridge: Cambridge University Press, 1983).

Sevak, L., *Black People and Homelessness*, unpublished MSc report (Department of Human Nutrition, London School of Hygiene and Tropical Medicine, University of London, 1987).

Sharp, I., *Nutrition Guidelines for School Meals: Report of an Expert Working Group* (London: The Caroline Walker Trust, 1992).

Shipley, J., *Social Assistance. Welfare that Works* (Wellington: Budget Statements, 1991).

Shookner, M. and D. Pfrimmer, 'Canadian Alternative Statement', *World Summit for Social Development* (Copenhagen, 10 March 1995).

Signpost, (Wellington: New Zealand Council of Christian Social Services, March 1994), pp. 1–2.

Simpson, T., *The Sugarbag Years* (Wellington: Allistair Taylor Publishing, 1974).

Sloggett, A. and H. Joshi, 'Higher Mortality in Deprived Areas: Community or Personal Disadvantage?', *British Medical Journal* 309 (1994) pp. 1470–4.

Smith, R., 'The Major Party Competition: Social Welfare since 1972', in M. Wearing and R. Berreen (eds), *Welfare and Social Policy in Australia* (Sydney: Harcourt Brace, 1994).

Snow, D.A. and L. Anderson, *Down on Their Luck: A Study of Homeless Street People* (Berkeley, CA: University of California Press, 1993).

Sooman, A., S. McIntyre and A. Anderson, 'Scotland's Health – A More Difficult Challenge for Some?', *Health Bulletin* 51:5 (1993) pp. 277–85.

SP Research Associates, *An Inquiry into Hunger in Regina*, The Mayor's Board of Inquiry into Hunger (City of Regina, 1989).

SPA, *Foodbanks in New Zealand: Patterns of Growth and Usage* A report on a short term research investigation (Wellington: Social Policy Agency Research Unit, 1994).

SPARC, *Food Bank Users: A Profile of the Hungry in BC* Social Planning and Research Council of British Columbia (Vancouver, 1986).

Statistics Canada, *Labour Force Information* Catalogue 71–001P (Ottawa, 18 February 1995).

Stilwell, F., 'Work, Wages, Welfare', in A. McMahon, J. Thomson and J. Wilson (eds), *The Australian Welfare State: Key Documents and Themes* (Melbourne: Macmillan, 1996 forthcoming).

Stitt, S. and D. Grant, *Poverty: Rowntree Revisited* (Aldershot: Avebury, 1993).

Sutch, W.B., *The Quest for Security in New Zealand 1840–1966* (Wellington: Oxford University Press, 1966).

Sutch, W.B., *Poverty and Progress* (Wellington: A.H. and A.W. Reed, 1969).

Tarasuk, V.S. and H. MacLean, 'The Institutionalization of Food Banks in Canada: A Public Health Concern', *Canadian Journal of Public Health* 81 (1990) pp. 331–2.

Taylor, I. (ed.), *The Social Effects of Free Market Policies* (New York: Harvester Wheatsheaf, 1990).

Taylor, J. and A. McClelland, *Poverty and Inequality* (Fitzroy: Brotherhood of St Laurence, 1994).

194 *References*

Taylor-Gooby, P., 'Ideology and Social Policy: New Developments in Theory and Practice', *Australia and New Zealand Journal of Sociology* 30:1 (1994) pp. 71–82.

Tennant, M., *Pauper and Providers. Charitable Aid in New Zealand* (Wellington: Allen and Unwin/Port Nicholson Press, 1989).

Ternowetsky, G. and G. Riches, 'Labor Market Restructuring and the Public Safety Net: Current Trends in Australian and Canadian Welfare States', Paper presented to the Australian, Canadian and New Zealand Studies Association Conference (Victoria University Wellington, 1992).

Thomson, N., 'A Review of Aboriginal Health Status', in J. Reid, and P. Trompf, *The Health of Aboriginal Australia* (Sydney: Harcourt Brace Javonovich, 1991) pp. 37–79.

Toronto Board of Education, 'The Relationship Between School Feeding Programs and School Performance', *Scope* 6:2 (1991) pp. 1–4.

Toronto Food Policy Council (TFPC), *Developing a Food System which is Just and Environmentally Sustainable* (Toronto: Toronto Food Policy Council, 1994a).

Toronto Food Policy Council (TFPC), 'Reducing Urban Hunger In Ontario: Policy Responses to Support the Transition from Food Charity to Local Food Security', Discussion Paper No. 1 (Toronto: Toronto Food Policy Council, 1994b).

Toupin, L., 'National Groups Go to the United Nations to Save Rights in Social Safety Net', press release (Ottawa: National Anti-Poverty Organization, The Charter Committee on Poverty Issues and The National Action Committee on the Status of Women, 27 April 1995).

Townsend, P., *Poverty in the United Kingdom* (Harmondsworth: Penguin, 1979).

Townsend, P., P. Corrigan and U. Kowarzik, *Poverty and Labour in London* (London: Low Pay Unit, 1987).

Townsend, P., N. Davidson and M.Whitehead (eds), *Inequalities in Health* (Harmondsworth: Penguin, 1982).

Townsville Bulletin, 'Aboriginal Children Go Hungry in the Territory' (17 April 1995).

Travers, P. and S. Richardson, *Living Decently: Material Well-being in Australia* (Melbourne: Oxford University Press, 1993).

Trethewey, J., *Aussie Battlers* (Melbourne: Collins Dove and the Brotherhood of St Laurence, 1989).

UNCHR, Correspondence of Professor Alston, Chair of Committee on Economic, Social and Cultural Rights, with H.E. Ambassador G. Shannon, Permanent Mission of Canada to the United Nations Office, United Nations Centre for Human Rights (Geneva, 4 May 1995).

UNICEF, *The Progress of Nations* (New York: UNICEF, 1994).

UNESC, 'Concluding Observations of the Committee on Economic and Social and Cultural Rights: Canada', Committee on Economic, Social and Cultural Rights United Nations Economic and Social Council, E/C. 12/1993/5 (10 June 1993).

United Nations, *International Covenant on Economic, Social and Cultural Rights* General Assembly Resolution 2200A (XXI) (16 December 1966).

United Nations, *UN Monitoring Committee on the Convention on the Rights of the Child* (1989).

United Nations Development Programme, Human Development Report 1994, (New York: Oxford University Press, 1994).

United States Senate, Select Committee on Nutrition and Human Needs, 91st Congress, 1st Session, *The Food Gap: Poverty and Malnutrition in the United States* (Washington, D.C.: US Government Printing Office, 1969).

USDA, 'Food Program Update: A Review of FNS Food Assistance Program Activity', Fiscal Year 1994, Third Cumulative Quarter (Washington, D.C.: Food and Nutrition Service, 1994).

US General Accounting Office *Public and Private Efforts to Feed America's Poor* (Washington: GAO, June 1993).

VanAmburg Group, Inc., *Second Harvest 1993 National Research Study* (Erie, PA: VanAmburg Group, revd edn 1994).

Voichick, J. and L.T. Drake, 'Major Stages of U.S. Food and Nutrition Policy Development Related to Food Security', in N. Leidenfrost and J. Wilkins (eds), *Food Security in the United States: A Guidebook for Public Issues Education* (Washington, D.C.: Cooperative Extension System 1994) pp. 17–23.

Waldegrave, C. and R. Coventry, *Poor New Zealand* (Wellington: Platform Publishing, 1987).

Walker, A., 'Blaming the Victim', in C. Murray, *The Emerging British Underclass* (London: Institutue of Economic Affairs, 1990) pp. 49–58.

Warnock, J.W., *The Politics of Hunger* (New York: Methuen, 1987).

Watson, P., *Community Health Initiatives and Food: An Information Pack* (London: National Community Health Resource, 1991).

Webber, M., *Food for Thought* (Toronto: Coach House Press, 1992).

Wheler, C.A., R.I. Scott and J.J. Anderson, 'The Community Childhood Hunger Identification Project: A Model of Domestic Hunger – Demonstration Project in Seattle, Washington', *Journal of Nutrition Education* 24:1 (1992) Supplement, pp. 29S–35S.

Wilkinson, R.G., 'Income Distribution and Life Expectancy', *British Medical Journal* 304 (1992) pp. 165–8.

Williams, C., *Eating for Health – A Costings Exercise: Homeless Families in Bed and Breakfast Accommodation* (London: Riverside District Health Authority Health Promotion Service, 1989).

Williams, C., *Healthy Food: A Guide for School Governors and School Boards* (London: School Meals Campaign, 1994).

Williams, C. and E. Dowler, *Identifying Successful Projects on Diet and Low Incomes: A Review of the Issues*, Working Paper No. 1 for the Low Income Project Team to the Nutrition Task Force (London, Department of Health, 1994).

Wilmott, P. (ed.), *Urban Trends 1* (London: Policy Studies Institute, 1992).

Wilson, J., *Lori* (Broome: Magalala Books, 1989).

Wilson, J., 'Social Work Practice and Indigenous Australians', in P. Swain (ed.), *In the Shadow of the Law* (Annandale: The Federation Press, 1995) pp. 263–74.

Winnipeg Harvest, *The Report of the November 1989 Hunger Survey* (Winnipeg: Inter Agency Food Network, 1989).

Winson, A., *The Intimate Commodity* (Toronto: Garamond Press, 1993).

World Summit for Social Development, *Copenhagen Declaration and Programme of Action* (United Nations: Copenhagen, 6–12 March, 1995).

York, G., 'UN Poverty Report Dismissed By Tories', *Globe and Mail*, 1 June 1993.

Young, M., 'Starving in the Shadow of the Law: A Comment on *Finlay v. Canada (Minister of Finance)*', *Constitutional Forum* 5:2 (Winter 1994) 31–5.

Index